Preying Indians

Thomas Medonis

Good Word Books
2014

Praying Indians

    As man, non-fiction is flawed. The possibility for a flawless rendition is no possible feat. Nevertheless, all intentions within this work are to provide an enjoyable time quest. In the work that follows I have compiled a microscopic amount of amazing local history, in order to depict a past we know very little about. What if the truth we have been taught for hundreds of years has been tainted?

    Numerous events are thus shared throughout the story portraying the downfall of the Southern New England Indian civilization. The hospitable Plymouth welcome the English settlers received, provided by Massasoit in 1621, is the foundation for the necessity of our ongoing diplomacy. Truth be told, Massasoit, the great Wampanoag Sachem, had a son named Metacomet, or King Philip, and his boy to this day has the first civil war in America in 1675 named after him. And, his role was not favorable to the English. Yes, Massasoit was imperative for colonial existence. But, in contrast, his son was tired of the settlers expanding upon land that was rightfully his. Metacomet, ultimately, was killed for standing up against the expansionist conquest forced against his people. Is he wrong for this?

Such an ill character has been molded by a power whose actions demand no accountability.

The past several years have been spent researching why White and Redmen couldn't coexist. Was it the Redman's self-sustaining nature? Was it the Whiteman's shrewd nature? Hence, I began to dig as deep as literature would permit. I didn't have to look far. The Indians that have previously lived where I have lived, Hartford, Wethersfield, and Springfield, more or less, experienced the beginning and end of my inquiry. Turbulence that led peaceful beginnings to a bitter violent end has consumed my energy. The most fascinating of all facts I uncovered was that there were Christian Indians! Yes, praying Indians. And these very men were at the heart of the colonial dysfunction.

Spreading Christianity amongst the Indians was a commitment made by two special English missionaries and a magistrate. Thomas Mayhew Jr. and John Eliot were missionaries to the Indians, while, Daniel Gookin, was superintendent to the Indians. The missionaries, small in number, held Christian motives toward transforming the heathen. Of these motives there were three of most importance:

First, the glory of God, in the conversion of some of these poor desolate souls.

Secondly, his compassion and ardent affection to them, as of mankind in their great blindness and ignorance.

Thirdly, and not the least, to endeavour, so far as in him lay, the accomplishment and fulfilling the covenant and promise, that New England people had made unto their king, when he granted them their patent or charter, viz. That one principal end of their going to plant these countries was, to communicate the gospel unto the native Indians.[1] [Daniel Gookin]

Convert the New England Indian? Where did this silly idea come from?

Actually, the answer lies in the beginnings of the Massachusetts Bay Colony. It was in 1629 that Governor John Winthrop and the Massachusetts Bay Company held the hope of creating a Christian state within the New World. A feat believed to become possible through the conversion of the heathen toward the Gospel. Before Winthrop left England on board the Arbella, he had promised in the governor's oath of office in 1628-29 to bring the natives of this new country to the knowledge of the true Christian God. It was truly believed that the Indians wanted the English to "come over and help us."

Travelling even further back, missionary labor upon aboriginal species began earlier than those of the colonies. Columbus believed the Indian was capable to adopt the Catholic faith. Columbus reported in a letter "many beautiful and pleasing things" given "in order that I might the more easily make them friendly to me, that they might be made worshippers of Christ. ... Let Christ rejoice on earth, as he rejoices in heaven, when he foresees coming to salvation so many souls of people hitherto lost."[2]

In the late sixteenth century the Christianizing of the Indians was both a religious hope and an act for the glory of England. Religious reform for the Indians became one of the strongest motives for expansion. Men intending to come to New England felt it was part of the "divine plan". The "glory of God" and the "glory of England" became one.[3] In 1609 Prince Henry declared:

You will make a savage country to become a sanctified country; you will obtain the saving of their souls, you will enlarge the bounds of this kingdom, may the bounds of Heaven, and all the angels that behold this if they rejoice so much at the conversion of one sinner, O what will be their joy at the conversion of so many.

Nonetheless, no conversion was soon made after Governor Winthrop settled in the Massachusetts Bay. The plantations constructed, beginning in 1630, spawned the great migration of Englishmen into Massachusetts Bay, forever changing the vast wilderness America once was. Obviously, such an influx set in motion the removal of aborigines from their homeland. A continual influx of planters amid the 1630s caused overcrowding throughout the eastern coastline of Massachusetts.

The wealthy men involved with the Massachusetts Bay Company seriously believed that the New England aborigines were the degenerate descendants of the ten lost tribes of Israel, and it was hoped that they might be reclaimed from this strange backsliding.[4] A writer described that the Indians and Jews shared similarities in rites, ceremonies, and opinions.

With these intentions it nevertheless took sixteen years after Winthrop's arrival to just begin conversion efforts within Massachusetts Bay. Sidetracked, the planters were busied in safety, education for their children, building towns, and prosperity. Concerns so great placed the Indians in their shadow.

The first to truly convert an Indian in this country was Thomas Mayhew Jr. in 1646. It was on the infant island of Martha's Vineyard, not the mainland, where a man's beliefs were peacefully transformed. An Indian plantation developed practicing Christian and Puritan tradition. This evolution was only made possible through the conduct of Mayhew and his father, Thomas Mayhew Sr. Mayhew Jr. not only shared the Gospel with the Martha's Vineyard Indian, but made it his life's work. Undoubtedly, one of the most divine men I have ever read of. In this most righteous labor something much more important than the necessity for expansion transpired. Mayhew's work was for the improvement of his neighbor.

A feeling of sympathy for the redmen has always existed within myself as well, especially for the fact that my grandmother has told me we have some Indian blood in us. Nevertheless, as abovementioned, I was most taken aback the moment I discovered there were some among the Natives that had become Christian. Passionate for an understanding into our history, this discovery magnetized my focus.

If Mayhew felt comfort amongst them they couldn't have been that diabolical. A young man, in his twenties, dedicated his life for their improvement. It took a while for some native islanders to become familiar with Mayhew's purpose, as he taught the concept of sin and proper conduct. Providence, nonetheless, worked rather quickly for Mayhew.

Christianity was also attempted in the Massachusetts Bay. Change for a man dependent upon his natural environment, however, was a far different process on the mainland than on Martha's Vineyard. John Eliot was the missionary who spread his message toward the Indians of Massachusetts, Rhode Island, and Connecticut. There is a strong debate to be had whether there were any successful conversions within Massachusetts Bay under John Eliot. There were none in Rhode Island or Connecticut.

Eliot's great failure was his ignorance in the distrust that his fellow Englishmen held toward the Indian. Eliot spent such great effort on the advancement of the Indian that he lost sight of educating the English on the transformation of the Indian. Without a doubt, though, Eliot felt great sympathy for the Indians. He was very troubled during the outbreak of King

Philip's War in 1675, in which his very own Christian Indians were rebelling. He felt the war would not have occurred if Plymouth had honest land dealings with Philip. Eliot wrote to John Winthrop, Jr., "I humbly request that one effect of this trouble may be to humble the English to do the Indians justice and no wrong about their lands."[5]

It must be said that the term Christian, or praying, Indian is a great hypocrisy in the literal sense. The planters on the mainland used Christian Indians more as tools for warfare rather than pillars for the word of the almighty Lord. Many years removed from the arrival of John Winthrop with his proclaimed missionary intentions, there developed preying Indians and praying Indians. For many praying Indians the term preying would apply just as appropriately. To determine any difference, if one exists, we must first understand the difference between the two conflicting roles, why Indians chose one path or the other, and how they were driven toward that particular carriage.

Was there an earnest collective effort for the successful transformation of the heathen toward Christianity? If so, was it a sincere effort by the missionaries? It is true the conversion of the native was one of the first justifications as to the purpose for New England. Why, though, would a group of wealthy merchants even consider having the ability to transform a savage?

These converted natives known as the praying Indians were also variously called friendly Indians, Christian Indians, Converts, Red Puritans, or peaceful Indians. They were on the side of the English, though some rebelled at the time of King Philip's War. And so, the Praying Indians would ultimately sacrifice their lives for the colonies very own survival amid New England's second war. There existed some supernatural strength within these Indians that fostered a vigilance to fight at any moment upon the colonies request, even as they were sent against relatives.

The other group of Indians I will distinguish were unfavorable to the English. I define this group as preying Indians, non-converts, rebellious Indians, neutral Indians or hostile Indians. These were the Indians who did not align with the colony nor the culture, rebelled from Christian conversion, or simply manifested hatred toward the colonization of their homeland. Moreover, they did not understand the legal system of the English and were severely punished for the lack of understanding.

The Christianizing of Indians consequently stirred rage in other Indians on the mainland. In the past it was customary for individuals or broken tribes to be accepted into larger tribes, yet, once Christian conversion grew in numbers and praying villages, it became viewed by non-converts as simply the adoption of Indians into white settlements. Ultimately, the transformation increased the foreigners' strength[6].

To confuse matters, there were tribes, such as the Massachusetts, Wampanoags, and Nipmucs, whose members separated, either remaining peaceful or rebelling. The Mohegans of Eastern Connecticut held a strong alliance with their colony throughout many years, and greatly influenced the outcome of the two Indian wars of New England. The Mohegans preyed upon tribes unfavorable to the English or themselves. You will become quit familiar with Uncas the Mohegan Sachem.

Tribes most resistant to Christianity were those with the strongest leadership. Indeed, the Sachem's role was threatened by the objective of their colony. The two most influential chiefs in promoting the colonies growth, ironically, also denied the conversion of their tribes: Massasoit of the Wampanoag Confederacy, responsible for the original peaceful settlement of

Plymouth in 1620-21, and Uncas, chief of the Connecticut Mohegans.

There are many interpretations as to what or who was responsible for the creation of Indians preying upon the colonies or their own kind, but the one certainty for the Indian is the change to their lifestyle that disease and the arrival of the English spawned.

A vast loss to the Indian culture and property was undoubtedly the result of illness. Death because of foreign diseases became a common occurrence to the native families of the Massachusetts, Wampanoag, and other surrounding tribes. It was written by an Englishman that "the good hand of God [swept] away great multitudes of natives by the small pox, a little before went thither, that he might make room for us there."[7]

Around 1612 in Norumbega, what New England was once called, a lethal strain of infectious fever first spawned through fisherman and explorers infecting the coast. The illness decimated the coastal Wampanoag and Massachusetts tribes for many years and the mighty sachems could offer no protection for their tribes. The arrival of European diseases permitted the Plymouth settlers to set up camp on the uninhibited fields of the Wampanoags' land called Patuxet in 1620.

Henceforth, new neighboring settlements would form on the Atlantic Coast- Providence Plantation, Hartford, Fort Saybrook. All this development, in my estimation, was the greatest of insults applied to the aborigine. Yes, many Indian relatives perished, clearing vast amounts of land, but the surviving tribes still held entitlement to their land. The planters displayed superiority toward the inferior Indian through legal measures.

Massachusetts Bay decreed that Indians could be executed for blasphemy, a crime interpreted to include denial or cursing of the true God, and derogation of the Christian religion. On another instance, one Indian was fined forty shillings for breach of peace because he traveled from Springfield to Hartford on a Sunday. Another was punished for firing a gun on Sunday.[8]

I would not like that conduct from my neighbor either. Moreover, there was no intention to accept or learn native tradition. At first, the Indian lived perfectly fine in the wilderness with no dependence upon any foreign entity. We, on the other hand, depended upon the Indian for our very own survival in a desolate wilderness. Subsequent to the expansion of colonies it appeared necessary to censure every aspect of the Native lifestyle.

When we look back on this age of the true natives, their existence may be described as one of no importance. Their lives, on the contrary, are of the greatest significance. The advance for a Christian country and what has become of America is all the result of a Puritan design for civilization first enforced upon the aborigine.

Does regulating actions of a man from a different theology establish civility?

Whatever the answer, transforming the Redmen toward Puritan conduct would be a familiar struggle amid the formation of the colonies. The one tribe that caused the most grief for the colonies during the early stages of colonization would be the Pequots. Pequot defeat in the Pequot War of 1637 would serve as the first military step in order to open the gates for Christian Indians. To find the answer as to why these Christian Indians held so much rage to the point of revolt in 1675 we must first understand the Pequot War. Bigotry began far before 1675.

The Relocation

The Pequot invasion of 1637 in considered the first war of Connecticut. Passionate interest has sparked towards this event, as the Pequot demise was the first indicator of what the colonies were capable of, in terms of removing unwanted residents. This war, though more of an invasion in nature, is the first major incident which increased the separation and fear between the colony and the Indian.

The Pequots were a branch of the great Muhhekanew (or Mohican) nation. Their main seat had been on the east bank of the Hudson River, in the area of Albany, but the Pequots were driven from their country by the Mohawks (Iroquios). The Pequots next chose to call eastern Connecticut home.

The Pequots settled near the seacoast, on territory formerly occupied by the Niantics, which was on both sides of the Mystic River. Not content with the conquest of the coastal tribes, the Pequots made war on the Sequins of the central

Connecticut valley around the area of Hartford and Wethersfield. According to the Dutch account, the Sequins were beaten in three encounters, and they thus became tributary to the Pequots. This was some years after the first visit up the Connecticut River by the Dutchman Adriaen Block in 1614, but probably not earlier than 1630.[9] The Dutchman's visit marked the beginning of the end for the River Indians and Pequots, as the river would no longer be theirs.

"In 1626 a Pequot war party had defeated the Wongunk sachem Sequin (Sowheag), the leader of the loose alliance of River Indian bands, and finally after three defeats in battles with the Pequots, the Connecticut River Indians thereafter agreed to pay annual tribute to the Pequot Grand Sachem Tatobem and received in return a pledge of Pequot protection."[10]

Ironically, this method used by the Pequots, as the powerful exacted tribute from the inferior, is comparable to the conduct of the English upon the natives, in which strength enabled conquest.

In the meantime, high hopes were held by English settlers' of becoming associated with the great merchants of England who had moved around the Watertown area- bounds within the Massachusetts Bay Companies jurisdiction. No simple tradesmen those merchants, but persons who dealt in a wide assortment of goods, such as linen cloths, buckrams, fustions, satins, fine woolen, and other commodities. Nevertheless, if success did not first come in Watertown, labor could be found in neighboring Medford, which would be found on the private estate of Mathew Craddock.

Thomas Mayhew Sr. called Medford home during his early stages of life in New England. Previously, in business at Southampton in England, Thomas Mayhew, Free Commoner and Merchant, followed the colonizing ventures of the great mercantile companies. Southampton was filled with merchant adventures concerned in the first settlement and maintenance of plantations in the West Indies and on the mainland of America.

A gentleman named Mathew Cradock at some point discovered the abilities of Thomas Mayhew. Cradock was a successful London merchant and the first governor for the company of the Massachusetts Bay, as Mayhew's stature had grown through successful dealings. His standing was shared through the reports and intelligence of others, but the most important information told to Cradock about Mayhew was from the mouth of John Winthrop, with whom Mayhew had been acquainted.

Cradock was a potent merchant within England who traded in all the oceans. He invested in trade with Persia and the East Indies, and also sent ships to the Levantine, the Mediterranean, and the Baltic provinces. As Governor he was financially invested in the Massachusetts Company, in which he supported John Endicott as the chief authority of the small colony at Salem. Cradock wrote a letter to Endicott stating, "omit no good opportunity that may tend to bring [the heathens] out of that woeful state and condition they now are in."

As early as 1629 Cradock sent over shipwrights, gardeners, coopers, cleavers, and a wheelwright to the new plantation. In that year he would settle his personal estate at Medford on the banks of the Mystic. The estate would need management. Thus an appointed agent or a factor would be appointed to have oversight and supervision of his shipping, fishing, trading, and plantation interests.[11]

Mayhew would become one of these factors. Thus, one of Thomas Mayhew's first New England residencies was in Medford. Medford, the private plantation of Mathew Cradock, was not considered a township at this time. The plantation was situated upon a grant of thirty-five hundred acres. As Cradock's factor, Mayhew became the foreman for a large number of employees, who were occupied to develop Cradock's business interests in numerous fields. In 1634, Mayhew built a brilliant water mill in Watertown, which Mayhew would eventually buy for himself, and then sell it and receive great profit.

A crew took two days to help carry the timber for building the mill at Watertown. "The mill, which was the first in Watertown, was built at the head of tide-water on the Charles River at Mill Creek, which was a canal, leaving the river at the head of the falls, where a stone dam was built." [12]

Crossly for Mayhew, Cradock, in London, had become frustrated with Mayhew's results as the Medford factor. Cradock believed his investments in New England should produce great revenue. But New England wealth did not grow over night, "nor did it contain the wealth of the Caribbean". New England timber and the fish caught in abundance did not reach profitable markets in the home country.

Cradock blamed Mayhew's bad dealing for his financial misfortunes and he was released as factor. It also meant removal from Medford for Mayhew and his family. Nevertheless, things remained amicable, and Mayhew took up residency in the nearby village of Watertown, where he held economic interests.[13]

Mayhew quickly became one of the landowners in Watertown, wherein his land consisted of a large farm of two hundred and fifty acres. Thereupon he held a prominent role as he was elected one of eleven selectmen to dispose of civil matters. Watertown colonists weren't confident, however. A man innocently 'fired his musket into the air to scare wolves away from his cattle and the whole colony went on alert. People who lived within earshot spread the alarm and before morning drums were beating in Boston and planters were grabbing their weapons'.[14]

What happened subsequent to the Watertown colonization, however, would change the landscape and the Pequots forever.

The idea for migration to the south was planted in Watertown as well. John Oldham, a Watertown Deputy, began exploring the Connecticut River Valley and the Indians who lived there. Oldham was described as "a crusader for Presbyterianism against the Pilgrim subversives of the Church of England."[15]

Through Providence Oldham was led toward Connecticut. Oldham had grown a reputation as "a colorful and controversial trader". Oldham first came to Plymouth in 1623, on the ship Ann, and, nevertheless, trouble quickly began for Oldham in 1624. There was no favor in his active involvement with Rev. John Lyford, in plotting both here, and by correspondence with a faction in England, against the interests of the Plymouth Company. Further follies ensued, which caused his arrest and expulsion from the Colony- his defiance of and drawing a knife on Captain Standish when called upon duty of watch, and ward; his outrageous conduct towards the Governor himself and his cursing. Thus Oldham received great indignation from the highly dignified within Plymouth.

In the spring of 1625, although Oldham had been forbidden, he came back to Plymouth and again misbehaved, whereupon he was jailed until he had relinquished his anger. In March of that year he was again expelled. Oldham left for Virginia, and had there a great sickness, but recovered and came back up again to his family in the Bay, and lived there whilst the population greatly increased.

By 1629, as again a resident of Massachusetts, he made himself obnoxious to the Governor and Council. Oldham felt he was owed something, yet his persistent pressing upon their notice of plans and claims were considered to be more for his benefit than for the Company's. These stirrings were apparently based upon a patent, which Oldham had obtained, or in which he was somehow interested. He claimed a title based upon a patent and right by grant which the council felt was void by law. Oldham professed to have been issued a patent "under William Gorges, son of Ferdinando, covering part of the region around Boston."[16]

Oldham admitted no terms of agreement, unless he had liberty to trade for beaver with the natives, which the company denied even to the best of their own planters. He was satisfied to trade for himself with his own stock and means, which was so small that it would not much hinder Plymouth or the Bay. However, Oldham's trade did interest other men, who were never likely to reap any benefit from the planting of the country, but their chief aim and intent was their own profits from Oldham's intercourse with the natives.

Subsequent to his return to New England in the late summer of 1629, foiled of his great plans for a land patent in Massachusetts, Oldham would finally become admitted a freeman of the Massachusetts Colony, May 18th, 1631, whereupon, he was an early planter at Watertown and acquired church membership with a grant of 500 acres.

In May 1632, Oldham was one of the two Watertown deputies chosen to advise with the Governor and Council about raising a public stock. Sadly, in the summer of that year he had a small house near in Watertown, made all of clapboards, but it burnt down by making a fire in it when it had no chimney.

In May, 1634, he was one of Watertown's three representatives to the first General Court of Massachusetts, in which he had fairly earned the reputation of a fearless, enterprising, and successful trader and explorer among the Indians of the New England coast, and in the Connecticut Valley. Evidently, he was now sharing the better side of his nature within the Bay.[17] Oldham was now a highly respected citizen.

Influential in opening trade relations with the Narragansetts, as he travelled into Rhode Island for a trading expedition, Oldham was also one of the first Englishmen to venture into the Connecticut River Valley in 1633, with three other men. Subsequent to these visits with the Indians, smallpox appeared and spread through the valley tribes, halting trade. The disease had spread among the Dutch trading houses along the Connecticut River and then around the trading houses of the English. Soon the disease spread to Rhode Island and Massachusetts. Amongst the Narragansett, 700 had died. Oldham had traded with all of these tribes before the outbreak, and the coastal tribes expressed to the River Indians along the Connecticut that Oldham had been amongst them. Thus, some of the natives laid blame for the outbreak of disease on Oldham.

According to William Bradford:

> For it pleased God to visit these Indians with a great sickness. (...) This spring those Indians that lived about their trading house there, [the Plymouth trading house at the site of Windsor], fell sick of the small pox and died most miserably; for a sorer disease cannot befall them, they fear it more than the plague.[18]

Despite the Indian claims, the trip was productive for Oldham. During the visit to the Connecticut River Valley, he obtained some black lead, as well as hemp, all of which was much better than the English product.

In consideration of the promising goods available, Oldham estimated he would establish a southern plantation in the near future. In order for the plantation to progress "he had to secure at least ten men to go with him the next year, but only in time to prepare the soil for the following year's crop." Thereupon, those who came with Oldham to Pyquag, also known as Wethersfield, were from the Watertown church.[19]

At this time in their lives they were ready to leave Watertown and acquire their own land. Oldham clearly presented the prospect for a successful enterprise, which he could lead for the well being of many families.

This rich land bordering the river also attracted others within the Bay. Such vast "numbers had come over from England, and planted themselves in the vicinity of Boston, that the people at Watertown, Dorchester, and Newtown, began to find themselves crowded into such close neighborhoods, that they had neither land enough fit for culture, nor pastures for their cattle. Especially they were in want of meadow lands." [20] Impressed by reports of the rewards within the Connecticut River valley, where meadows were said to be far more fertile than the stony soil of the bay, residents of Dorchester, Watertown, Roxbury, and Newtown looked toward Connecticut.[21]

In the fall of 1634, Oldham and nine companions made another overland journey by land, through the forests, and settled in a rude manner on the Connecticut River. A small trading post was established in Wethersfield, putting up temporary cave dwellings and houses, and spending the winter trading from that location.

It was precious land before they arrived. Maples, beeches, giant oaks, all stood out among the trees that kept their greens throughout the winter. The land was a forest of trees of every size and species. The Sequins, the largest of the river tribes, had their homes on the banks of the river, while another had built a palisade to ward off a Pequot attack.

"There was plenty of clay and ample limestone on every side, yet we could have no brick and no mortar; grand boulders of granite and rock were everywhere, yet there was not a single facility for cutting, drawing, or using stone. These homeless men, so sorely in need of immediate shelter, were baffled by [the] conditions, and had to turn to many poor expedients, and be satisfied with rude covering. Some reverted to an ancient form of shelter: they became cave-dwellers; caves were dug in the side of a hill, and lived in till the planters could have time to chop down and cut up trees for log houses."

Men worked fast, and without a sawmill, brick kilns, or stone cutters, he relied on his broadax. Within a couple months he constructed a log house. He first dug a square trench two feet deep, "of dimensions as large as he wished the ground floor of his house, then setting upright all around this trench (leaving a space for a fireplace, a window, and a door) a closely placed row of logs all the same length, usually fourteen feet long for a single story. The earth was filled in solidly around these logs, and kept them firmly upright; a horizontal band of puncheons, which were split logs smoothed off on the face with the ax, was pinned around within the log walls to keep them from caving in. Over this was placed a bark roof, made of squares of chestnut bark. A bark or log shutter was hung at the window, and a bark door hung on withe hinges, with a rough puncheon floor, hewed flat with an axe." Mother's sought the house would be "rolled up around a splendid flat stump; thus she had a good firm table. The chinks of the logs were filled with moss and mud, and in the autumn banked up outside for warmth."[22]

All able bodies also assisted in planting a small crop of winter wheat. In terms of commerce, Wethersfield settlers had learned from Dutch reports of Indians coming down the River with canoes overflowing with furs. The Dutch, at first, felt there was more than enough trade available on the River for both European powers that they made aware all the trade opportunity.

Still, the planters were truly in a difficult situation. The great hardships of cold and hunger spawned with the first winter's arrival. Nevertheless, for the whole of that season, the Watertown planters, in little parties of a few families, continued to make additions to the little company of pioneers at Wethersfield. Oldham planted Wethersfield in 1634, and in 1635, near eighty men, women, and children arrived from Massachusetts to settle. And so, from this time the colony of Connecticut was recognized

Many would have perished if it had not been for the friendly Indians during these first few years. They gave maize to be dried and eaten during the difficult months. They also shared the fishing holes along the river. The greatest of all, nature, provided wild berries, wild birds, wild fish, herbs, nuts, and roots.

John Oldham, as the Bay agent, held peaceful trade with the Pequots in accordance with a treaty formed on November 7, 1634. He traded outside the Connecticut River during the year 1635, and returned to the Connecticut from Boston in April 1636.[23]

Wethersfield was known as Pyquaug to the Indians, and at first, was named Watertown by the planters. Soon thereafter, however, the settlement became Wethersfield. Providentially, "the Indians received [the whitemen] joyfully, and their sachems, Sehat of Poquonnuc, Arramament of Podunk, and the more famous Sowheag and Sequassen, sold land without stint or hesitation. Sequassen sold Hartford and the whole region westward, including the territories of the Tunxis."[24] However, the first Indian deeds of sale at Windsor, Hartford and Wethersfield were never preserved.

It was a new experience for everyone at hand and quickly turned difficult. By the first December famine began to set in with the cold. Father's measured out the bread and meat to each of his young, until both bread and meat were gone. Corn was bought in small quantities from the Indians, but these neighbors hadn't enough to spare[25]. Only a few hundred acres were cleared and the remainder was forest, wherein divers wondered how this land was to support them.

There was never grave concern until the massacre. Confidence rested in the dealings of fur, as there was a great interest for pelts in Wethersfield and abroad.

Vigorous labor on the cabins continued as they began setting up expeditions with trustworthy river Indians to secure fur relations along the river. Fear for the Indian neighbors didn't exist. The planters had no reason. They never had experienced problems to the north. Some men wanted to deal solely with the Massachusetts Bay Company, in which the Bay Colony in turn would ship out the goods directly to England as payment for colonial expenses. However, trade upriver to Springfield became the best route to achieve a rewarding enterprise.

William Pynchon who was one of the founders of that city established the earliest fur trade operation in Springfield in 1636. Pynchon had been a prominent eastern Massachusetts figure who had held a number of positions in the Massachusetts Bay government. In the 1630s he was one of the Bay's leading merchants whose commercial activities   included fur trade in Massachusetts Bay and Maine. William Pynchon rapidly cornered the Connecticut River Valley fur trade market. [The Massachusetts Historic Commission][26]

Success thereupon arose for those that chose to join in a partnership with William Pynchon upriver in Springfield. Agreements were made with sub-traders to collect fur from Wethersfield and other River Indians, and simply ship it up river or out into the Atlantic. Men would travel to and from Springfield often- a location where they could export all of their pelts. The timing was just right as Springfield propelled into the leading fur trade center upon the Connecticut River Valley.

      The location of Springfield assured its rapid growth as a fur trade center. The adjacent Connecticut River and nearby Westfield River provided access to natives of the middle Connecticut River and Hudson River valleys, and the Bay Path assured contact with the colonial settlements of eastern Massachusetts, particularly Boston. Thus William Pynchon and his son John had established and maintained regular trade contacts with Agawam, Norwottuck and Pocumtuck hunter trappers and middlemen. These natives acquired furs and pelts either by hunting or trapping in the uplands.

      From Springfield the native furs and pelts were transported to Boston by boat on the Connecticut River and along the Southern New England coast. These goods were then shipped on to England and Europe where they were prepared for sale in the European, English, and colonial markets. [The Massachusetts Historic Commission][27]

When the Indians first learned that the white men were willing to trade all sorts of wonderful items for a skin that was caught so easy as the beaver, they began to hunt and trap the animals with reckless abandon. There was an abundant supply of beaver at first, but the beaver population would quickly diminish. Beavers did not migrate and when the population within a wetland was all killed, they became extinct in that area.

      Success in Wethersfield was great early on as was the quantity of pelts, but a few years after they settled anger would begin to develop. Misunderstandings of agreements would take precedent. Maybe the planters should have been more conscious of the tension cultivated in the wilderness with the Indians.

With the arrival in Wethersfield, yes, peace was welcomed, first by the Wongunk tribe along the beautiful river. This same tribe was the first to introduce the availability of pelt.

The Confederacy of the Wongunks, also known as the Sequins, had many smaller bands related to them. The Wongunk's were a branch of the Mahicans of the upper northwest, who were pushed out of that region by the Mohawks. They moved into Wethersfield because the Nipmucks of the Massachusetts central hill country denied any entry into their country. The Pequots were also related to the Mahicans, but still oppressed the Wongunk's.

The River Indians in the Wethersfield area- known as the Wongunks- were led by their sachem Sequeen or Sowheag, whose son Sequassen was sachem to the Hartford Indians known as the Suckiaug. The Suckiaug of Hartford, the Wongunks or Sequins of Wethersfield, the Matianucks of Windsor, the Hockinums, living on the east side of the River, and the Podunks, all spread throughout the river coast. They were all considered River Indians. The tribes held bounds around Hartford and into Wethersfield. River tribes were willing to provide beaver skins, corn, and fertile land for the English settlers' new homes. In exchange, the settlers and their powerful guns could provide protection from the Pequots.

The Wethersfield Massacre

English land sales along the river promptly began when the planters arrived in Wethersfield, wherein Bay planters and the Wongunks had their agreements handled by qualified agents. Interpreters and witnesses for both parties were present. The sachem of the Wongunk tribe, Sowheag, added his mark if he agreed. At this time, the redmen felt they were getting the best of the bargain, as they retained rights to hunt and fish on the land.[28] For the Wongunks, alliance with the planters had become more favorable an option than paying an annual tribute to the Pequots.

The Wongunks, like other River tribes, had long resented the harsh domination that the Pequots held over them, and it was in hope of ending their subjection to the Pequots that the river tribes had openly welcomed the English. The group who settled Wethersfield, interestingly enough, left Massachusetts without a clergyman to lead them. Of all the townships belonging to the Connecticut Colony, Wethersfield seems from the first to have been most involved in difficulties, civil and ecclesiastical. The plantation had been commenced by a high-spirited and very excitable people, impatient of control, delighting in the most daring enterprises, and stimulated rather than alarmed at the dangers that harassed them.[29]

During this early period of settlement, there had been some murders of sea traders. These men were adventuring along the coasts or rivers, and being not sufficiently manned, and lacking caution, they became the easy victims to the Indians. But these, after all, seemed random cases in nature, isolated instances, having no special relation to one another, and therefore the murders did not arouse the fears of the Wethersfield community, who went on peacefully- planting their fields, raising their houses and getting to feel more and more at home in their New World.[30]

However civil the beginnings in Wethersfield hostility soon arose. Sowheag learned that his new English neighbors were no better than the Pequots. Either the settlers in Wethersfield didn't seem to understand the terms of the purchase agreement or they simply chose to ignore the arrangement. Misunderstanding occurred when Sowheag set up a wigwam in Wethersfield in early 1637, and as a result, was then driven out by force. In frustration the Wongunk chief thus turned to his former enemies, the Pequots, for assistance in resolving the matter.[31] "At first Sowheag turned to the English for protection against Sassacus, the Pequot Sachem; now he turned to Sassacus for protection against the English."[32] Sowheag would become the one to plant the seed for open warfare.

By this time, the River Indians in the vicinity of the Wethersfield Plantation—those Indians from whom the settlers had bought their land and with whom they were in daily contact—had so far proved friendly, and though recently there had been some disagreement with them, still there was no reason to consider them hostile.

The Pequots, conversely, had of late shown much restlessness and suspicion of the white man's presence among them. Yet no one in Wethersfield expected what was to occur. A record of the event was written the same day the massacre occurred:

> *On the morning of April 23, 1637 during the time of prosperous work, there fell, like lightning from a clear sky, a disaster so great that paralyzed the hearts and energies of the Wethersfield settlers. A party of Pequots, some say two hundred, came up the Connecticut River in canoes as far as The Island and, from that standpoint, watched through the forest for their opportunity to attack, probably in the early morning, upon the Wethersfield people who were at work in the meadows on the adjacent west bank of the river. The unfortunate settlers were clearing and preparing their lands there for the spring plowing, men and women being busy and unsuspicious of danger. They were suddenly surprised by the savages and in the quick disorder and struggle that ensued, six men and three women were killed and two maids were carried away. [Adams and Stiles]*

Henceforth, this is what transpired whilst the Pequots left Wethersfield with the two maids, and, furthermore, what ultimately happened to the captives:

> *Having done this, the savages left as fast as they had appeared. Thrilled with their performance, they attracted the attention of the garrison down the Connecticut River called Fort Saybrook, which they sailed past near the mouth of the River. They hoisted up poles in their canoes upon which they hung the clothes of their slain victims, mocking the sails of the white man's ships. There was nothing that could be done by the soldiers in the fort to*

rescue the two captive maidens, who could plainly be seen in the savage's canoes. Captain Lyon Gardiner in command of Fort Saybrook, did order a cannon to be discharged at the fleet of canoes, which came near putting the captives in even more danger than before.

I was told that the Dutch governor, in the most noble of all efforts, sent a sloop to Pequot to redeem the two English maidens, though it violated their peace with the Pequots. The sloop offered a lot for the maids' ransom, but nothing was accepted. Therefore the Dutch, who had many Pequots on board, kept six of them and with them, exchanged the Pequots for the two maids, who had no violence committed to them. [Adams and Stiles][33]

What occurred in Wethersfield is what we call the Wethersfield Massacre. The great irony in this mess is that the woman who chiefly saved those two maids from death was wife of Pequot sagamore Mononotto. The Pequot wife's humility later "attracted admiration" from the English. Nevertheless, imagine the fear within the two kidnapped girls, daughters of William Swaine. Much anger was to be felt toward the Indians, especially the Pequots, as the word spread that they were the offenders.

Sowheag's revenge against the settlers through the Pequots' invasion would force the young New England colonies into forceful action. It is a fact that actions of the Pequot before the massacre had the Bay already preparing for war against that tribe. Massachusetts had declared war upon the Pequots two weeks before the Wethersfield Massacre, but her forces hadn't yet taken the field. The Connecticut General Court hadn't even made a formal commitment to war, but suddenly provoked by the disaster in Wethersfield, the general court, on May 1st, 1637, voted for an offensive war against the Pequot.[34]

The Connecticut general court represented the little republic of less than three hundred and an excited session ensued subsequent to the massacre. It was filled with doubt and considerations for the survival of the colony. There was no fear within the General Court, which was comprised of the fifteen picked men, six magistrates and nine committee men- two magistrates and three commissioners from each of the three river towns. These men had the fate of the English throughout New England in their hands. The first written memorial of their doings is in the following words: "It is ordered that there shall be an offensive war against the Pequot, and there shall be ninety men levied out of the three plantations of Hartford, Wethersfield, and Windsor." [35]

It was as early as 1636 that the three river towns, Hartford, Windsor, and Wethersfield, had established a General Court, but it wasn't until 1637 when the court made their most momentous decision. It was felt that the Pequot raid on Wethersfield showed the need for a combined force. Under this General Court the first military conscription, the first levy of taxes and the first declaration of war took place. Thus the first raising of a company to attack the Indians took place in Connecticut. [36]

Although the three towns together contained no more than 250 inhabitants, the court ordered the enlistment of an army of ninety men, with forty-two to come from Hartford, thirty from Windsor, and eighteen from Wethersfield.

Each soldier was to provide himself with a pound of gunpowder, four pounds of shot, twenty bullets, and a musket for the trip downriver. A barrel of powder per man would be issued once the company reached the English Fort Saybrook. The planning for the invasion of the Pequot village was finalized by the force at the mouth of the river in neighboring Fort Saybrook.

As mentioned above, the Massachusetts Bay Colony made preparations to wage war against the Pequots before Connecticut did. The Bay's General Court on April 18, 1637, had authorized a levy of 160 men, passing an emergency tax measure to raise 160 pounds to pay some of the anticipated costs. But the court directed the magistrates to enlist the help of the Plymouth Colony in bearing the burden. Plymouth, however, felt they had reasons to not endorse the cost of the war, possibly because of the Bay Colony's earlier refusal to aid Plymouth in its struggle with the French in Maine, where in 1633 Plymouth's prosperous fur trade become short lived as their Maine post fell to the French.[37]

The Treaty of 1634

To understand Massachusetts necessity to declare war upon the Pequots before the Wethersfield massacre I must ask a couple questions: Why was the declaration of war against the Pequots being called for by the Massachusetts government prior to the Wethersfield Massacre? Why was the Pequot Tribe so violent toward the Wethersfield Settlers? Might the massacre have been part of a larger retaliation effort to obtain justice according to Indian custom? Was the invasion of the Pequot fort by the sanctioned Connecticut force, known as the Pequot War, necessary?

There were many factors, as with any war, which determined the invasion of the Pequot fort by our force. The Wethersfield Massacre simply expressed to the Connecticut colony the necessity to eliminate the Pequots. To the north, the necessity to declare war upon the Pequots by Massachusetts Bay was, in part, a result of the actions by the Pequots in retaliation to the invasion of their village in 1636 by a force led by John Endicott. This invasion was legally justifiable due to two previous murders committed by Indians, as well as the possible alliance between the Pequots and Narragansetts.

One of the murders by hands of Indians was of the founder of Wethersfield, John Oldham, who may be a larger part of why I lived in Wethersfield. The Block Island Indians killed him in 1636 and it was a great conflict to the Massachusetts Bay. However, there was a prior murder of a seaman that was committed by some Pequots, but this murder would receive a much greater retribution for the English than true justice called for. In 1633, the Pequots and Niantics killed a drunkard Englishman named John Stone, who was already unfavorable to the Massachusetts colony.

John Stone was killed in retaliation for the murder of the Pequot Sachem Tatobem, who was killed by the Dutch on the river. It is told that Sassacus's father, Tatobem, was lured aboard a Dutch vessel to trade, but was murdered. Thus, Sassacus, sought revenge, and when the next trading vessel arrived he boarded it and found the Captain's cabin. The ship was English, not Dutch, but because the Indians could not tell the Dutch from the English, the Pequots consequently murdered all of the Englishmen onboard.

Following these murders, a fear for the Pequot began to loom over Massachusetts Bay. In October 1636, following the murder of Oldham which was committed by a tribe not even of the Pequots, a plan for invasion of a Pequot village was prepared by Massachusetts Bay as a disciplinary expedition. The plan was to first strike the sub-tribe of Narragansett Indians on Block Island for their role in the murder of Oldham, and then the next blow was to be forced upon Pequots in their home territory

This was an unfortunate situation for the Pequots, they did not do much wrong. A different tribe had killed Oldham, and Captain Stone as you will see had already been banished from the Bay Colony for ill conduct. The Pequots committed Stone's murder in accordance with their retaliatory customs, not the way in which the white men would prosecute murder.

Stone would become more valuable dead than alive to the Bay as his murder had occurred during a time when the white men began a great interest in the rich Connecticut River land.

There were many seeking the supreme authority for the bounds held by the River Tribes- the Europeans consisting of the Dutch and the English, and the Indians, consisting of the Pequots and the Narragansetts. The English claimed, through right of discovery, grant from their monarch, and subsequent purchase of the Indians, the possession of most of the country, and have kept it ever since.[38] The Pequot Indians, on the other hand, who had claimed the valley earlier than the Europeans, claimed supremacy by right of conquest over the tribes living around the river whose right of discovery was best of all.

The Dutch briefly held a fortification on the river before the English and negotiated a commercial agreement with the Pequots concerning freedom of trade. "The territory purchased by the Dutch was to be freely used by Indians of all nations, and was to be a territory of peace. The hatchet was to be buried there. No warrior was to molest his enemy while within its bounds."[39] The Pequots bound themselves to respect the Dutch and allow all Indians, regardless of tribal affiliation, access to the Dutch trading post. The Dutch obviously sought Narragansett trade, who held an abundance of currency known as wampum. The Pequots quickly realized that their Narragansett rival, who was independent traders with the Dutch, could use the Europeans to drive them back out of their tributaries bounds.[40]

Thus, the peace declared in the Dutch-Pequot Agreement of 1633 would be short-lived. The Pequots, who guarded the river tribes rights against both the Narragansetts and the Dutch, felt proper in wanting to remove the Narragansetts from their tributaries' land in order to control trade. Thereupon great interest was held in eliminating the Narragansetts from encroaching on their territory.

The Pequots wouldn't allow a rival to challenge their livelihood upon the river, whereupon, in the fall, a group of Pequot warriors ambushed and killed several Narragansetts tributaries along the path toward the House of Good Hope, which had barely been completed. The Dutch felt this act broke their peace agreement made with the Pequot Sachem Tatobem.

The Pequots chose murder to show their dominance over the Narragansetts, wherein, the Dutch retaliation was immediate and severe. When the Pequot principal sachem, Tatobem, boarded a Dutch vessel to trade, he was seized and held for ransom. The Dutch informed his tribe that they would never again see their leader unless they pay a bushel of wampum to his abductors. The Pequots immediately sent the payment to the House of Good Hope and demanded Tatobem's freedom, but instead they received his corpse in return.

One large war party of the Pequots could have easily driven the Dutch from the Connecticut Valley following the murder of their sachem. Surprisingly though, Tatobem's murder didn't ignite a deadly assault on the tiny and exposed Dutch trading house. Despite the loss of a sachem, the Pequots didn't want to give up trade with the Europeans. They wanted to control trade, not end it.

In murder committed by someone outside their family, according to Pequot tradition, the tribe obtained retribution by killing the villain or someone of relation to justify the wrong. The act of retribution toward the Dutch for Tatobem's murder was committed through a band of Pequots accompanied by some western Niantics, but, regrettably, the Indians found victims who were to be English, not Dutch.

Pequots who later described the circumstances of Stone's murder, during a visit for aid in Boston in 1634, reported that Stone had first abducted two Indians near the mouth of the Connecticut River in territory occupied by the western Niantics. He then forced his captives to guide him upriver and intended to kidnap them for ransom. As Stone's ship anchored for the night, a band of twelve Indians boarded it and pretended to be interested in trade. While this Indian band diverted the crew above deck, the new Grand Sachem of the Pequots, Sassacus, visited the captain in his cabin. Stone, a drunk, had drank himself into a stupor and collapsed to his bunk. The new sachem split Stone's head with a hatchet and threw a blanket over his body. In the violence that followed, the Indians cornered the ship's crew in the kitchen, seized some loaded muskets, and fired into a supply of gunpowder, which exploded. They then killed the remainder of the crew, looted the cargo, and set the ship ablaze.

The Pequots may have thought nothing would result due to their revenge as it fit in their customary defense for avenging murder. Consequently, by the fall of 1634, Pequot control of the trade throughout the Connecticut valley was weakened. Their trade with the Dutch collapsed through the killings of the Narragansetts at the House of Good Hope and the assault on Stone's trading ship. They faced not only the hostility of the Dutch and their Indian neighbors to the east, but now an Englishman had been murdered.

The murder of Tatobem, therefore, marked the beginning of disorder for the Pequots. Tatobem previously already had many of his Pequot allies and river tribe tributaries withdrawing from his authority, and his son and successor, Sassacus, was unable to hold together even those who were supposedly Pequot. It was Uncas, a Pequot exile, who was the great force that divided the Pequot and unified the white man with the Mohegan to ultimately bring the Pequot to an end.

Uncas the great; the only redman who held such undaunted self-preservation whilst obtaining an advantage over his kinsmen comparable to no other native. How was this possible? Through a most slanderous and untrustworthy nature! I swear to you kind reader, the most ill precedent will haunt this land forever.

"In person, Uncas is said to have been a man of large frame and great physical strength. His courage could never be doubted, for he displayed it too often and too clearly in war. (...) No sachem, however, was ever more fond of overcoming his enemies by stratagem and trickery. He seemed to set little value upon the glory of vanquishing in war, compared with the advantages it brought him in the shape of booty, and new subjects, and wider hunting grounds. He favored his own men and was therefore popular with them; but all others who fell under his power he tormented with continual exactions and annoyances. His nature was selfish, jealous and tyrannical; his ambition was grasping, and unrelieved by a single trait of magnanimity. He was [at the time of the Pequot War], it is probable, in the prime and vigor of early manhood."[41]

Uncas was the sachem of the Mohegans, a Pequot tributary through intermarriage. He claimed birth by both Mohegan and Pequot sachemships. Even as it was the daughter of Tatobem, the Pequot Sachem, who had married Uncas, the Mohegan had still quarreled with his father-in-law. Begging and obtaining Tatobem's and then Sassacus's forgiveness, Uncas received a pardon from the existing sachem and was allowed to return to his village at least five separate times.

Whilst exiled among the Narragansetts many of his his Mohegan warriors fled with him and remained in Narragansett country. In this manner he lost many of his followers and his land. "His territory was so small, and his men so few, that he was unable to make a grand hunt alone."

"[Other] Mohegans, therefore, and, according to one author, fifty of them, took up their residence on the Connecticut River, chiefly in the township of Hartford. (...) It is possible, also, that some of these men were not native

Mohegans, but river Indians, who had attached themselves to an adventurous and warlike chief like Uncas, and had thus acquired a title to the name Mohegoneak. Uncas, himself, probably lived in this part of the country, as it is not at all likely that he would be allowed to continue at Mohegan. Mohegan was the ancient burying place of the Pequot sachems; and would Sassacus, the descendant and representative of that race of heroes, allow their graves to be polluted by the foot of one who had made himself an alien to his tribe?"[42]

Subsequent to Tatobem's murder, Uncas saw a chance to succeed him as Pequot Grand Sachem. To become Grand Sachem, the candidate needed to be a member of one of a small number of prominent families- hence Tatobem's son Sassacus was chosen after the murder. Uncas denied acceptance of the Grand Sachem and sponsored the removal of Sassacus. His efforts didn't work, and once again Uncas fled, but would return and humble himself to the Pequot sachem, as he wanted to live in his own country again. Sassacus granted the request on condition that Uncas would remain loyal, terms which Uncas agreed to, but soon again broke his oath. However, this crusade against Sassacus would slowly gain impetus.

One reason for Uncas's rebellious nature may have been the tribute the Pequots sought from the Mohegans. Pequot tributaries remained greatly distanced from the Pequots because of the tribute sought. For example, it was Sassacus's challenge to Mohegan hunting grounds that eventually drove their members away, and through this pressure by the Pequots, Uncas also began winning over some of the River Indian Bands also unfavorable to the Pequots terms. All these factors led Uncas to position himself in a war that would enable him to replace Sassacus as Pequot Grand Sachem. Thus, the Pequots' destructive force threatening the colonies existence may have been exaggerated, as Pequot power was in decline.[43]

Nevertheless, Stone's murder had begun the momentum against the Pequots. Uncas' unconfirmed tales also further strengthened the anger toward the Pequots, as exaggerations would strengthen colonial fear whether the statements were true or false. Colonists accordingly accepted the statements from their faithful friend.

Originally, the Pequots had sought early intervention amongst the English. In 1634, the Pequots sought Englishmen for aid against the Dutch and Indian rivals, but most importantly, they sought some portion of trade. Sassacus turned to Boston. Not to mention, shortly after Stone's murder, the Pequots sent a trading party to the House of Good Hope and within a short time, the Dutch killed a Pequot with a blast of cannon shot. Now, not only were the Pequots threatened by the Narragansetts, but they no longer held tidings with the Dutch. Aside from seeking protection, they were also becoming very dependent on foreign trade. The Pequots, though, didn't think anything of an English ill will toward their tribe after killing Stone. Conversely, "The English held themselves free from any peace with the Pequots as a people guilty of shedding English blood."[44]

In October of that year, one Pequot messenger arrived in Boston and made a proposal for peace.

> The messenger brought a present for Deputy Governor Ludlow from his sachem. He laid down before the governor two bundles of sticks, indicative of the number of beaver and other skins which the Pequots would give the English, and promised also a large amount of wampum, and therefore requested a league between his people and the pale faces. Ludlow accepted the presents thus made to himself, and gave him in return a moose coat of equal value for the Pequot chieftain; but the

governor kindly told the messenger, when he took leave of him, that Sassacus must show his respect for the English by sending deputies of greater quality than he was, and enough of them, before a treaty could be made with the colonies. [Robert Boodey Caverly][45]

"The messenger, rather humbled in being the bearer of his own disgrace at a foreign court, [was dismissed without answer and] seems to have done his errand faithfully, for in due time two Pequot counselors appeared, carrying presents, and of character requested to the business in hand. Deputy Governor Ludlow said he was not against peace, but that there were some old scores to be settled between the two powers."[46]

A fortnight afterward, otter skin, beaver coats, and skins of wampum, accompanied a new group of Pequot envoys to the residence of Roger Ludlow. The magistrate would however declare the gift inadequate and in turn request four hundred fathoms of wampum, forty beaver skins, and thiry otter skins. The English sought a substantial amount of tribute for their hand in trade and partnership. Another major condition was delegated-the Pequots were expected to deliver the murderers of Stone. It became understood also that if those men in Massachusetts chose to plant in Connecticut the tribe was to relinquish their rights to the English, which encouraged the English to plant in Connecticut. The English would sign a treaty with the tribe in which Sassacus's envoys made their marks- a bow and arrow and a hand on the document- but there came many uncertainties.

Yes a peace and friendship briefly formed being that the English " should be at peace with them, and as friends to trade with them, but not to defend them," as there was no intention by the Bay Colony for military assistance.[47] The Pequot envoys were proposed a trade agreement, yet the English asked such a high price for trade and friendship that the Pequot ambassadors were not entitled to accept any tributary request. The English demands failed acceptance when the Pequot Envoys returned home and presented the terms to Sassacus and his council. The treaty demands far exceeded anything Sassacus was willing to send forth. The Pequots would now become aware of the ill feelings the English held because of Stone's death.[48]

The agreement reached at Boston would fall short of Pequot hopes and expectations. "The English were to send them a vessel immediately, not to defend them, but to trade with them."[49] Magistrates, also, declined to pledge themselves to defend the Pequots, even with the understanding that the English could use as much land as they needed in the country of the Connecticut, provided they would form a plantation. The Pequots too were to give them all possible assistance in their tidings. Furthermore, the magistrates of Massachusetts Bay were already of the conclusion that they would not assist the Pequots in any future Indian trade war, as the Narragansetts not only were more powerful but were also closer to the Bay settlements. The Pequots thus failed to find a European confederate in Boston.

Sequentially, through the treaty's terms, in 1636-1637 more settlers came to Connecticut, "bringing their wives and children, and the Indians received them with joy. The sachems of the Poquonnucs and Podunks, as well as Sowheag or Sequin of the Wangunks, willingly sold them all the land they could use. Sequassen, sachem of the Hartford Tribe, sold them Hartford and the whole region westward, including the territories of the Tunxis, as far as the country of the Mohawks. Nassecown of Windsor, was so taken in love with the coming of the English that, for some small matter, he turned over to them all the land on the eastern side of the Connecticut to which he laid claim."[50]

A most important Puritan requirement for a treaty of peace with the Pequot would ultimately become the surrender of those who were guilty of Captain Stone's death, albeit the Pequots knew Stone held an unrighteous manner and was worthy of death. Those in Boston, had no reason to mourn or seek retribution for Stone's murder, as he was banished from the colony for unfavorable conduct. Massachusetts Bay, however, came to realize in time that Stone was worth more dead than alive. Stone's reported death at the time seemed to be petty retribution for the Pequots, and his death would lay dormant with no punishment for two years. Insistence prevailed, nevertheless, as it became of the greatest necessity to discipline the Pequots.

The treaty request by the magistrates for the men who killed Stone and his crew was more than simple Puritan justice. Some of the murderers were not Pequots. The other Indians involved belonged to the Western Niantics, who were easily confused with the Pequots. As the Bay demands for the killers were part of the treaty, it formed a situation the Pequots weren't accustomed to. If the Pequots seized the persons of the Niantic tribe involved with the murder and delivered them to Massachusetts, it would have violated Indian custom and honor. Thus, the Pequots would refuse to make decisions of which outside sachems hadn't held knowledge, but most importantly, their sachem Sassacus was a main actor in the murder of Stone. The Pequots didn't threaten to stand in the way if Massachusetts should send its own men to do Puritan justice on the Western Niantics, but Sassacus wouldn't be surrendered.

This treaty conference satisfied both the Bay magistrates and the Pequot ambassadors initially, though in time, the treaty would cause more harm than good. The colony would send no vessels for a long time to trade with the Pequots. It was John Oldham who would finally trade with the tribe along the Connecticut shore in 1636. The trade mission was a success, but Oldham would be killed when he stopped on Block Island thereafter quite possibly because he traded with the Pequots.

Ultimately the treaty failed, the gifts received by the English from the Pequot envoys in Boston would eventually be returned to the Pequots at a later time, which was a show of great disrespect. Nevertheless, the Pequot land concessions would never be returned. English migration thus swept into the Pequot tributaries land, which were the bounds of the River Indians. One area along the River particularly became of great interest for the English. The home of the Pequots neighboring the mouth of the Connecticut River held a great value. Control by the English of a main entrance by water into and through central Connecticut and into Springfield, Massachusetts became a subject of great importance. An English plantation there would have an effect on both the Dutch who held the region prior and the Pequots who considered the area home.

Fort Saybrook

In the course of the year 1630, the famous Plymouth Company, a corporation that initiated the New England grants, granted the whole territory of what was subsequently called the colony of Connecticut, and much more, to Robert Rich, Earl of Warwick. The patent confirmed this grant to him from Charles I in that same year, and expressed the assignment to the proprietors with a description of the boundaries.

On the 19th of March of the year 1632, Robert Rich, Earl of Warwick and the president of the Council for New England, executed under his hand and seal the grant since known as the old patent of Connecticut, wherein he granted his existing territory to Saye, and Sele, and Brooke, and ten of their friends.[51] The grantees however did little about their rights until 1635, when the patentees of Connecticut Lord Saye and Sele, Lord Brooke, and their other associates, commissioned John Winthrop, Jr., to be governor of that territory for a year. His commission included constructing a fort and settlement at the mouth of the river.[52]

The idea for Saybrook first arose when two of the few Puritans in the English House of Lords, Saye and Sele and Brooke had constant reminders that they might soon need a haven abroad in order for safety outside of England. Thus they had granted to other Puritans a small tract of land around the Connecticut River, which would produce a fortification at the mouth.

Recruiters in England during 1635 recruited a company of men for erecting a fort and building houses. The fort construction also brought responsibility on the governor of the colony for securing at least 1,000 to 1,500 acres for the fort, food production, and dwellings.

After being sent to England to carry recruits, the ship Abigail returned on October 6, 1635, and arrived in Boston with John Winthrop Jr. The Abigail carried with her the commission from Lord Saye and Sele and Lord Brook, to begin a plantation in Connecticut, and make Winthrop Jr. governor there.

In March 1636, Lieutenant Lion Gardener arrived for his command at the mouth of the Connecticut, and would construct Fort Sayebrook. Within the fort's grounds were a small freshwater pond and space for both a garden and an orchard. Gardener also erected a wooden hall subdivided into living quarters, as well as a barracks and small storehouse. The placement of the two cannons on Fort Hill and a ten-foot-high mound within the palisade allowed Gardener command upon the treacherous, sand-clogged channel at the river's mouth. The plantation was named Saybrook in honor of the two prominent patentees.

Fort Saybrook, "at the mouth of it, was a place of a very good soil, good meadow, all sorts of good wood, timber, variety of fish of several kinds, fowl in abundance, geese, ducks, deer, and squirrels, which were as good as English rabbits. Its location was on a fair river, fit for harboring of ships, and bounds with rich and godly meadows. This lied thirty miles from the upper plantations on the river Connecticut."[53]

The ever-changing state of the Indian on the river through all the land advance, along with the resulting anger that intensified through circumstances unfamiliar to the Pequots, forced the whole region into a most unstable state. Fort Saybrook, soon after its formation in 1636-37, was troubled by rumors of a Pequot attack. The Pequots, additionally, had made no intention to pay the full wampum tribute mandated in the treaty agreement at Boston in 1634, nor did they fulfill the English demands that they apprehend and deliver the murderers of Captain John Stone and his crew.

When John Oldham pressed them on those matters, the Pequots replied that the tribal elders hadn't approved the treaty, whereupon Oldham declared them a very false people. There were numerous sources throughout the valley that intensified rumors of a Pequot uprising. English suspicions and anxieties about Pequot motives were steadily increasing, especially through reports from friendly Indians who warned of Pequot plans to destroy the plantations.

A Plymouth Indian agent at Windsor named Jonathon Brewster sent a letter to John Winthrop Jr. (acting Governor of the Connecticut Colony) reporting that Uncas told him that the murder of Stone had been planned in a Pequot council of war and that Sassacus orchestrated the affair:

To the worll John Withrop Govr at the mouth of the river Coniticutt (...)

Woncase (Uncas), sent me word that upon the 23rd of May of last, Sasocuse, chiefe sachem of the Pequents, with his brother, Sacowauein, and the old men held consultation one day, and most of one Night, about cutting off of our Plymouth Barke, being then in their harbor weakly manned, who resolving thereupon appointed 80 men in Armes beforc Day to surprise hir;

but it pleased the over Rueling Power of god to hinder them, for as soone as these bloody executioners arose out of Ambush with their canoes, they discerned her under sayle with fayre winde returning home. (...)

I understand likewise by the same messenger (Uncas) that the Pequents have some mistrust that the English will shortly come against them, and therefore out of desperate madnesse doe (the Pequots) threaten shortly to sett both upon Indians, and English jointly. Further by the same Sachem, I am enformed that Sasocuse with his Brother, upon consultation with their own men, was an actor in the death of Stone, and these men being 5 of the principal actors alive, 3 living at Pequent, and 2 at Ma ham le cake...

Yours in all love and service
Jonathon Brewster.
Plimouth House in Cunitecutt:
This 18th of June 1636

In Uncas's statement it appears that the Pequots were certain of orchestrating an English attack. Reaction to the Pequot threat justified the river towns' prior requirements to hold training days and deliver powerful speeches. A state of preparedness was considered to be that of greatest necessity, and to that end it was regulated in the first year's records, June 7th 1636, that every man must have ready for the constables' inspection once a month a gun, two pounds of powder, and twenty bullets, or be fined ten shillings, and there must be monthly training. No firearms should pass to natives under any circumstances. [The Pequot] could only rely on the knife and tomahawk, arrow, and ambush.[54]

The Pequots were likewise alarmed by rumors of an impending English attack on them that they were too preparing for war. The Pequots fully honored their promise concerning English settlement within Connecticut, but their failure to obey the more demanding provisions of the 1634 treaty developed deep suspicions that Indians were the devil's agents. "Indian diplomacy apparently did not require promptness in fulfillment."[55]

At first, the distance between Puritan and Pequot territory prevented immediate intercourse on the matter. Yet once English migration into Connecticut expanded into Saybrook, renewed efforts were made to secure Pequot submission to Puritan demands. The interaction between the Puritan and Pequot would also lead to many more misunderstandings.

In Saybrook space between the Puritans and Pequots didn't exist. The rumors of the Pequot planning an invasion against Fort Saybrook alarmed the authorities in Boston as well as Connecticut Governor John Winthrop Jr. Winthrop would thus become informed of Governor Vane's ultimatum from the Massachusetts Bay. In early July 1636, Governor Vane notified John Winthrop, Jr., that he had been commissioned by the Bay Colony to investigate Pequot conduct and to secure both the surrender of the murderers of Stone and the full wampum payment discussed in 1634. Winthrop's instructions requested that he first begin by asking the Pequot's Principal Sachem, in a civil manner, for a meeting to discuss central matters. Winthrop's instructions were to threaten war if he could not secure Pequot submission.[56] The Pequot, though, had no intention of paying the full wampum tribute requested in the treaty agreement in Boston in 1634, nor were they going to hand over the murderers of Stone.[57]

In Saybrook, Lieutenant Gardener was dismayed by the Massachusetts Governor's intentions to pressure the Pequots. He exclaimed to the commissioners from Boston, "I know you will keep yourselves safe in the Bay, but myself, with these few, you will leave at the stake to be roasted, or for hunger to be starved; we being so few in the River. They must consider that there were only twenty-four people at the fort, men, women, boys, and girls, and not food for more than two months, unless we saved our corn field, which could not possibly be if they came to war, for it is two miles from our home."

Gardener later claimed that Winthrop and his commissioners promised him that they would do their utmost to make an effort to persuade the Massachusetts authorities to resist from war for a year or two, until Saybrook could be better provided for it.

If Sassacus wouldn't give in to any of the demands within the treaty's terms, the colonial emissary's declaration to the tribe was to be that the Bay would take Pequot lives, not their presents. Thus the Pequot sachem was called for, to come to Saybrook. An unnamed Pequot representative spoke with Winthrop through an interpreter in July 1636, and the presents—otter skin coats, beaver, and skins of wampum—that were presented to the Boston magistrates in 1634 were returned sorely against Gardener's will. The return of the presents was practically a declaration of war by the English. Having placed Gardener and his garrison in jeopardy by provoking the Pequots, John Winthrop Jr. then left Saybrook, disregarding his promise to return promptly to his duties there.

Several days after Winthrop's departure, an Indian named Cocommithus appeared at the gates of Fort Saybrook. In fluent English, he explained that he had once lived at Plymouth but had joined the Pequots and now came bearing a message from Sassacus that the Pequots held two of the English horses and wished for trade. The Grand Sachem, despite the previous ultimatum, wanted trade with Saybrook. Lion Gardener of Saybrook would penne his decision to proceed in trade with the Pequots:

Mr. Steven Winthrop would go to Pequot with
trucking cloth and all other trading ware, for they knew
that we had a great cargo of goods of Mr. Pincheon's, and
Mr. Steven Winthrop had the disposing of it. And he said
that if he would come he might put off all his goods, and the
Pequot Sachem would give him two horses that had been
there a great while. So I sent the Shallop, with Mr. Steven
Winthrop, Sergeant Tilly, and Thomas Hurlbut and three
men more, charging them that they should ride in the
middle of the river, and not go ashore until they had done
all their trade, and that Mr. Steven Winthrop should stand
in the hold of the boat, having their guns by them, and
swords by their sides, the other four to be, two in the fore
cuddie, and two in aft, being armed in like manner, that so
the out of the loop-holes might clear the boat, if they were
by the Pequots assaulted; and that they should let but one
canoe come aboard at once, with no more but four Indians
in her, and when she had traded than another, and that
they should lie no longer there than one day, and at night
to go out of the river, two of them go ashore to help the
horses in, and the rest stand ready with their guns in their
hands, if need were, to defend them from the Pequots, for I
durst not trust them. [Lion Gardener]

It seemed reasonable for those at Saybrook that Sassacus
had taken in two English horses and would return them if the
English would send a trading party to the Pequots, yet, upon
their return to Saybrook after the trade expedition to the
Pequots, Gardener was angered to learn that his men hadn't
done what he ordered. With Saybrook's men sailing into the
harbor, the Pequots didn't seem aggressive and were hesitant
to board the shallop in the manner Gardener specified. The
Pequot's still had Tatobem's death aboard a Dutch ship and the
threats of revenge for Stone's murder in mind and did not

board the English shallop. Two of the Englishmen therefore went ashore. One of the men entered the sachem's wigwam not far from the shore. Wincumbone, the sachem's wife, was present in the wigwam and made signs for the English to leave, as if they would cut off his head; which, when the Englishman recognized this, he drew his sword and sprinted to the others. They then boarded the shallop as the abundance of Indians immediately came to the water-side and called them to come ashore. Instead, the traders immediately set sail and returned to Saybrook. Upon Gardener hearing the result, he assumed the Pequots planned for Saybrook's destruction.

The Invasion of Block Island and The Pequot

In 1636 another murder would occur, but this time the killers were not Pequots. In late July 1636, John Oldham visited Saybrook to trade with Gardener and then with the Pequots. He sold a few items to Lieutenant Gardener which cost five pieces. He then set sail for the final time toward Block Island accompanied by two Narragansett Indians and two English servant boys.

On July 29, another trader, John Gallop, happened to be on a trade mission to Long Island in a small bark but was brought toward Block Island because of a change in wind. Near the island, he spotted a pinnace at anchor, which he knew was Oldham's. As Gallop came closer he saw that the deck was filled with fourteen Indians. He and his men pursued the scene and began firing with his only two muskets at the Indians on the deck. Gallop then rammed the pinnace, frightening the Indians so that six jumped out.

Gallop continued to damage Oldham's ship and five more Indians jumped off into the sea and drowned. With the fleeing of so many Indians, Gallop and his companions boarded Oldham's ship. One Indian appeared from a hatch and surrendered. He was tied up and thrown into the hold. Then another surrendered. Gallop, fearing their skill to untie themselves, had one of the two Indian captives thrown, still bound, into the sea. Gallop and his men then searched the ship. They found the body of Oldham hidden stark naked, his head cleft to the brains, and his hands and legs cut as if they had been cutting them off. The corpse was still warm. After burying Oldham at sea, Gallop then unloaded what remained of Oldham's cargo, took his sails, and tried to tow his ship. But with night coming and the wind rising, they let it go and the wind carried her to the Narragansett shore.

The murderers belonged to the Block Island Indians who were affiliated to the Eastern Niantics, themselves tributaries to the Narragansetts and not the Pequots. A short time after Oldham's murder, "three Narragansetts appeared in Boston with a message from Canonicus, their head sachem- two of these men had been with Oldham. The sachem, in the message written for him by Roger Williams, denied that any member of his tribe had participated in the crime. From the one Narragansett who had not been with Oldham, however, the colony authorities got, either by force or willingly, a different story. He stated that the Narragansett sachems, except for Canonicus and Miantinomo, were aware [of] the murder, that they had plotted to kill Oldham because he was trading with the Pequots.

It was also alleged by the Narragansett envoy who visited Boston after Oldham's death that the two Narragansett Indians who sailed with Oldham and joined him in Boston participated in the fatal assault on Oldham. The magistrates were enraged by that revelation but refrained from arresting the two presumed villains because they were sent as messengers from Canonicus and were therefore entitled to diplomatic immunity. The next day Governor Vane of Massachusetts Bay wrote to Canonicus. He informed the sachem that he suspected his Indian envoys of involvement in Oldham's murder and that he had refrained from arresting them because they were on a diplomatic mission, but that now he expected the Narragansetts to send them back to Boston for investigation.

Miantonomi also sought to deflect English wrath and suggested that Oldham's murderers had taken refuge with the Pequots. It became understood that all sachems of the Narragansetts, except Canonicus and Miantonomi, organized Oldham's death, yet nevertheless, "the Massachusetts Bay Colony accused the Pequots of harboring Oldham's murderers, and of having participated in the crime. The only evidence they could possibly have had for this rash accusation was that the Pequots had harbored other killers, as was the case of Captain Stone."[58] The Narragansetts also sent word that they had recovered and would return near one hundred fathoms of wampum and other goods of Mr. Oldham's. The Bay Colony discovered that three of the seven Indians that had drowned after participating in this grave crime were Narragansett sachems. While the Bay didn't hold Canonicus or Miantonomi responsible, the Narragansetts were to surrender all those who played a role in the murder.

There would be no decisive measures taken by the Narragansetts to revenge the death of Captain Oldham, whereupon Bay Colony officials subsequently took action. They also took into account the Pequots' refusal to obey the renewed demand that the terms of the treaty of 1634 be honored by payment of wampum accompanied with surrender of the murderers of Stone. The magistrates interpreted both Oldham's murder and Pequot noncompliance as evidence of an

Indian uprising. One of the greatest colonial follies now lay ahead.

Rather than waiting for any more Indian outbreaks of violence, the Puritans decided to eliminate the savages before they struck and threatened the new plantations. The Bay Colony believed that a preventative strike would secure their safety, and, thus, the Indians would become terrified into obedience by the example of violence towards those who had murdered Englishmen.

The governor and council of the Massachusetts Bay Colony consulted with the colony's clergy about doing justice upon the Indians for the death of Mr. Oldham. Assured that the Lord would smile upon a raid, the Bay Colony sent off a force of ninety men, to Block Island, under the command of John Endecott and Captain John Underhill, who then were the military trainers in the Colony. The military commission also called for the Pequots to surrender all who had a part in the Stone murder, the Oldham murder, and other murders during the recent past. They also intended to bring back women and children as slaves or hostages.

The relationship between Pequot and Puritan was no longer one of a mutual understanding through a treaty. Endicott's orders in 1636 were to take possession of Block Island by force, kill all of its adult male inhabitants, and enslave their women and children. After punishing the Block Islanders, Endecott was to sail to the Pequot village near the mouth of the river, demand the surrender of the murderers of Capt. Stone and other English, exact from the Pequots a payment of damages to the colony of a thousand fathoms of wampum, and take some Pequot children as hostages to assure the tribe's future good behavior. If the Pequots refused to supply those children for shipment to Boston, they were to be taken by force.

Endicott's accompanying force consisted of ninety soldiers who were all volunteers. They served under the command of two captains, John Underhill and Nathaniel Turner. Accompanied by two Indian guides, Endecott's little army embarked in three pinnaces on August 22, 1636. Reaching Block Island just before dusk, the ships encountered rough waves and the landing proved difficult. An Indian walking the Block Island shore saw the English party, while the other warriors were hidden behind the embankment near the shore. Fifty or sixty able fighting men, with arrows notched, awaited the English landing.

The men in the first detachment struggled through the pounding surf toward shore to hit the beach, while the Block Islanders began to shoot their arrows. Other detachments were unable to land and jumped overboard. They waded through the shallow but rough waters to the beach and a few men were left behind to guard the boats. Once on firm ground, the Bay Company began firing at the Indians. As bullets flew over their heads, the Block Island warriors quickly fled and were not to be found during the two days Endicott's party remained on the island.

The island contained two Indian villages, which the war party found deserted. Endicott's men saw little action on Block Island. Although they spent the day on the island, putting cornfields and wigwams to the torch, Endicott's troops weren't able to kill and enslave Indians as ordered, as the Block Islanders were hidden very well. Leaving the blazing village, Endecott and his men travelled through narrow and overgrown paths in search of the tribe, but the natives remained invisible. Finally, in anger, Endicott admitted he could not find them, and then gathered his forces at the close of the second day of the campaign.

They then sailed away from Block Island toward the mouth of the Connecticut River and stopped at the small

Saybrook Fort, where they would stay four days because of poor weather. The few men under the command of Gardener joined Endicott's force before that company travelled to the second destination of this campaign-the Pequot village.

The brief stop at Saybrook fort concluded and Endicott and the force then sailed along the coast. They passed the domain of the Western Niantics, and the tribesmen shouted from the shore, "What cheer Englishmen? What do you come for?" When the Indians ashore got no answer, they became alarmed and cried, "Are you angry, Englishmen? Will you kill us? Do you come to fight?"[59] The Indians, at first, hoped that they had come to trade. The English, however, remained silent and dropped their anchor in the mouth of the Pequot River, in the center of Pequot country. The Indian greetings met with no response and their once welcoming mood changed. That evening, as the fleet remained anchored at the mouth of the Pequot River, the Pequots and their western Niantic allies stayed on the shore as a lookout having made fire on both sides of the river, they feared the war party would land during the night.

Early in the morning after the all-night anchorage in Pequot River, an elder Pequot statesman paddled out to Endecott's shallop by canoe to inquire why the English remained in the water. Aboard Endicott's boat, the elder Pequot sagamore requested the reason for the visit. The Puritan officers informed him that the governors of the Bay sent them and demanded the heads of those persons who had killed Englishmen. To their surprise, the Pequot elder responded with a confession: The Pequots, he admitted, killed Stone. He told the English it was a just act of retribution, for Sassacus had intended to avenge the death of his own father. Even with Tatobem kidnapped by the Dutch and after his kinsmen had paid the ransom demanded for his life, the Europeans betrayed all decent custom and put the Grand

Sachem to death. "Who," the Pequot elder cried, "could blame us for avenging so cruel a murder?"

The elder Pequot representative justified Stone's murder; "We know not that any of ours have slain any English. True it is, saith he, we have slain such a number of men; but consider the ground of it. Not long before the coming of these English into the river, there was a certain vessel that came to us in way of trade. We used them well, and traded with them, and took them to be such as would not wrong us in the least matter. But our sachem or prince coming aboard, they laid a plot how they might destroy him; which plot discovereth itself by the event, as followeth. They keeping their boat aboard, and not desirous of our company, gave us leave to stand hallooing ashore, that they might work their mischievous plot. But as we stood they called to us, and demanded of us a bushel of wampam-peke. This they demanded for his ransom. This peal did ring terribly in our ears, to demand so much for the life of our prince, whom we thought was in the hands of honest men, and we had never wronged them. But we saw there was no remedy; their expectation must be granted, or else they would not send him ashore, which they promised they would do, if we would answer their desires. We sent them so much aboard, according to demand, and they, according to their promise, sent him ashore, but first slew him. This much exasperated our spirits, and made us vow a revenge. Suddenly after came these captains with a vessel into the river, and pretended to trade with us, as the former did. We did not discountenance them for the present, but took our opportunity and came aboard. The sachem's son, Sassacus, succeeding his father, was the man that came into the cabin of Captain Stone, and Captain Stone having drunkmore than did him good, fell backwards on the bed asleep. The sagamore took his opportunity, and having a little hatchet under his garment, therewith knocked him in the head." [John Underhill][60]

The English objected, but the Pequot representative added that the Pequots thought that Stone was a partner in the murder of Tatobem, "for we distinguish not between the Dutch and the English, but took them to be one nation, and therefore we don't feel that we wronged you, for they slew our king, and thinking these captains to be of the same nation and people of those that slew him, made us choose this revenge."

The English commanders may have respected the elder for coming aboard, but they still accused him of being a liar. They argued the Pequots could easily tell an Englishman from a Dutchman, as they have experienced both nations. With an increase in anger, the Puritan commanders rejected the explanation, declaring that if they were not given immediately the heads of those persons that have slain their own, they would attack. The Pequot representative calmly responded, "Understanding the ground of your coming, I will entreat you to give me liberty to go ashore, and I shall inform the body of the people what your intent and resolution is, and if you will stay on board, I will bring you a sudden answer." The English did grant permission for the elder to go ashore. The Pequot also asked the English not to come ashore until a conference was held on the matter.

Endicott, wary of the elder Pequot's true intentions upon reaching shore, disregarded the request to stay offshore and immediately landed his forces in armor and full battle array. At once, they were lined up in military order. The elder seeing the English land their forces, came pleading not to advance any closer, but stand in a valley. Suspecting an ambush, Endicott marched the soldiers up to a hill.

The English saw that between the lower point they had stood and the Pequot encampment there stood a small hill which the Indians could use to their advantage. Instead of holding a disadvantage, the English chose to move to gain an advantage, and Endicott marched his troops to the higher ground. Soon after they had taken possession of the hill, the elder reappeared, joined by three hundred men who surrounded the English. However, most of the men were unarmed. Some of the Pequots recognized the Saybrook troops and conversed with them. The Pequots told them there was no one there to answer the war party's demands. The elder told them that neither of the princes were home because they had gone to Paumanok [Long Island], so no tribal business could be conducted.

The Pequots cleverly delayed any battle by means of conversation for an hour or so, while in the meantime, they managed to have their wives, children, and most of their belongings sent out of the plantation. Some Pequots were standing remotely off and did begin to laugh at the English for their patience. Endicott finally became impatient and he told the Indians, "Begone, Begone! You have dared the English to come and fight with you, and now we are ready." Thus the Indians retreated and were chased by Endicott who ordered his soldiers not to open fire. The Pequots, feeling secure, laughed and let arrows fly, but hit none. The whites opened fire and killed one, but the rest of the Pequots scattered out of range with their families and belongings secured. Endicott, on the other hand, was furious at being outsmarted by the Pequots.

Again, as with Block Island, Endicott found himself reduced to an infuriating hunt for fractional bands. The Pequots took occasional potshots from rocks and thickets.[61] Marching into the village, Endicott and his men set fire to the wigwams and the corn harvest and dug up and destroyed the goods that the Pequots had buried.

Now the English had truly started a war with the invasion of the Pequot Village. The unlucky expedition of John Endicott was soon followed by months of violent events, as the wolves were now roused.

The first attack was made upon the Saybrook Fort, to which place some of the corn taken from the Pequot village had been transported. "Perhaps the Pequots reasoned as the ministers and magistrates of Massachusetts had done with the murders of Stone and Oldham- they who shared the plunder were responsible for the bloodshed."

> The Connecticut plantation, understanding the disrespect of the enemy to now be so great, sent down a certain number of soldiers, under the conduct of Captain John Mason, to strengthen the [Saybrook] fort. The enemy had began hovering about the fort, continually took notice of the supplies that were come, and forebore drawing near it as before; and letters were immediately sent to the Bay, to that right worshipful gentleman, Master Henry Vane, for a speedy supply to strengthen the fort. For assuredly without supply suddenly came, in reason all would be lost, and fall into the hands of the enemy. This was the trouble and perplexity that lay upon the spirits of the poor garrison. Upon serious consideration, the governor and council sent forth in February 1637 the following year, Captain John Underhill, with twenty armed soldiers, to supply the necessity of those distressed persons, and to take the government of that place for the space of three months. [John Underhill][62]

Pequot Retribution

My knowledge on the facts of Endicott's failed invasion have come from various works. Sympathy increased for the redmen with nearly every tale I read, once the occurrence that preceded the premeditation was discovered. It was not fair that the colonies were rousing the Pequots into war. Early in October 1636, an incident transpired, which was an indication of what the colonists would now continually face at the hands of the Pequots.

As five men belonging to the Saybrook garrison were carrying home hay from the meadows, the Pequots concealed themselves in the tall grass, surrounded them, and took a man by the name of Butterfield prisoner. The rest escaped. Butterfield was roasted alive, with the most brutal tortures. Nothing could stop the activity of these Indians, now that they were provoked. They lurked in the lowlands that surrounded the fort. They stole up and down the river by night and day, watching for victims. A house had been built for the uses of the garrison about two miles from the fort, and six men were now sent to guard it. Three of them went out upon an errand, when one hundred Pequots rose against them and took two of them. Success finally made them so bold that they destroyed all the store-houses connected with the fort, burned up the haystacks, killed the cows, and ruined all the property belonging to the garrison that was not within the range of the garrison guns.

There existed no sympathy for the Indian, and they no longer thought of them as peaceful servants, they now thought of them as savages that must be disciplined and disposed of- in February 1637 the Pequots killed some English at Saybrook. With all the ire I still feel the Pequots did not deserve their fate. It was in that same month, the court met at Hartford, and ordered that letters should be sent to the governor of Massachusetts, denouncing the evils resulting from Endicott's expedition, and calling on the governor for men to help prosecute the war with vigor, in which John Underhill and twenty armed soldiers were sent.

Lieutenant Gardiner went out one day in March, with about a dozen men, to burn the marshes. The Indians lay in wait for him, and as he passed a narrow neck of land, the Indians killed three of his men, and mortally wounded another. Gardiner himself was also wounded. The Pequots pursued him to the walls of the fort, and, surrounding it in great numbers, mocked the fugitives, imitating the dying groans and prayers of the English whom they had taken captive and tortured. The tribe also challenged the Saybrook men to leave the fort and come out and fight like men.

Soon after that incident, the Pequots in canoes would board a shallop as she was sailing down the river. She had three men on board. The Englishmen made a bold defense, but in vain. One of them was shot through the head with an arrow, and fell overboard. The Indians took the other two and killed them. They then split the bodies in twain, and suspended them all by their necks over the water, upon the branches of trees, hideous spectacles, to be gazed at by the English as they passed up and down the river.

Was the Pequot rage a result of Endicott's foiled expedition? If their home was not invaded would any of this have happened?

It appears the Bay magistrates failed to grasp how dreadfully they had exposed their peers along the river to Pequot revenge, as well as establishing the possibility for a united tribal formation against all the plantations. The Block Island Indians, who were tributaries to the Narragansetts, and the Pequots, were both invaded by Endicott's force. The Puritans had a trading house not only on the Connecticut but also at Sowams and various other points in Indian country and quickly perceived there was an ultimate threat to the colony.[63] The Bay Colony, though, blamed the Pequots for the warlike climate; this was believed because the Pequots didn't provide the requests desired by the English in terms of the treaty.

It was evident that the river towns of Connecticut were furious by Endicott's actions, complaining their lives had been placed in danger. To make matters worse, the Pequots would send a representative to the Narragansetts claiming that the English were minded to destroy all Indians. Rumors spread that the Pequots and Narragansetts had concluded a peace after four years of hostilities. Sources mentioned that Pequot ambassadors were already on Narragansett Bay urging Miantonomo to ally the Narragansetts with the Pequots and to form a numerically superior force with which to annihilate the barely four thousand English in all of New England.[64]

Narragansett Alliance

The Narragansetts kept neutrality with the colonists, which was very favorable to the young colonies, since a Narragansett-Pequot alliance would be disastrous. Instantly grasping the possible doom of Massachusetts in an alliance of the Pequots and Narragansetts, especially following all the Pequot attacks, Governor Vane of Massachusetts and the Council rushed a frantic appeal to Roger Williams, who lived among the Narragansetts. Williams commission was to use his utmost and speediest endeavor to break and hinder the league labored by the Pequots and work for a league between the Narragansetts and English instead.[65]

Within a few days an embassy hurried from Boston to Narragansett bounds. Roger Williams first entertained the Massachusetts embassy at his house in Providence, sent word to Canonicus, then escorted the delegation as interpreter to see the sachem. An imposing assembly received the English at Narragansett, where proceedings opened with a feast of white chestnuts and cornmeal mush with blackberries mixed in. The "grave old" Canonicus was joined by his "touchy, haughty giant nephew", Miantonomo, who shared the sachemship.[66] The parley took place afterward in a state-house. Canonicus, well stricken in years, lay on his side on a mat, his warriors sitting on the ground with their knees doubled up to their chins as they listened intently to Williams' translations.

Canonicus amazed the English by his wisdom and discreet answers. Miantonomo, though more forward in siding with the English, was struck as a very stern man, of a great stature, of a cruel nature, and with all his nobility, he caused his guests to tremble at his speech. He was, though, a friend to the English. The Bay emissaries actually believed at that time the two Narragansett Grand Sachems could field thirty thousand fighting men. Though the number was nearer four thousand, which would still have been formidable for Massachusetts.

At the time of this meeting, Williams had already won Canonicus to neutrality but quickly transformed this neutrality to active alliance. He did it by working on Miantonomo more than Canonicus, as Canonicus was always shy of the English. While he was a prudent and peaceable prince, he never cared to court the English, never feared them, and never acknowledged any precedence of their government over his own. Albeit, the two sachems weighed William's argument and chose to favor with the whitemen.

One-way Williams sweetened Canonicus's spirit was by gifts of sugar, for which the sachem had a great fondness. Roger Williams wrote to Governor Winthrop: "Sir, if any thing be sent to the princes, I find Canonicus would gladly accept of a box of eight or ten pounds of sugar; and, indeed, he told me he would thank Mr. Governor for a box-full."[67]

Frequently the sachem harassed Williams to ask Winthrop to send more. Canonicus must have been around seventy years old at this time, and he lived to be past eighty. In 1636, he had turned over the active administration of his government to Miantonomo, who had exercised equal authority since 1632. Canonicus had sons to inherit his sachemship, but the nephew Miantonomo appeared far more impressive; the arrangement seemed to be best for the tribe and entirely acceptable to the sons.[68]

The answer to the English Colonies' dilemma of the Pequots was to be found in the Narragansett-Mohegan-Connecticut-Massachusetts alliance and was the first Indian-Englishman confederation formed.

Miantonomo told Roger Williams that the Pequots "labored to persuade"[69] him that the English were going to kill all the Indians. Subsequent to the meeting, Miantonomo was sent for by the governor again concerning an alliance. John Winthrop wrote on the matter:

> He came to Boston with two of Canonicus's sons, and another sachem, and near twenty sanaps. Cutshamakin, the Massachusetts Sachem, gave notice the day before. The governor sent twenty musketeers to meet him at Roxbury. He came to Boston about noon. The governor had called together most of the magistrates and ministers, to give countenance to our proceedings, and to advise with them about the terms of peace. It was dinner time, and the sachems and their council dined by themselves in the same room where the governor dined, and their sanaps were sent to the inn. After dinner, Miantunnomoh declared what he had to say to us in propositions, which were to this effect:—That they had always loved the

English, and desired firm peace with us: That they would continue in war with the Pequods and their confederates, till they were subdued; and desired we should so do: They would deliver our enemies to us, or kill them: That if any of theirs should kill our cattle, that we would not kill them, but cause them to make satisfaction: That they would now make a firm peace, and two months hence they would send us a present.

The governor told them, they should have answer the next morning.

In the morning we met again, and concluded the peace upon the articles underwritten, which the governor subscribed, and they also subscribed with their marks, and Cutshamakin also. But because we could not well make them understand the articles perfectly, we agreed to send a copy of them to Mr. Williams, who could best interpret them to them. So, after dinner, they took leave, and were conveyed out of town by some musketeers, and dismissed with a volley of shot.

THE ARTICLES.

1. A firm peace between us and our friends of other plantations, (if they consent,) and their confederates, (if they will observe the articles, etc.,) and our posterities.

2. Neither party to make peace with the Pequods without the other's consent.

3. Not to harbor, etc., the Pequods, etc.

4. To put to death or deliver over murderers, etc.

5. To return our fugitive servants, etc.

6. We to give them notice when we go against the Pequods, and they to send us some guides.

7. Free trade between us.

8. None of them to come near our plantations during the wars with the Pequods, without some Englishman or known Indian.

9. To continue to the posterity of both parties.[70]

The Pequot War

Negotiations amongst the Massachusetts Bay delegation and the Narragansetts were a success as the Narragansett sachem, Miantonomi, stated he would continue in war against the Pequots and their confederates until they were subdued. Uncas, the Mohegan sachem, also, wanted to contribute to an alliance that would force war with the Pequots.

The attack on Wethersfield solidified an attack upon the Pequots. It brought the river valley and the General Court into a state of war. There was great outrage at the violence they withstood and sought revenge.

Reverend Thomas Hooker and the leaders of Hartford Colony commissioned ninety-odd planters to take this fight to the enemy. Captain John Mason, 'a man tall and portly, but nevertheless full of Martial Bravery and Vigour'[71], was in command. All but Mason were civilians, and not being soldiers, they had nevertheless been drilling as a trained band through the latest hostilities.

Mason's commission requested that the forces would gather in Hartford to embark to Saybrook. Uncas "was at the Podunk fort across the river, where he was assembling a Mohegan contingent- he reported the joy of the Pequots over their success in Wethersfield."[72] Seventy warriors would accompany Uncas when his band would depart Hartford toward Saybrook. Most were Mohegans, but some of his followers were drawn from the neighboring River Indian villages.

The soldiers from the several towns joined in Hartford and after religious exercises their hearts were reinforced by a counsel from the Rev. Thomas Hooker, in the course of which he said to them, "although gold and silver be wanting to either of you, yet have you that to maintain which is far more precious, the lives, liberties and new purchased freedoms of the endeared servants of our Lord Jesus, and of your second selves, even your affectionate bosome-mates, together with the chief pledges of your love, the comforting contents of harmless prating and smiling babes."

It was on Wednesday, the 10th of May, that the trained men crowded into ready boats embarked at Hartford and set sail for the mouth of the river. John Mason was Captain, and Samuel Stone, was his chaplain. The three river plantations force formed following the massacre with a hundred sixty men-ninety English levied from the plantations, and seventy Mohegan Indians. They set sail from Hartford in a fleet comprised of a pink or narrow-stern rowboat, a pinnace or eight-oar rowboat with a small sail, and a shallop."[73] The colonial men were also accompanied with many Indian canoes on their journey past wounded Wethersfield.[74]

"The water was so shallow at this season of the year that the vessels several times ran aground in dropping down the river. This delay was so irksome to the Indians, that they begged to be set ashore, to which Mason consented, on their promising to meet the English at Saybrook. 'Despite suspicion, it became impossible to refuse the request of the Indians that they be landed and take the familiar trail where progress would be faster.'[75]

The Dutchmen crowding at the shore of the River witnessed the meager display of force with amusement and probably with doubts of success. The Dutchmen did hold neutrality; nevertheless, there was kinship by color of skin, but there was also Dutch opportunity to be gained if we were to be defeated.[76]"

It was not until the 15th of May that Mason and his men arrived at Saybrook, having spent five days in sailing about fifty miles, "adverse wind, sluggish current and inexpertness of oarsmen delayed the stronghearted little party."[77] Uncas led his men overland as Mason and the English floated clumsily down river. "On the early arrival of Uncas at the fort, Gardiner put him to the test."

Near Saybrook fort, six Pequots were lurking in a nearby cove. Uncas with twenty of his braves were obligated to bring them in, dead or alive- four Pequots were killed, one escaped, and the sixth was made prisoner."[78] Uncas delivered the severed Pequot heads to the English at Saybrook. Upon hearing of this, all the men viewed the outcome as a special Providence.

Captain John Underhill, who joined with Uncas when the Mohegans reached Saybrook, verified the report of this skirmish. Upon Mason's arrival, Underhill, at Saybrook, would present his services to Mason, with nineteen men for the expedition if Lieutenant Gardiner would consent it. Mason was delighted with this and resolved to send back twenty of his own troops to protect, during his absence, the almost defenseless towns upriver.[79]

Mason reached Saybrook on a Wednesday and began discussion, at length, on how and what manner they should go forth into the Pequot's home, as they were unbeknownst of the country. They ultimately decided to sail for Narragansett Country and to then march through that country which bordered upon the enemy. The grounds and reasons of those actions are as follows:

First, the Pequots, the enemies, kept a continual guard upon the river night and day.

Secondly, their numbers far exceeded the English; the two Wethersfield captives who were taken by the Dutch and restored to Saybrook have mentioned the Pequots also having sixteen guns with powder and shot.

Thirdly, the Pequot being on land and being swift on foot, might much impede a landing, and possibly dishearten the army; invasion was expected only by land, there being no other place on shore but in Narragansett.

Fourthly, with the landing in Narragansett the force should come upon their backs, and possibly surprise them.[80]

Mason covered all this at a conference with Gardener at Saybrook upon arrival as they were stuck in five days of discussion at Saybrook. Mason invited Lieutenant Gardener to speak frankly, knowing that he refused war for at least a year or two- till better provided for it. Gardener wanted to let fortification alone awhile. Gardener first said that none of his men should go with them, neither should they go unless they, that were bred soldiers from their youth, could see some likelihood to do better than the Baymen with their strong commission last year. At last, even though Gardener knew the "war is best won away from home, contributed four of Saybrook's soldiers, but he refused to go."[81]

Trust had now been established with the Mohegans and a well-orchestrated plan to invade the two main Pequot forts was established. Sassacus' Weinshauks Fort and Mamoho's Mystic Fort were the biggest palisaded villages in the region. Sassacus at age seventy-seven also held twenty-six villages tributary to his influence. Native people as far away as Wethersfield turned to him in appeal, and as we have seen he responded in force. His reputation in war had been known throughout. However, Indian warfare held strict rules against killing anybody but enemy braves. The Indian fort is where women, children and valuable stores were kept from being adopted by the enemy tribe, while the braves would fight it out with little harm done.[82] For war against the English, the Indians would divide themselves into small bodies, so that the English were forced to change their usual stance.[83]

"In Saybrook, Mason urged the scheme of sailing past the Pequot country, as far as Narragansett Bay, and, there land, they would then march through the Narragansett country under the protection of the old hereditary enemies of the Pequots, steal upon the Pequots in the night and crush them."[84]

They set sail Friday morning. These ships, with seventy-seven soldiers and some sixty Mohegan warriors aboard, sailed out of Saybrook Harbor bound for Narragansett. At this time the Massachusetts men had been summoned for war. The Bay Colony voted to raise two hundred men and the Plymouth Colony fifty- to go to the aid of Connecticut. The Plymouth Colony never did raise its fifty men, but forty of the Bay Colony soldiers, under Captain Daniel Patrick, were sent at once to join the Narragansetts, where they could obtain canoes in which to visit Block Island. Rumor had it that the Pequots had moved their women and children there for safety. When Block Island was conquered, Patrick was to go back to the mainland and join up with the Connecticut troops against the Pequots.[85]

Upon arrival on the Narragansett coast the men from Saybrook could not land until Tuesday at sunset because of severe wind, at which time Captain Mason landed and marched up to the residence of Miantonomo. Mason told the sachem that he had not an opportunity to acquaint him beforehand of his coming armed into his country. Mason considered the alliance held with the Narragansetts and knew the sachem would approve the object to avenge the wrongs and injuries received from the common enemy. Miantonomo expressed himself pleased with the design of Mason, but thought his numbers were too few to deal with the enemy, who were, as he said, "very great captains, and men skillful in war."[86]

The first requirement for the attack on the two Pequot forts worked accordingly as they were seen by the enemy passing the forts by sail as if the company were leaving the region. The next step, once the war party was established in Narragansett, had the other men travel westward to attack the forts at night. Moreover, respecting Miantonomo's stature, experience, and power in numbers of braves, Mason requested only free passage through his country.

"That same evening a Narragansett runner arrived at the camp with a message from Captain Patrick. Marching overland, Patrick had gotten as far as Providence with his forty men, and he urged Mason to await his arrival before moving on. Helpful and necessary this added strength would prove, Mason decided against waiting, as such a delay was strongly opposed by his men, who had now been two weeks away from home and wanted to get back to their farms and families. In addition, the Narragansett and Pequot tribes were not now openly at war and there was some intercourse between them. Word

might get through to Sassacus of the march of the colonists."
[Chandler Whipple][87]

It was on Wednesday, the 24th of May, that the little army of seventy-seven Englishmen and sixty Mohegans and river Indians began their march for the Pequot forts. The force headed west with Uncas and his braves; the force received no promised guides or auxiliaries from Miantonomo's village. The trek started slow through the wilderness paths, and that day they journeyed twenty miles out of Narragansett country to the home of the Eastern Niantic.

These Eastern Niantics offered no assistance to our inadequate force. The eastern Niantic was a country that bordered on the Pequot territory and it was the seat of one of the Narragansett sachems. But the sachem refused to meet with us, or let us enter his palisades to pass the night.

Mason, upon questioning their conduct, felt these Indians were in a partnership with the Pequots. The Eastern Niantics set a strong guard about their fort, and would not allow one of their own to escape from it during the night. But the conduct of the Niantics was truly the result of fear, rather than an alliance with the Pequots. In the morning, several of Miantonomo's men, that he sent overnight, caught up to the column, the Narragansetts were smiling and intended to join the force in their expedition. For when the Niantics saw that the Narragansetts desired to assist the English, they took heart, and, forming a circle, declared that they too would fight the Pequots, and boasted how many they would kill. When Mason resumed his march on Thursday May 25th, he had about five hundred Indian warriors.[88]

"These new friends became loud with loyalty-oaths, signs and ceremonies that swore to their cooperation ahead.[89]"

The force was now accompanied by 500 Indians, consisting of Mohegan and river Indians, Narragansett, and Eastern Niantic warriors. The massive force then headed west to the Pequot village. Wequash, a Pequot who defected from Sassacus to the Narragansett and became a Niantic Sagamore, guided the party toward his former tribe. He spoke that the Pequots mainly retired into two forts for security.

Along the trek westward toward the two forts the force reached a shallow crossing and stopped on grounds where the Pequots would fish. Groups upon groups of Narragansetts began to manifest great fear, and great numbers started deserting; returning home because of a great concern of Sassacus and the Pequot fort. They had now come into the country of Sassacus, and found that they were within a few miles of his principal fortress. The expedition seemed no longer pleasant for them, but a violent fate grew more and more realistic with every step closer toward neighboring Pequot. Mason called Uncas to him, and asked him what he had to expect from the Indians. The chief replied that the Narragansetts would all drop off and leave, but that he and his Mohegans would never leave the English. Uncas's Mohegans stayed.[90]

After the reduced force refreshed themselves, they marched three miles and came to a field which had lately been planted with Indian corn and with this find they presumed they were very close to the enemy. At first the force was motivated to reach both forts, but understanding that one of them was so remote that they could not come up to it before midnight, they chose, with extreme heat exhaustion and want of necessities, to invade the nearest of the two forts, the one to be known as the Mystic Fort, not Fort Weinshauks, Sassacus' fort.[91]

In the morning of the 26th of May, 1637, they encamped in Groton, between two rocks. We were now so near the enemy, that the advanced lookout could distinctly hear the savages singing and dancing within their fort with great merriment.

The night prior to the attack proved to be comfortable, being clear with moonlight. The English appointed guards and placed sentinels at some distance; they heard the enemy singing at the fort, who continued on until midnight. The force was informed that as the Pequots saw the pinnaces sail by them some days before, it was concluded the English were afraid of them and were to not come near them; the message of their song was to that purpose.

In the morning, the force awoke and saw it very light. The men rose, commended themselves to God, and then thought immediately to move toward the assault. The allied Indians who remained showed a path and told the English it led directly to the fort. They held their march about two miles, wondering that they came not to the fort, and fearing they might be deceived, but seeing corn newly planted at the foot of a great hill, supposing the fort was not far off, a champion country being round about; then making a stand, Mason gave the word for some of the Indians to come up. Uncas and Wequash appeared. The English demanded of them, where was the fort? They answered it was on the top of that hill. Then the English demanded where the rest of the allied Indians were? They answered, "Behind, but afraid."

The English told the Indians they should not fly, but stand and watch whether the English would now fight. Then Captain Underhill came up, who marched in the rear, and commending themselves to God, divided the men. There being two entrances into the fort, they intended to enter both at once.[92]

The attack was now set on this morning. Thus the seventy-seven Englishmen under Captains Mason and Underhill charged their long sought target, nevertheless frustrated by fleeing Native allies. Improvising on the original plan greatly changed it, they failed to strike their target in the night, and were not able to set up the crippling ambush they planned.

Up and then along the flanks of the sloping wooded hill the English charged. Above in the trees they could see smoke from campfires inside Mystic fort, but not a living soul. Swords drawn, their muskets primed and fuse-matches struck alight, the armored English labored up through the trees and formed two files rushing to surround the Mystic palisade- they did not bring along their Narragansett and Mohegan allies. Mason and Underhill waved Uncas, his Mohegans, and the remaining Narragansetts to the side, into an exterior circle. The Narragansetts were of very little service in the attack upon the Pequot fort, holding themselves distant.

The captains, leading the colonies in its first war, would determine the fate of the young plantations, especially with the disappointments of Block Island and the first Pequot invasion.

The fate of Connecticut was now to be decided with Captain Mason leading his company up to the northeast side. The first real obstacles for the English at the Mystic fort were a dog within the fort barking and a Pequot lookout crying out, "Wanux! Wanux!" meaning, English! English! The English then commenced their assault on Mystic with a booming, all together volley into its massive palisade. The English fire and then the fort's silence drew the English in. The captains each gathered half of the men and entered separate entrances.

The Pequot braves—"the amount will be forever unknown because truly only 'Pequots knew how many bodies were in Mystic,'" [likely under 100][93] —stayed in the Mystic fort and lured their enemy in, as their people escaped prior to the invasion.

The entrance near which Mason stood was blocked up with bushes about breast high. Over this petty obstruction he leapt, sword in hand, shouting to his men to follow him. But Seely, his lieutenant, found it easier to remove the bushes than

81

to force the men over them. When he had done so, he also entered, followed by sixteen soldiers. It had been determined to destroy the enemy with the sword, and thus save the corn and other valuables that were stored in the wigwams. With this approach, the captain, seeing no Indians, entered one of these wigwams. Here he found many warriors who crowded hard upon him, and beset him with great violence; but they were so amazed at the strange spirit that had so suddenly thrust itself upon them, that they could make but a feeble resistance. "There, Mason is 'beset with many Indians,' in such close quarters. "'They, are many, yet they cannot prevail."[94] Mason was soon joined by William Hayden, who, as he entered the wigwam through the breach that had been made by his captain, stumbled against the dead body of a Pequot, whom Mason had slain.

Mason, still intent on destroying the Pequots, and at the same time saving their property, now left the wigwam, and passed down one of their streets, driving the crowd of Indians from one end of it to the other. The Mystic Fort had embraced a large area of about twenty acres and housed more than seventy houses in this space, with lanes or streets passing between them. "Mason saw many Indians in the lane; and he went towards them, but they fled." At the lower extremity of this lane stood a little company of Englishmen, who, having entered from the west, met the Indians as they fled from Mason, and killed about half a dozen of them. The captain now faced about, and went back the whole length of the lane, to the spot where he had entered the fort. He was exhausted, and quite out of breath, and had become satisfied that this was not the way to combat the Indians.[95]

"We shall never kill them in this way," said the captain, and then added, "We must burn them!"

With these words the request of the council of war to save the prizes of the enemy was annulled.

Before the wigwams were ignited, the Englishmen inside with the captains searched around to see if they'd been mocked. With the unlikelihood of Pequots sleeping in their lodges through the commotion, incessant destruction manifested and the captains lit firebrands from the Pequots' campfires. Almost in an instant, the little village was wrapped in flames, and the Pequot warriors fled in dismay from the homes that had just before sheltered them. The mat-roofed lodges of Mystic kindled so fast into flames that the English were forced back outside the fort.

Outside, facing the wooded hills now, the company found themselves in a situation where they became trapped between the two Pequot forts and many angered Pequot warriors. The existing Pequots were now to be joined by their relatives from the other Pequot fort Weinshauks, who were immediately coming in from the west. The combined Pequots then charged upon the force with their prime men, and let fly their weapons, at which time Mason's force set forth to Pequot harbor. Underhill's men managed to volley, and they killed enough Pequots to break their first charge with bullets that outreached the arrows. But the real battle was just beginning. More and more warriors would attack the isolated English, exceeding their shot and might. Around three hundred is the presumed amount of braves that had joined the conflict from the other Pequot Fort Weinshauks.[96] It was assumed that the English ships were a great distance and most of the Indians but Uncas, his men, and a few Narragansetts had deserted.[97]

The English force also now became aware of Indian conduct in war. The Indians fell out amongst themselves, the Pequots, Narragansetts, and Mohegans were changing a few arrows together, and after such a manner, it seemed as if they fought seven years they would not kill seven men. They came not near one another, but shot remote, and not point-blank, as the English do with bullets, but at rovers, and then they gazed up in the sky to see where the arrow fell, and not until it is fallen do they shoot again. But spending a little time this way, the English were forced to cast their eyes upon their poor maimed soldiers, many of them lying upon the ground, wanting food and such nourishable things as might refresh them in this faint state. But the English were not supplied with any things to help them, but only were able to look up to God.

Some of the English-allied Indians, who had stood close to them, fell into confusion, and were determined to leave the English in a land they knew not which way to get out. Suddenly fifty of the Narragansett Indians fell off from the rest, returning home. The Pequots spying them, pursued after them. Then came some of the other Narragansetts to Captain Mason and Underhill, crying, "oh help us now, or our men will be all slain." The Captains answered, how dare you crave aid of us, when you are leaving of us in this distressed condition, not knowing which way to march out of the country? But yet you shall see it is not the nature of Englishmen to deal like heathens, and the English aided them. Underhill pushing on with thirty men, in the space of an hour rescued their men, and in the English retreat to the body, slew and wounded above a hundred Pequots, all fighting men, that charged the rear and flanks.[98]

The English somehow survived the hundreds of braves from the other Pequot fort Weinshauks, who drove the English into the lower ground off the western side of Mystic Hill, whereupon the English endured the Pequot world of war. More braves poured into the fight, hundreds shot arrows with the English panic growing, yet there were not many casualties.[99]

While Mason's and Underhill's outnumbered English bled with their backs to the sea, the boats fortunately were spotted as the Captain on the boat eyed the smoke from the burning of Mystic Fort.[100] While debating what measures should be adopted, it was with delight that Mason saw his little vessels, their sails filled with the welcome gale that blew from the north-east, gliding into Pequot harbor. The non-injured colonists found themselves, among the maimed, wearied, and fainting soldiers and when they viewed the vessels they rallied to reach their rendezvous.[101]

The end of the colonial retreat was somewhere along the Mystic shore where they met their ships. The Pequots were playing upon the English flanks, and one Sergeant Davis, a strong soldier, spying something black upon the top of a rock, stepped forth from the body with a carbine of three feet long, and, at a venture, gave fire, supposing it to be an Indian's head, turning him over with his heels upward. The Indians observed this, and greatly admired that a man should shoot so directly. The Pequots were much daunted at the shot and refrained approaching so near upon the English. Coming forth to the Pequot River the English met with Captain Patrick, aboard the ship, who under his command had forty able soldiers who were ready to begin a second attempt. But the injured soldiers boarded the vessel and set sail for Saybrook fort with Underhill. Captain Mason and Captain Patrick chose to march over land, as they could not desert their Indian allies in Indian country. They proceeded and burned and spoiled the country between the Pequot and Connecticut River.[102]

Mason, with twenty of his men, and Patrick with his forty, set out to Saybrook fort by land, while Underhill with the wounded and the remainder of the Connecticut troops left onboard a vessel. The whole company, when received, was royally entertained by Lieutenant Gardener at the fort.[103]

In Wethersfield, everyone celebrated with glee, more so, as it was our small town that was struck by the most severe Pequot attack.

Victory brought about the birth for the Puritan to vindicate offensive warfare as a means for defensive measures.

This was made to appear as a decisive victory, and the Pequots were assumed ruined. Many were taken captive and many more were to be destroyed.[104]

Divers felt the Pequots were left in utter confusion, as many of the tribe's leaders blamed Sassacus for the defeat, and only special pleading by his councilors persuaded them to spare his life. Most of the Pequots agreed, however, that safety only existed in flight. The majority headed west for Mohawk country, where they hoped to find asylum, while others sought refuge with neighboring tribes.[105] Among those who fled west was Sassacus. Sassacus, however, fleeing to the Mohawks of New York for shelter, was slain and his skin and hair were brought to Boston. [106] So ended the great Pequot sachem.

The return of the colonists to their colony now granted "rights of conquest" within the Pequot bounds, and also, the safe return brought relief and inspiration for other Puritans. Thus, when the little army returned home, victorious beyond their hopes, it was a natural thing for the friendly Indians, in their gratitude over the destruction of their enemies, to surrender to the English the site of their village, and divide it among the soldiers, and themselves remove, as we know they did about this time. The River Indians ceded vast tracts of their land.[107]

> "It may be said that the annihilation of the Pequots can be condemned only by those (...) who suppose that savages, whose business it is to torture and slay, can always be dealt with according to the methods in use between civilized peoples. New England, with their virtues was bound to treat the red man with true justice and avoid cruelty in punishing his misbehavior. But if the founders of Connecticut, in confronting a danger which threatened their very existence, struck with savage fierceness, we cannot blame them. The world is so made that it is only in

that way that the higher races have been able to preserve themselves and carry on their progressive work." (John Fiske)[108]

Mason expressed:

"We were entertained with great triumph and rejoicing and praising God for his goodness to us in crowning us with success and restoring of us with so little loss. It was the Lord's doings, and it is marvelous in our eyes."[109]

Thus the enemies that had escaped scattered, and the Pequots now were a prey to all Indians. Happy were those that could bring in their heads to the English, of which there came almost daily to Windsor, or Hartford. The Pequots, though, growing weary of this, sent some of the chiefs that survived to mediate with the English. They offered that if they might but enjoy their lives, they would become the English Vassals, and to use them as they pleased, which was granted them. At which point, Uncas and Miantonomo were sent for, who with the Pequots met at Hartford. The Pequots were being demanded, how many of them were then living? It was answered, about one hundred and eighty, or two hundred. [John Mason][110]

Yet again, divers of men with substantial authority felt an invasion upon an Indian fortification would spawn peace. Why had anyone not told me that our sole purpose in warfare was to ignite anger, propagate conflict- to create war?

The Hartford Treaty of 1638

However wonderful it was for the colonies, the white-red relationship would gradually deteriorate following the war. A most influential demise through the legal system of the colonies would again arise five years later, which would set the stage for the slow Indian demise. Miantonomo's murder was all the result of a decision made by the general court. The arousal for my compassion is provided by the most daunting event an Indian could receive- the assassination of a Sachem. As you will see the death of Miantonomo through the United Colonies commissioners changed all Indian principles. The tragedy of Miantonomo's fate would thus quell any chance for justice. The legal system lost the recognition of true universal justice. There was great joy in the death of a sachem, one who recently assisted in the victory over the Pequots. This was so very confusing.

Problems for Miantonomo quickly spawned following the Pequot War, as Pequot outcast stirred contingency. The amicable surrender sought by the Pequots subsequent to their defeat would open the door for the Pequots to enter other tribes, whereupon the Mohegans and Narragansetts were compensated accordingly for their efforts during the previous war. The two increasingly powerful tribes would also vie for alliance with their own individual colony. The Narragansetts would be at a great disadvantage, however, as Rhode Island was not a member of the United Colonies, nor did the colony hold an armed force. Puritan guidelines and encouragement would thus conduct behavior between tribes.

A three-way treaty would be negotiated in hopes of a perpetual peace between the English, Narragansetts, and Mohegans. The Treaty of Hartford in 1638 resulted, with its purpose being to settle the scattered Pequots and arrange a system to advance Indian conduct within the colonies. On the 21st of September, Uncas and Miantonomo met the magistrates of Connecticut at Hartford. With about two hundred of the vanquished tribe still existing in the area, a treaty was entered into between the Connecticut Colony, the Mohegans, and the Narragansetts.

The Narragansett and Mohegan sachems agreed to capture and execute any Pequots guilty of disobedience, while the English gained most of eastern Connecticut, as Uncas ceded most of his land, aside from villages and fields- all for political strength. The treaty also forced the Narragansetts and the Mohegans to inform the Colony of any intentions of war against a rival tribe.[111]

The Treaty of Hartford, 21 September 1638 reads as follows:

ARTICLES BETWEEN THE INGLISH IN CONNECTICUT AND THE INDIAN SACHEMS

A Covenant and Agreement between the English Inhabiting the Jurisdiction of the River of Connecticut of the one part, and Miantinomy the chief Sachem of the Narragansetts in the behalf of himself and the other Sachems there; and Poquim or Uncas the chief Sachim of the Indians called the Mohegans in the behalf of himself and the Sachims under him, as Followeth, at Hartford the 21st of September, 1638.

Imp'r. There is a peace and a Familiarity made between the sd Miantinome and Narragansett Indians and the sd Poquim and Mohegan Indians, and all former Injuryes and wrongs offered each to other Remitted and Burryed and never to be renued any more from henceforth.

2. It is agreed there fall out Injuryes and wrongs for fuetur to be done or committed Each to other or their men, they shall not presently Revenge it But they are to appeal to the English and they are to decide the same, and the determination of the English to stand And they are each to do as is by the English sett down and if the one or the other shall Refuse to do, it shall be lawfull for the English to Compel him and to side and take part if they see cause, against the obstinate or Refusing party.

3. It is agreed and a conclusion of peace and friendship made between the sd Miantinome and sd Narragansetts and the sd Poquim and the sd Mohegans as long as they carry themselves orderly and give no just cause of offence and that they nor either of them do shelter any that may be Enemyes to the English that shall or formerly have had hand in murdering or killing any English man or woman or consented thereunto, They or either of them shall as soon as they can either bring the

90

chief Sachem of our late enemies the Peaquots that had the chief hand in killing the English, to the sd English, or take of their heads, As also for those murderers that are now agreed upon amongst us that are living they shall as soon as they can possibly take off their heads, if they may be in their custody or Else whensoever they or any of them shall come Amongst them or to their wigwams or any where if they can by any means come by them.

4. And whereas there be or is reported for to be by the sd Narragansetts and Mohegans 200 Peaquots living that are men besides squawes and papoes. The English do give unto Miantinome and the Narragansetts to make up the number of Eighty with the Eleven they have already, and to oquime his number, and that after they the Peaquots shall be divided as abovesd, shall no more be called Peaquots but Narragansetts and Mohegans and as their men and either of them are to pay for every Sanop one fathom of wampome peage and for every youth half so much- and for every Sanop papoose one hand to be paid at Killing time of Corn at Connecticut yearly and shall not suffer them for to live in the country that was formerly theirs but is now the Englishes by conquest neither shall the Narragansetts nor Mohegans possess any part of the Peaquot country without leave from the English And it is always expected that the English Captives are forthwith to be delivered to the English, such as belong to the Connecticut to the Sachems there, And such as belong to the Massachusetts; the sd agreements are to be kept invoylably by the parties abovesd and if any make breach of them the other two may joyn and make warr upon such as shall break the same, unless satisfaction be made being Reasonbly Required

The Mark of MIANTINOMMY

The Marks of POQUIAM alias UNKAS
JOHN HAINES
ROG'R LUDLOW
EDW'RD HOPKINS.[112]

And so perished the great Pequot tribe and Sassacus. The refugees without any tribal affiliation scattered here and there, and only Uncas keenly accepted and adopted several of them into his tribe of Mohegans. Thereupon Miantonomo believed Uncas was using his share of the Pequot prisoners to increase his own power and in October a feud between Miantonomo and Uncas became apparent, denying any possible peace between the two.

At a private conference in Hartford, Miantonomo, gave the Council the names of all the remaining members of the Pequot tribe who had been guilty of killing Englishmen. A list of these names was read to Uncas who admitted that it was correct. Miantonomo said that of the remnants of the Pequot tribe, Canonicus had few, as Canonicus had ten or eleven out of the seventy who were submitted to him, the others never having come in, or having returned to their old hunting grounds after coming in. Old Pequot territory was now considered Mohegan country.[113]

John Winthrop wrote on Uncas harboring the Pequots:

Unkus, alias Okoco, the Monahegan sachem in the twist of Pequod River, came to Boston with thirty-seven men. He came from Connecticut with Mr. Haynes, and tendered the governor a present of twenty fathom of wampom. This was at the court, and it was thought fit by the council to refuse it, till he had given satisfaction about the Pequods he kept, etc. Upon this he was much dejected, and made account we would have killed him; but, two days after, having received good satisfaction of his innocency, etc., and he promising to submit to the order of the English touching the Pequods he had, and the differences between the Naragansetts and him, we accepted his present. And, about half an hour after, he came to the governor, and entertained him with these compliments: This heart (laying his hand upon his breast) is not mine, but yours; I have no men; they are all yours; command me any difficult thing, I will do it; I will not believe any Indians' words against the English; if any man shall kill an Englishman, I will put him to death, were he never so dear to me. So the governor gave him a fair, red coat, and defrayed his and his men's diet, and gave them corn to relieve them homeward, and a letter of protection to all men, etc., and he departed very joyful.[114]

"Uncas became furious with Miantinomo for having informed the English magistrates of secretly harboring Pequot refugees. Miantonomo and his Narragansetts were considered favorable to the English during the Pequot invasion, however that relationship would slowly change through the work of Uncas. In October the feud between Miantonomo and Uncas became apparent, denying any peace between the two. Miantonomo set out with an imposing group composed of his wife and children, several of his sachems and not less than one hundred and fifty warriors. Roger Williams and two other Englishmen also accompanied him. Before reaching Hartford they were met by a number of Narragansetts returning to their own country from Connecticut, the group complained that the Pequots and Mohegans robbed them. Close behind the heels of this complaint came another from a Nipmuck band who said they had been plundered shortly before by a band of six or seven hundred Indians of the Mohegans and their confederates. They reported that this band had spoiled twenty-three fields of corn and robbed three Narragansetts who were staying with the Nipmucks, and also that this band was lying in wait for Miantonomo and his party; threatening to boil Miantonomo in a kettle.

Miantonomo was not to be discouraged by threats of this character and pressed on, upon reaching Hartford he would describe his case against the Mohegans. Divers grievances were presented before the council against Uncas, who was not present. Uncas was subsequently requested and came to Hartford to answer the complaints against him. He brought an Indian to testify that the party which had been in Nipmuck country consisted of only one hundred and not six or seven, and that they took only a little corn for roasting and did a few other harmless things but no damage. The magistrates would attempt reconciliation between the two. Uncas was invited to dine with Miantonomo over some venison the Narragansett hunters brought in. This invitation was refused despite the urgent request by Hartford that he accept the offer.

Interestingly enough, the division of the remaining Pequots made the Mohegans under Uncas the most deadly enemies of the Narragansetts, even with the elimination of the Pequots, the Narragansett greatest former threat. The combination of Pequots and Mohegans, thus, became the dominant tribe in old Pequot. The Pequot consolidation also gave Uncas authority over the surrounding tribes, with the exception of the Narragansetts. He now declared to be Sachem of the Mohegans, and all the tribes formerly subject to the Pequots. This included the River Tribes living around us.[115]

The Pequot destruction did not halt fear as the colonists had continued to fear an Indian insurrection. Uncas spread the rumor that Sequassen had conspired with Miantinomo to make Miantinomo the Grand Sachem of all the New England tribes, and then declare war upon the whites. Hearing this rumor, the magistrates summoned Miantinomo to Boston to answer accusations."[116]

Similarly to the colonists, the Indians also formed a grim perception of their permanent neighbors. A lingering memory of the Pequot destruction made Indians wary to engage in conflict with the colonists. Any conflict for Indians solely existed between rival tribes vying for English protection and allegiance; hence the Mohegans against the Narragansetts.

Sowheag (Sequeen), who greatly provoked the Pequot uprising in Wethersfield, was a great problem for the Puritan authority following the Pequot war. The Wethersfield planters wanted justice, but Sowheag argued he had acted against the injustice. Wethersfield men did feel they did a minor wrong to Sowheag by not allowing him to settle within the jurisdiction of his own home, yet he still was presumed responsible for causing the Wethersfield Massacre. Endicott's failed raid upon the Pequot tribe in August 1636 brought no consideration for Pequot retaliation on Wethersfield in April 1637.

The leaders of the River colonies had to write to the Massachusetts magistrates for assistance on how to handle Sowheag. The Massachusetts magistrates' answer was that Sowheag was the receiver of the first wrong and had been justified by his act. The outcome of his revenge was not relevant.

The conclusion reached was that Sowheag gave the English land there, upon contract that he might sit down by them, and be protected. When he came to Wethersfield and had set down his wigwam, they drove him away by force. Whereupon, he not being of strength to repair this injury by open force, he secretly draws in the Pequots.

Such of the magistrates and elders as could meet on the sudden, returned this answer: That, if the cause were thus, Sowheag might, upon this injury first offered by them, right himself either by force or fraud; and that by the law of nations, and though the damage he had done them had been one hundred times more than what he sustained from them; yet that is not considerable in point of a just war; neither was he bound to seek satisfaction in a peaceable way; it was enough that he had complained of it as an injury and breach of covenant. In accordance with this guidance, the Wethersfield people proceeded and made a new agreement with the Indians of the river.[117]

A deal was made favorable to both sides and a few years followed without injuries, and Sowheag eventually moved to Middletown. However, worry did begin to show as the settlers were unwilling to place confidence in a chief who indirectly caused the massacre.

In Wethersfield at this time, there was a growing suspicion of Sowheag's alliance to the settlers. Rumors ran rampant of Indian conspiracies in the 1640s and brought about investigation after investigation of tribal actions.[118]

River Indians, in hopes of protection and stability, would continue to offer land, but sadly for the Indians, the supply of furs eventually dwindled. Indians could not trade and lost ability to obtain foreign materials they had become accustomed to. From the English view, trade with the Indians became unnecessary. English planters therefore solely wanted Indian land, rather than trade goods or honor. A subtle peace somewhat calmed the colonies and at the same time threatened the long-term livelihood of many Indian communities. Private property in land thus became the foundation that allowed the young colonies to thrive, thereupon, eliminating the Indian.

1643

And thus, accompanying the great changes unfolding, conflict arose that ignited a flame only to be extinguished by a bloody unjust murder!

Jealousy and ancient enmity made [Uncas] an object of bitter dislike to the kinsman and ally of the Narragansetts, Sequassen, the sachem of the Connecticut River. This chieftain had doubtless strong hopes, on the overthrow of the Pequots, that he should recover his ancient influence, and perhaps become ever more powerful than before. But the sudden rise of Uncas blighted all these expectations, and ever afterwards he hated him with all the rancor of disappointed ambition. The events which followed, render the supposition probable, not only that Sequassen and the Narragansetts were acquainted with each other's sentiments towards the Mohegan chief, but that they had formed a conspiracy to overthrow and destroy him. Uncas, on the contrary, strove to defend himself and to injure his enemies, by spreading unfavorable reports of their feelings and designs with regard to the English. 'Miantinomo,' the Mohegans would say, 'wants to make himself sachem of all the Indians in New England. Miantinomo is trying to bring all the Indians into a great conspiracy against the white men.

These reports produced so much suspicion in the magistrates, that in November, 1640, they summoned the Narragansett chief to Boston. He obeyed immediately, thus at once producing a strong impression in his favor. When questioned, he was deliberate in his answers; would never speak except when some of his councilors were present that they might be witnesses; showed much ingenuity in his observations, and a good perception of what was wise and equitable in policy. He offered to prove that Uncas and the Mohegans alone had raised the reports against him; asked that his accusers might be brought before him, face to face; and demanded that, if unable to prove their charges, they should be put to death. His dignity, his frankness, and the justness of his remarks, silenced the complaints of the magistrates; they acquitted him of all suspicion of conspiracy, and he departed from Boston in peace.

This affair doubtless increased his hatred of Uncas; and, not long after, an event occurred which was said to be an effect of that hatred. One evening, as Uncas was passing from one wigwam in his fort to another, an arrow, discharged by some unseen marksman, pierced his arm. He reached the cabin to which he was going, without further injury, and entering it, was safe. The wound was slight and soon healed. The perpetrator of this attack tempted assassination was unknown; but a young Pequot, one of Uncas' subjects, being observed to have a large quantity of wampum, fell under suspicion. He was interrogated, and, as he could give no reasonable explanation of how he came by so much property, the suspicions against him were increased. Observing this, he stole away out of the village, fled over to the Narragansett country, and took refuge with Miantinomo. Uncas laid the matter before the magistrates of Massachusetts; charging Miantinomo with being the instigator of the attack on him; and the Narragansett sachem once more felt himself compelled to go to Boston. He carried the Pequot with him, and the young man was examined by the magistrates in the chieftain's presence. He told a most extraordinary story; how he was staying, at one time, in Uncas' fort; how Uncas engaged him to tell the English that he had been hired by Miantinomo to kill Uncas, and how Uncas then took the flint of his gun and cut his own arm on two sides, so as to make it appear as if it had been pierced by an arrow. This tale, improbable in itself, and unpleasing to the colonists, who already distrusted the Narragansetts, as well as favored the Mohegans, not only did not clear the culprit, but brought Miantinomo under deep suspicion. It seemed as if the story had been concocted between the sachem and his tool, for throwing off the guilt of a conspiracy from their own shoulders, and laying it on the intended victim of that conspiracy, who had barely escaped from it with his life. The magistrates expressed themselves convinced of the Pequots guilt, and declared that he ought to be delivered over to the vengeance of the Mohegan sachem. Miantinomo objected, arguing that the man was under his protection; but finally promised that, if he might only carry him back to his own country, he would then surrender him to Uncas. His earnest request was granted; he was allowed to depart with the prisoner; but on the way home he had him murdered by his own followers. (De Forest)[119]

The atmosphere concerning Indian affairs had become much disheveled in Wethersfield through all the mischief. They were now worthless as the fur trade was near obsolete. A decision would soon be made by the newly established United Colonies that distanced the Indian forever. The United Colonies murder of Narragansett Sachem Miantonomo in 1643 eliminated any common peace amongst neighbors. This was the most critical consequence that advanced the redmen to prey or pray.

The long chain of unjust legal measures subsequent to the Pequot War had become a burden to the Narragansett Sachem, along with colonial alliance to Uncas. The United Colonies' Commissioners approval for Miantonomo's death through the hands of Uncas felt it was just and necessary. I, on the other hand, feel it is the greatest injustice the young government had ever performed. This murder held such a significant role upon Indians because it implanted fear of the white man's authority upon someone who did no harm to the Whiteman.

In five years' time after the Hartford treaty of 1638, the Puritans finally settled their own colony's differences and formed a military alliance. The spirit of that union of the colonies became known as the United Colonies. The necessity to unite the colonies into overseeing commissioners was stirred when an accusation of war occurred in 1642.

John Winthrop wrote on September 1, 1642:

"There came letters from the court at Connecticut, certifying us that the Indians all over the country had combined themselves to cut off all the English, that the time was appointed after harvest, the manner also, they should go by small companies to the chief men's houses by way of trading, etc., and should kill them in the houses and seize their weapons, and then others should be at hand to prosecute the massacre; and that this was discovered by three several Indians. (…) Their advice was, that it was better to enter into war presently, and if we would send 100 men to the river's mouth of Connecticut, they would meet us with a proportionable number."[120]

To this the magistrates responded by taking away arms of the closest friendly Indians, and next summoning Miantonomo once again to the charge of inciting a confederacy. Winthrop then wrote on September 8, 1642:

> The general court being assembled, we considered of the letters and other intelligence from Connecticut, and although the thing seemed very probable, yet we thought it not suffiecient ground for us to begin a war, for it was possible it might be otherwise and that all this might come out of the enmity which had been between Miantonomi and Onkus, who continually sought to discredit each other with the English. Besides we found ourselves in very ill case for war, and if we should begin, we must then be forced to stand continually upon our guard, and to desert our farms and business abroad, and all our trade with the Indians, which things would bring us very low; and besides, if upon this intelligence we should kill any of them or lose any of our own, and it should be found after to have been a false report, we might provoke God's displeasure and blemish our wisdom and integrity before the heathen.
>
> When [Miantonomi] came, the court was assembled, and before his admission we considered how to treat with him. Being called in, and mutual salutations passed, he was set down at the lower end of the table, over against the governor, and had only two or three of his counselors, and two or three of our neighboring Indians, such as he desired, but would not speak of any business at any time before some of his counselors were present, alleging that he would have them present, that they might bear witness with him at his return home of all his sayings.

In all his answers he was very deliberate and showed good understanding in the principles of justice and equity, and ingenuity withal. He demanded that his accusers might be brought forth. He gave divers reasons why we should hold him free of any such conspiracy, and why we should conceive it was a report raised by Uncas, and therefore offered to meet Uncas at Connecticut, or rather at Boston, and would prove to his face his treachery against the English. We spent the better part of two days in treating with him, and in conclusion he did accommodate himself to us to our satisfaction."[121]

Uncas would never meet with Miantonomo in Hartford. He would meet with the Connecticut magistrates alone. Tension between the two also increased because of the scramble for wampum. One reason for Connecticut's behavior toward Uncas was his willingness to pay large quantities of the shell currency in return for Pequot exiles. The method was simple and plain- as more Pequots found their way under Uncas to strengthen the Mohegans, more wampum tribute was sent to Connecticut.

Miantonomo would soon too feel the wrath of Uncas and the United Colonies. Consequently, with this paranoia of Indian attacks, the English force formed the "Union of the Colonies of Massachusetts Bay, Plymouth, New Haven and Connecticut, [which] was formed (1643) under the title of the United Colonies of New England. This was the to be the strongest league of the colonies. The object was a common protection against the Indians, and the encroachments of the Dutch and French settlers."[122] No war was to be commenced by any general court without approval of the United Colonies. Moreover, there is no doubt that the United Colonies Commissioners foremost intention was for obtaining Indian land.

Sadly, both the 1638 Hartford treaty and the United Colony Commissioners would not insure any peace for Miantonomo. The Narragansett Sachem, however, may have angered the colonies most severely on a subject not covered by the treaty or an incident involving Uncas. He sold valuable Narragansett land to Englishmen not of the Puritan theology, wherein Massachusetts Bay was not pleased. Those who bought the land within Rhode Island bounds were highly unfavorable to the Bay Colony.

Originally, the beginnings of Providence were through the Narragansetts who gave refuge to the persecuted Quakers from Massachusetts Bay. It was to Narragansett that Roger Williams fled when he was banished from Salem in 1636 and it was among them that Williams lived. The beautiful land within Rhode Island would soon thereafter be occupied by men of non-Puritan denomination- adventurers, religious dissidents-, as the territory had never been granted to any colony by royal charter.

And so, as the Narragansett allowed Williams to settle Providence, it was there that a non-Puritan named Samuel Gorton fled with his increasing band of freethinkers after they were fined and whipped and banished from Plymouth in 1638 for defending a young widow whom the court wished to deport. Before Gorton and his party arrived in Providence, "from Plymouth he went to Newport in June of 1638; but again a disturber of the peace, he was whipped and banished from the Rhode Island Colony and went to Providence. His offenses were in the nature of religious contentions. In Providence, 'that shelter for persons distressed of conscience', he had no fear of prosecution, but he settled in Pawtuxet."

Gorton stirred dissent within the Pawtuxet Settlement in 1642, described in John Winthrop's recordings: "Gorton instructed and captained a party of Providence Anabaptists who denied, not only infant baptism, but also all the authority of magistrates and churches."[123]

Henceforth, four of the town's freemen, William Arnold, Robert Cole, William Carpenter, and Benedict Arnold, "could not consort with Gorton and that company and therefore were continually injured and molested by them' went and offered their lands to the Bay Colony and were accepted under its government and protection."

Governor Winthrop justified the motive by the four men as to their submission toward the Bay:

'partly to rescue these men from unjust violence and partly to draw in the rest in those parts either under ourselves or Plymouth, who now lived under no government but grew very offensive; and the place was likely to be of use to us, especially if we should have occasion of sending out against any Indians of Narragansett and likewise for an outlet into Narragansett Bay; and seeing it came without our seeking and would be no charge to us, we thought it not wisdom to let it slip.'[124]

The formal complaint against Gorton and his associates led to their removal from Pawtuxet, and in January 1643 he moved once again, this time to an area south of Pawtuxet along the Narragansett Bay. There he purchased a tract of land at Shawomet from the Narragansett Sachems, Miantonomo, Pomham, and another minor sachem, for forty-four fathoms of wampum. Pomham was the local sachem who held the land and signed the deed under pressure, but he would soon quickly flee to Massachusetts and submit all his land to the colony, as the four in Pawtuxet had. Thereupon, objections of the Shawomet chief Pomham and the Cowesset chieftain Socononoco, permitted Massachusetts to remove the unwanted squatters, known as the Gortonists, who now dwelt in Massachusetts bounds.[125] Massachusetts, angered by the

Narragansett land dealings, would ultimately deny
Miantonomo the help he would legally need to keep his life.

Miantonomo, by selling the Shawomet peninsula to
Samuel Gorton, who the Puritans viewed as a spirit struck
dumb with blasphemies and insolences, now involved himself
in the quarrel between Massachusetts and the Gortonists.
Gorton knew, as many others felt in Rhode Island, their
independence would vanish the moment Massachusetts or
Connecticut obtained the rights of conquest over the
Narragansetts. This awareness made a Narragansett conquest
much more difficult than the Pequot conquest, as the Rhode
Island planters held strong ties and communication with
England. Massachusetts would thus engage in drawing in the
last of those parts who now live under another government,
but grow very offensive. Gorton, as a result of the ill nature he
received, would write to the court four pages justifying his
beliefs-"A True Complaint of a Peaceable People, Being Part of
the English in New-England, Against Cruell Persecutors".

Simply, Massachusetts greatly desired the acquisition of
the territory of Narragansett Bay! Urged by the English
enemies of Gorton, the Massachusetts authorities relied on
Pumham, the local sachem, who laid claim to the ownership of
Shawomet and pleaded the inability of Miantonomo and
Canonicus to give valid title to the lands they had sold. This
scheme was successful, and a group composed of citizens of
Rhode Island, standing ready to purchase the land in question,
as it was conveyed to them by Pumham and Sacononoco,
offered their allegiance to the Massachusetts colony.

Miantonomo would again be summoned to Boston, and
could not prove, in the opinion of the authorities, his authority
over Pumham and Saconono, despite the declaration of
Roger Williams, that the authority of the Narragansett sachems
over the lands and chiefs in question, had existed as far back as
the settlement in Plymouth." Miantonomo on his return home,

learned that one of his relatives, Sequassen, had been roughly handled by Uncas.

Rumor has it; Sequassen chose to involve himself with the Mohegans and challenged the life of Uncas. It is said that Sequassen was related to Miantinomo by blood, as well as by alliance to the Narragansetts, wherein any of Sequassen's ill acts would be considered part of Miantonomo's conspiracy. A leading Mohegan was assassinated through an ambush by Sequassen's warriors, as Uncas and the Mohegans paddled a canoe down river, whilst attempts were also made to kill Uncas. Uncas quickly appealed to the magistrates in Hartford in response to the murder, whereupon he was told that it was wisest for the clans to reach some understanding. But, if necessary, the magistrates granted Uncas the right to avenge Sequassen's wrongs.

Uncas did not perform the peaceful reconciliation that the magistrates suggested for his lost Mohegan. He chose revenge. An invasion into the Sequins home was performed, killing seven and wounding around twenty men, burning wigwams, and carrying away great plunder. This act against Miantinomo's relatives occurred in the early summer of 1643. "This brought Miantonomo to the Hartford authorities in accordance with the 1638 treaty, who assured him that [the colony] could take no part for or against the Mohegans and matters must be settled peacefully amongst themselves."[126].

Governor Winthrop of the Bay was also asked by Miantonomo if the Sachem could use force against Uncas, wherein Winthrop responded, "if Uncas did him or his friends harm and would not give satisfaction, we shall leave him to take his own course."

Thereupon, he gathered a large force and marched toward the home of the Mohegans. Thus the year sixteen hundred and forty-three was the year Miantinomo invaded Uncas's fort.

Miantonomo gathered a huge force of six or seven hundred warriors and marched into the center of the Mohegan around Norwich, Connecticut. Uncas heard of the invading force from outlooks stationed in the direction of the Narragansetts. The Mohegan sachem learned from the scout that Miantonomi's force outnumbered his, yet he still chose to prepare his warriors. The Mohegan force left Shantok, the largest Mohegan fortification, with four hundred warriors and they met Miantonomo at the Great Plain, four miles from Shantok. There, Uncas would use trickery to compensate for being so greatly outnumbered.[127]

The Narragansetts appeared after crossing the fords of the Yantic, wherein the two forces quickly opposed each other. Uncas sent forward a messenger to ask for a conference. It was accepted and the Mohegan went out to meet Miantonomo, whilst both sides stood as spectators within a bow shot of each other. At the meeting between Uncas and Miantonomo the two faced each other between the two opposing forces. Uncas suggested the two settle this matter in one on one battle, and the winner would gain control of the loser's warriors. "Let us fight it out, if you kill me, my men shall be yours; if I kill you, your men shall be mine." Miantinomo, however, would not accept it. The Narragansett refused holding confidence in his superior numbers, "My men came to fight and they shall fight." Uncas, at that time, gave a pre-arranged signal and fell to the ground, thereupon, a surprise shower of arrows from three hundred Mohegan bows flew against their unprepared enemies who were within easy shot and unsuspicious of any such act.

The shower of arrows fell upon the helpless Narragansetts and Uncas sprang up, and with his warriors yelling their battle cry and holding their tomahawks, rushed upon the astonished enemy.[128] The Narragansetts fled panic-stricken. As Miantonomo's men broke and ran, the Mohegans pursued them through tangled thickets. Thirty Narragansetts died and many more were wounded in route. Miantonomo was wearing an English suit of armor which delayed his flight, and some pursuing Mohegans satisfied themselves with getting in his way, in order that Uncas himself, who was not in the front ranks of the pursuers, had the honor of facing his great enemy.[129] Uncas now held the shamed Miantonomo and brought him as a prisoner in Shantok.

The Narragansetts hoped a truce could be formed between the two warring tribes, and the Narragansetts quickly collected forty pounds worth of wampum for the return of Miantonomo. The wampum packages were sent to Uncas, some to Uncas's wife, and some to his favorite counselors; but Uncas would not free his captive.

Whilst Miantonomo was held prisoner the two sachems spoke at length.

Miantonomo supposedly proposed that Uncas join him in an alliance against the newcomers. However, in accordance with Indian custom Miantonomo's life was forfeited upon capture. Uncas' subsequent action was based on how Connecticut and Massachusetts would regard the handling of Miantonomo. Uncas knew there were whitemen that favored Miantonomo, therefore, he chose to do nothing with the captive without instruction from the Connecticut magistrates. When word came to Rhode Island, Gorton would write a letter to Uncas demanding the safe return of Miantonomo. If the sachem was to be harmed, Gorton threatened that great harm would also come to the Mohegan Sachem. Furthermore, Uncas did not want to enter a war against the Narragansetts without colonial support,[130] as he did not want to remove himself from the good graces of the white man.

In the end Uncas took his prisoner to Hartford for advice, which reflected the respect Uncas held for English law. The English held him prisoner at Hartford, and his case was put at the top of the schedule for the first meeting of the Commissioners of the United Colonies on September 7, 1643. Many things were set in motion with this decision- the character for future policy on Indian affairs, the ability to gain success through deceit and preferential treatment as Uncas had, and the establishment for the conduct of the general court to be driven by land and greed. All were of the opinion that "it would not be safe" to set the Narragansett Sachem "at liberty"[131]. The commissioners felt that Uncas could not be safe whilst Miantonomo lived. Those distinguished men of the United Colonies legally decided to have Miantonomo murdered by the hands of Uncas.

The sentence of Miantonomo is one of the most unjust decisions that stand recorded by the Colonial Courts. He had shown many acts of kindness towards the whites; in all his intercourse with them he had demonstrated a noble spirit, and only six years before his death had assisted Mason and his little band of soldiers from Hartford in their conquest against the Pequots.[132]

Why did the English intervene in the affair at all? The only answer could be that they sought to make an example of Miantonomo to terrify the natives as well as punish him for ill land dealings. The people of Rhode Island, who lived near Miantonomo, and whom he had often befriended, took sides with him while he was a prisoner, believing him to be in the right. Uncas and his constituents, on the other hand, brought up another piece of evidence as to why Miantonomo should sustain colonial punishment. They told the authorities at Hartford that Miantonomo had engaged the Mohawks to join him and that they were then encamped within a day's journey, and were awaiting Miantonomo's release.

The authorities apparently believed this, without making any attempt to verify it, and used it as a piece of evidence. The most significant justification for the punishment of Miantonomo, however, was because he was a treaty violator. They revived the Hartford treaty of 1638 with its stipulation that neither Uncas nor Miantonomo should war against the other until they had first protested, and that the English had heard their grievances. The language of the treaty may have been viewed as, "The English of Connecticut are to decide," not those of Massachusetts who Miantonomo received council with in regards to a retaliation against Uncas for his acts against Sequassen and his men.

The unfortunate Miantonomo had brought himself to his own doom. The hatred between the rival sachems, Uncas and Miantonomo, was deep and finally turned deadly for one of the two. Surprisingly though, Miantonomo's fate was to be determined by the clergy of the United Colonies Commissioners, because the commissioners were confused. According to English law there was no good reason for putting Miantonomo to death. The question was whether they should interfere with the Indian custom by which his life was already forfeit to his captor. The magistrates, however, suspected the Narragansetts of hostile intentions and in their time of confusion the commissioners sought spiritual guidance. A council of forty or fifty clergymen (elders), from all parts of New England, were in session at Boston, and the question was referred to a committee of five of their number. Thus the question of life or death was left to five men who were willing to be made the scapegoats. "These same men belonged to the profession that showed itself to be made up of the most bloodthirsty of all the English, and even more so than any of those whom they delighted in calling savages."[133]

Whilst the question was discussed whether Miantonomo should be put to death, the charges brought forward against him were these: that he had killed a Pequot who had testified against him in reference to his treatment of Uncas; that he had again and again tried to take the life of Uncas by assassination and poison; that he had broken his league in making war upon the Mohegans without taking his appeal to the English; and lastly, that he had conceived the horrible design of cutting off the whole English population, and had hired Mohawks and Indians of other tribes to assist him in its execution.

> Thus Uncas imposed upon the commissioners by acting upon their fears in this delicate matter, and that several of these charges were sustained by the most wicked perjury, I can't doubt. The several accusations in most of their details, I believe to have been a Mohegan fabrication and backed up by the testimony of Mohegan witnesses. It seems that the commissioners questioned its truth, and hesitated to act upon it. At last it was referred to five principal clergymen of the several colonies, who, after a solemn, and I doubt not an honest debate, advised that sentence of death should be passed upon the accused. The commissioners followed this unfortunate advice, and assigned Uncas to execute the sentence. [Hollister][134]

The commissioners directed that Uncas should bring his captive "Into the next part of his government, and there put him to death, provided that some discreet and faithful person of the English accompany them and see the execution, for our more full satisfaction."

The decision was prompt and the sentence was authorized that Miantonomo must die. Roger Williams was at this time in England and unable to speak in behalf of the Narragansett Sachem. Uncas promptly obeyed the directions given, taking with him two Hartford men as witnesses. Miantonomo was brought between Hartford and Windsor, and it was Uncas's brother, following after Miantonomo, who clave his head with a hatchet.[135]

Hereafter, there was only one path for Indian leaders to follow for self-preservation, as Uncas displayed. With the final breath of Miantonomo, many others increasingly submitted to the English. Numbers of Indians transformed toward the English culture to further preserve their own and their group's lives, even going so far as to submit their land directly to a colony or to the king of England in order to receive the same rights as the colonists.

The major Narragansett sachems thereupon sought a way to preserve their independence and to protect themselves succeeding the execution. The Narragansett leadership chose to deal directly with the King of England having observed Rhode Island residents' success in appealing to a distant royal authority for protection.

The land issue that arose from Gorton's purchase, along with the treats and reaction in Rhode Island regarding the sachems death, led Gorton and the grieving Narragansetts into direct conflict with the United Colonies. To increase tension, the Massachusetts authorities sent an armed force to remove the Gortonists. With no backing, as Rhode Island was not a member of the United Colonies, Gorton sailed across the Atlantic to London in order to discuss matters with the King, concerning both himself and the Narragansett struggles. Thus in 1644 a previous minor land dispute now blossomed into an affair to be dealt with by royal authority. A letter delivered to the King on April 19, 1644, shared that the Narragansetts, seeking relief for all their pain and grief, willingly decided, and most humbly, to submit, subject, and give over themselves, peoples, lands, rights, inheritances, and possessions unto the protection, care and government of that worthy and royal

Prince, Charles, King of Great Britain and Ireland. Subjection was the only solution as the Narragansetts held great suspicion of some of His Majesty's subjects.

The written act of submission made it clear as to what the Narragansetts hoped to gain- allegiance upon condition of his Majesties' royal protection. Submission to the king legally protected them from other subjects of the king living in the colonies: "Nor can we yield over ourselves unto any, that are subjects themselves in any case." The sachems understood they now employed the English crown in hopes of gaining advantages in their local struggles with the colonial authorities and other Indians. The Narragansetts wished to continue as equals not subjects to the United Colonies.

There were other Indians who chose to form an allegiance with Massachusetts Bay, contrary to the Narragansetts' and the compact they had formed with the King. On June 22, 1643, as abovementioned, Indians within Rhode Island considered tributaries of the Narragansetts, Pomham and Socononoco, had journeyed to Boston and submitted themselves and their lands to the government of Massachusetts, ignoring any reference to the king. Massachusetts Bay then laid claim to Shawomet, but requested Miantonomo, prior to his death, to appear before the authorities to decide the ownership of these lands and to prove his claim of authority over the other two sachems who claimed the land theirs, as Pomham was sachem of Shawomet, and Sacononoco sachem of Patuxet.

Narragansett land at issue was thinly settled by a colony of unchartered squatters, some of whom had made purchase from Miantonomo. In Massachusetts's view, many of these purchasers were undesirables for several reasons and all of them were establishing independent title to land that Boston wanted, and a majority of the squatters disregarded certain religious practices.

As Samuel Gorton and his associates were these independent residents at Shawomet, it would seem that Boston became very angry at that transaction and predicted that Miantonomo would lose his head for it.[136]

Before the certainty of the prediction by Boston, Miantonomo promptly appeared in Boston, and was demanded in open court- whether he had any interest in the said two sachems as his subjects, he could prove none. The two Indians of Rhode Island, Pomham and Socononoco, sought protection against the Narragansett, protecting their interest against Gorton, who had taken away their land in agreement with Miantonomo. The two submitting sachems were forced to appear before the governor of Massachusetts and sign a form, which they did and then departed joyful and well satisfied. This instance gave encouragement to many Indians to come in and submit to the Massachusetts government, in expectation of the like protection and benefit. Governor Winthrop considered the submission of Pomham and Socononoco, "a fruit of our prayers and the first fruit of our hopes that the example would bring in others."[137]

Before Pumham and Socononoco submitted land, there already existed great confusion by the fragmentation of lands in Rhode Island. The settlers planned and struggled against each other, and some chose to scheme with other Puritan colonies.[138] The submission by the four Pawtuxet men toward the Bay is the principal illustration of the disorder within Rhode Island. "Governor Winthrop evidently did not consider Pawtuxet as part of Providence, a settlement on part of the land purchased by Williams of the Indians, and intended by him always to be part of the plantation. But the four men of Providence must have so known and so understood."[139]

The Narragansetts became very cautious with all whitemen. "The Narragansetts had by no means remained quiet under the loss of their sachem, they were continually harassing the Mohegans with their war parties. Miantinomo's authority was inherited, at least to some degree, by his brother, a young man of about twenty, named Pessicus. Within a month after the death of Miantinomo, and also in the following March, Pessicus sent presents to Boston, with messages that he wished peace with the English, but was still determined to make war upon Uncas. His presents were refused; unfriendly answers were returned to him, and he was told that the English would stand by Uncas whenever he should be attacked.

Twelve or fourteen Englishmen, sent by Hartford to protect Uncas, probably had enough and more than enough to do, all summer, in keeping watch, and running about from this point to that, to chase away the intruders. Things finally became so troublesome, that the Commissioners determined, [September, 1644,] that both parties should be summoned to Hartford, and plead their case before the Court.

Notwithstanding the restrictions which the English had been continually putting upon the Indians since their settlement of the country, the independent spirit of the Narragansett sachems was not quelled in any degree. Whatever externals of submission might have been apparent, underneath was a current of unrest and a harboring of revenge. [Herbert Milton Sylvester][140]

Yet no Narragansett uprising arose!

"In the years following, various regulations were adopted by the Connecticut government by which the intercourse between the Indians and the whites was to become more limited. The Indians were not allowed to live within a quarter of a mile of any English settlement; and if they brought their guns into the settlement they were to be confiscated. One tribe was not allowed to entertain wandering members of other tribes; and in no case was a strange Indian to be admitted to the settlements, unless fleeing from his enemy. Drunkenness prevailed among the savages, and the settlements were at times disturbed by their attempts to obtain liquor, and all Indians were forbidden to walk about the streets after nightfall, under penalty of a fine or flogging. The English were not allowed to take the property of an Indian for debt without consent, or upon legal warrant; and later it was enacted that such as trusted an Indian with goods were deprived of all right to appeal to law for the recovering of the same. It was during these years that the efforts for the Christianizing of the Indians were going on under the auspices of the Society for Propagating the Gospel in New England; and it is noted that at this time the Mohegans, as well as the other Connecticut tribes, had little if any knowledge of Christianity, and were still to be regarded as among the heathen." [Herbert Milton Sylvester][141]

The event of Miantonomo's death was so historic for the colonies' growth, as his fate proved why Indians should not dissent against any portion of the English power. He was punished even after bringing his intentions of war against Uncas to the authorities—in other words, he had followed the rules. The legal effort by Massachusetts for the acquisition of some Narragansett land may have been the main factor of his fate, and ironically, the results initiated the first steps for the missionary program on the mainland. The death of the great Narragansett sachem also signified the diminished protection a sachem provided for the tribe, which forced the Indian to depend on another form of authority outside the tribe for leadership. As easy as this sachem was destroyed, the scattered

Indians now had to find protection and support in a new source and they had no problem in giving up their land for it.

His punishment set the stage for the submission of lands by the Massachusetts Sachems and their affiliates in 1644. These submissions opened the possibility of praying Indian villages sanctioned by the court, which came fifteen years after John Winthrop first proclaimed the missionary purpose. Miantonomo's death finally initiated the conversion of Indians toward the Gospel! The submission of Massachusetts sachem Cutshamekin and four others to colonial authority in March 1644 approved the General Court to direct the county courts to instruct the Indians in knowledge and worship of God and to take care that the Indians should be civilized.

Christian practices thus became an obligation for Massachusetts tribes when they ceded their land. The door finally opened for the development of a new Indian society with religion leading those living within the bounds of the Massachusetts Bay colony. The Puritans believed that their government extended to all within the colony's borders, whereupon the Christian Indians, were now also lawfully obliged to and protected by the same laws that governed English settlers. There existed a parallel between Narragansett land submission to the king and Massachusetts Indians submitting themselves to the colony: both submissions were for protection.

It was in 1644, March 7- Nashowanon (Nipmuc Sachem at Washekim), Cutshamekin, Masconnamet, Massasoit (Wossamegon), & Squaw Sachem (Nipmuc leader near Mount Wachuset), voluntarily submitted themselves to the authority of the Massachusetts Bay government:

The submission of 1644, reads as follows:
Wee haue & by these presents do voluntarily, & without any

constraint or pswasion, but, of or owne free motion, put orselues, or
subiects, lands, & estates under the government & jurisdiction of the Maisachusets, to bee governed & ptected by them, according to their just laws & orders, so farr as wee shalbee made capable of understanding; & wee do pmise for orselues, & all or subjects, & all or posterity, to bee true & faithfull to the said government, & ayding to the maintenance thereof, to our best ability, & from time to time to give speedy notice of any conspiracy, attempt, or evill intension of any which wee shall know or heare of against the same; & wee do pmise to bee willing from time to time to bee instructed in the knowledg & worship of God. In witnes whereof wee have hereunto put or hands, 1643-1644.

"Cutshamache,
Nashowanon,
Wossamegon,
Maskanomett,
Squa Sachem."

Before submission was allowed to be accepted, the Indians were examined as to their religious belief and moral attitude. This examination was as follows:

"F. To worship ye onely true God, who made heaven & earth, & not to blaspheme him.

Answer: We do desire to revrence ye God of ye English, & to speake well of him, because wee see hee doth better to *ye* English than othr gods do to others.

2. Not to swear falcely.

An: They say they know not wl swering is among ym.

3. Not to do any unnecessary worke on ye Saboth day.

An: It is easy to ym ; they have not to do on any day, & they can well take their ease on yl day.

4 To hono' their parents & all their superiors.

"An: It is their custome to do so, for the inseriors to honor their superiors.

5. To kill no man without just cause & just authority.

An: This is good, & they desire to do so.

6. To comit no unclean lust, or fornication, adultery, incest, rape, sodomy, buggery, or beastiality.

An: Though sometime some of ym do it, yet they count that naught, & do not alow it.

7. Not to steale.

An: They say to you as to ye 6th query.

To suffer their children to learn to reade Gods word, yl they may learn to know God aright, & worship him in his owne way.

They say, as oportunity will serve, & English live among ym, they desire so to do.

That they should not bee idle."

To these statements the Indians consented, acknowledging them to be good. The authorities were satisfied with the result of the examination and accepted their allegiance. The general court ordered the colonial treasurer to give each of the Indians a coat of red cloth— two yards of material in each, and a pot full of wine. The Indians presented the members of the court with twenty-six fathom of wampum.[142]

Was this an absolute submission to the colony? Massachusetts perceived the treaty as that, but were the sachems voluntarily relinquishing their lands, freedom to worship, and subjects? Or, in fact, was the sachems aim to have their estates governed and protected by the Bay Colon, wherein they were willing subjects to be instructed in the knowledge of God from "time to time."

Missionary Mayhew Jr.

A feeling of uneasiness was felt in the mid 1640s, as many various difficulties would reign upon wary minds-unbeknownst Indians, premature death, Narragansett invasion, civil obedience. Whitemen were no longer concerned of his trade or relations with the Indians. His fur enterprise was rapidly decreasing in revenue and his opinion on the redmen diminished after the Wethersfield massacre. Altogether, the fur supply had vastly diminished. There was such a great depletion of furs in the area since the planters first arrived in Wethersfield that it was no longer a profitable trade in 1645. There was little civil tidings with the River Indian, which removed any value the planters held toward the Pynchon Springfield fur enterprise.

"The Indian wampum soon became a too uncertain quantity except in dealings with the natives themselves. This resulted in the early spread of warehouses. In 1645 each town had two fairs a year in addition to its public market on meetinghouse square. At these there was exchange of all manner of commodities that should be brought in, for cattle or any merchandize whatever. In the earliest days this was the custom in Hartford. Standards were fixed by the court and it was a duty of the town clerk to see that they were kept constant and observed."[143]

It so happened around this time in Martha's Vineyard, an area known as Capawock by the natives, was forming through the Mayhew family.

Mayhew's abode was at Watertown, where he had good accommodations of land, and built an excellent profitable mill there, which in those first times brought him in great profit. But it pleased God to frown upon him in his outward estate: so that he sold what he had in the Massachusetts, to clear himself from debts and engagements; and about the year 1642, transplanted himself to Martha's Vineyard, with his family.[144]

The first island plantation Thomas Mayhew established independently was named Great Harbor, which was also inhabited by twenty able bodied planters and their families. Three thousand Wampanoags, moreover, occupied the distant island. The elder Mayhew did not first settle permanently upon the island. It was a span of a couple years that Mayhew Sr. settled. Mayhew Jr. served as the plantation's governor until his father built his home.

The beginnings of Great Harbor, Martha's Vineyard, date back to 1641 when an emissary to the Right Honorable Earl of Stirling came in contact with Thomas Mayhew through a meeting in Boston. The emissary, with authority from the Earl of Stirling, was granted to dispose of lands for the colonization of Long Island and parts adjacent, and was encouraged to further his master's interests and to further the colonization of his lands. Negotiations were opened with the Puritan merchant Mayhew to accept a grant of one or more of the unsettled islands of Martha's Vineyard, Nantucket, and those adjacent, eastward of Long Island.[145] Thereupon, in a meeting in Watertown, Thomas Mayhew Sr. and Thomas Mayhew Jr. granted unto five of their neighbors a patent for the establishment of a large town upon the Vineyard with equal power in town government. A town proprietary was divided into shares.

At Great Harbor, newcomers were admitted into the proprietary from time to time, either by an increase in the number of shares, or the sale of a share or fraction of a share by an individual proprietor.[146] First, however, the land had to be obtained from the Indian proprietors, wherein Mayhew bought Martha's Vineyard, Nantucket, Muskeget, and Tuckenuck, from Tawanquatuck in 1641 for forty pounds.

At this time, new settlement had brought fresh excitement. When early planters arrived at Great Harbor in Martha's Vineyard there wasn't much to the plantation, as was the case in Wethersfield. The economy and structure on the island weren't much developed. Roads, paths, and bridges had to be built where nature held precedence. There was a lot of work on the bright side.

Felling trees with heavy tools, sawing lumber, building homes and a mill and public buildings, laying out roads and paths, removing rocks and stumps from the land, planting crops of corn and vegetables, pasturing horned cattle and sheep, and fishing, were tasks that required the labor of an entire community. Wherein men joined upon all tasks necessary in accord with erecting a township- the lots of Great Harbor were grouped together in a village style in order to coordinate military protection against possible Indian raids, and to grant the residents the advantages of a compact plantation. At all times, it was quite obvious, they were watched by lurking savages, who remained at a cautious distance and refused to hold much intercourse at first, as the memory of the Pequot invasion was forever stored.[147]

There was one Indian named Hiacoomes, however, who was the first willing to approach Mayhew Jr. Fortunate for Thomas, a friendship formed rather quickly between the two, as the Indian was willing to lend a helping hand. Hiacoomes was considered to be of the lowest kind of Indian in the Wampanoag Confederacy. The Wampanoags didn't have a need for Mayhew's friend. The tribe considered Hiacoomes as a harmless man- his speech was slow and his appearance unfavorable. Nevertheless, in such a close proximity to the whitemen, Hiacoomes would find an open door. Likewise, his wigwam would be visited, in which the Indian entertained the different race considerately. The whites began a discourse with him and soon the Indian would frequent their houses and attend the meetinghouse. By 1644 Hiacoomes obtained tools to read, while Mayhew developed his Wampanoag. This reception of knowledge would lead to a religious enlightenment on the island.

In contrast to the collective paranoia toward the natives, Mayhew began to wonder if it was at all possible to bring salvation to those that lacked vision. Hiacoomes example displayed an Indian eagerly accepting all the instructions Mayhew would share. Not to mention, within three years, Mayhew's tireless labor brought about a good understanding in Wampanoag tongue.

It was a laborious process that molded the first Praying Indian in Hiacoomes, and later his wife. A great deterrent arose consequently, the Sachems and powwows became quite alarmed of Hiacoomes new religion. Hiacoomes's former rulers tried to discourage his efforts, calling the Indian an Englishman, but all to no avail. These discouraging Indians, sadly, did not initially determine how righteous a man Mayhew Jr. was.

Contrary to the Pequots' loss of land and rights taken by the planters, Martha's Vineyard Indian rights were faithfully preserved. On the island, certainly, no effort was made to crowd the Indian out of his possessions. The Indians who lived in Martha's Vineyard were the Pawkunnawkutts, in which there were nine separate tribes holding membership in this confederation, each governed by its own petty sachem, but all subject to the Great Sachem Massasoit.[148]

Every plot within the bounds of Mayhew's patent was purchased from its lawful Indian proprietor, whilst Mayhew held an English title that professed acceptance from the crown, he chose to consider that title as granting him merely the right among Europeans to purchase lands from the aboriginal occupants. He held no control or ownership of any tract of land remaining in Indian ownership. When Mayhew sold land to a whiteman, which he himself hadn't purchased of the natives, he sold merely a right to the settler to obtain the title from the proper Indian sachem.

It was the general consensus of opinion in New England that a patent of land derived from the crown awarded upon the grantee the English title acceded upon by the Indian right of occupancy. It was the right of occupancy, which the English purchased from the Indians, even as the natives had no concept of acquiring a land title for a fee.

No man in New England was fairer to the Indians than both father and son Mayhew. A sense of obligation was held by both men to guide the Indians toward salvation. They established churches, courts, and civil governments among them. It was the total opposite of the hostility felt in Wethersfield, where men felt justified in land purchases for beads and other trinkets, while the Indians thought they were just signing over the right for the planters to share the use of the land.

On the matter of land transactions- "How could we blame the white man for giving the Indian what he wanted. Beads were desired as articles of ornament. Also, axes, firearms, and other items of hardware were wanted just as we need them."

From the Indian perspective, however, they would never fully understand the land titles. They couldn't comprehend that one man could become entitled to an estate so as to prevent others from using it- land to the Indian was as free as the water or the air. Nobody could have the private right to it. So, when the European came and obtained deeds from the sachems, it was merely the admission to share the land with the Indians on equal terms. It wasn't that the Indian had ceased to have the right to enjoy the land but rather share the same rights.

It is amazing to think the son of Mayhew with the same name, born about the year 1620-21, was the Mayhew who had first planted Martha's Vineyard in his early twenties, whilst never promoting the principles of coercion or material reward.

Thomas Mayhew Jr. put forth all of his energies on the island toward sincerely helping the Indians discover the Christian life. Endless labor ensued as a missionary among the native people, whom he could communicate with in their language.

Mayhew Jr. found the task of the native language tedious and laborious. Few English teachers existed among the Indians, for most of the educated English young men did not endeavor to learn or face the rigors of the Indian language. It was a disheartening work that had to be mastered at the outset, before much else could be done. Few of the English were able to speak it as the speech was a language that greatly used the compounding of words. The Indian language, moreover, offered no books, dictionary, or grammar. Not one printed word had ever before been printed.

Worst of all there was no aid by which the language could be learned, no grammar, no written specimens from which word sounds could be studied, for the language was an unwritten one. The only procedure open to one who sought to learn it was to strain one's ears in an effort to catch its sense in fragmentary bits from Indian companions, who knew little or no English.[149]

Nevertheless, Mayhew Jr. was not developing an untouched Island for his own benefit, but more so for the improvement of the Indian, as there was no interest in clearing land for his own benefit. His time was spent for the Indian. He would visit heir houses called "wetu's," which resembled a beehive, with saplings curved to form its fifteen foot diameter, with a hole in the roof center for smoke to go out. Mayhew would visit these wetu's quite often.

Thomas, Jr. was sympathetic to the Indian. Every action was for improving their material and spiritual life and I admire everything about him. In my opinion, the great achievement of his life was not the plantation upon the island, as he was very successful in this, but it was the peaceful development of the Indian toward the Christian conduct. His devotion made him known as a father, counselor, and sachem.[150]

There was no necessity for the missionary work at Martha's Vineyard to begin through force or fear. It began through the divinity within Thomas Mayhew whose spirit traveled into the soul of others. By exhibiting this righteous living and teaching, he shared with the Indians the Christian

God and a knowledge of civilized living, as many aspects of the religion were taught- love, salvation and everlasting life. Thus, through years under Mayhew's direction many Indians would pray to God.

There was a happy government settled among them, and Records kept of all Actions and Acts passed in their several Courts, by such who having learned to Write fairly were appointed thereto. The Princes with their Sachims made Publick acknowledgment of their Subjection to the King of England, being notwithstanding mindful to be understood as Subordinate Princes, to Govern according to the Laws of God and the King. [Mathew Mayhew]

Their church would first be the open field where the stage for Mayhew's sermon would simply be a nearby flat stone, whereupon the Indian Heaven was the same heaven all righteous men sought.

The successes of Thomas Mayhew Jr., as a missionary all became possible through his first convert, Hiacoomes. This was the initial Indian who held an interest in the Christian faith and desired to learn to read.

Observing in this Hiacoomes a disposition to hear and receive instruction; observing also, that his countenance was grave and sober he resolved to essay in the first place what he could do with him, and immediately took an opportunity to discourse him; and finding encouragement to go on in his endeavours to instruct and enlighten him, he invited him to come to his house every Lord's day evening, that so he might then more especially have a good opportunity to treat with him about the things of god, and open the mysteries of his Kingdom to him. Hiacoomes accepting his kind invitation, Mr. Mayhew used his utmost endeavors to enlighten him. And Hiacoomes seemed as eagerly to suck in the instructions given him, as if his heart

had been before prepared by God, and made good Ground,
in order to a due reception of his word sown in it.
[Experience Mayhew, grandson] [151]

At first, Hiacoomes felt the ridicule of his fellow-
tribesmen, who mocked him as he read while walking through
the wilderness. Laughter arose toward the new religion that
only worshipped one God, while those first in opposition to
Hiacoomes worshipped thirty-seven principal gods. However,
Hiacoomes would continue to gain knowledge on the faith
through the lessons taught to him on Sunday in the minister's
house at Great Harbor, which I attended. He learned fast, whilst
slowly the other Indians began to admire Hiacoomes, who was
once considered of little importance among them, but who now
gathered information unaware to all.

The decision by other Indians to consider taking toward
Mayhew began when masses of the Indians upon the island
caught the plague, probably beginning in the year subsequent
to Mayhew's arrival in 1642. Mayhew's party was most likely
the carriers of the germs and the missionary witnessed the
strange disease spread amongst them. To cure the plague, the
Indians would run up and down till they could no longer, they
made their faces as black as night, gathered every weapon,
spoke powerful words, but none of this worked and they were
punished by the ailment. The Indians blamed all their sickness
and death on breaking away from tradition. It was only
Hiacoomes who denied the Indian certainty that Christianity
was the cause of all the illness.

In 1646, sickness continued and swept through the
natives, but by this time it became obvious to other Indians
that Hiacoomes didn't suffer the plague. They mocked him as
an imitation Englishman at first, but he was somehow still able

to escape the severe wrath of the plague, whilst the traditional Indians who depended on mystical powwows were stricken. A small number of leading Indians upon the island, who had once excluded Hiacoomes when he was of their belief, slowly began to follow him as a Christian teacher.

Hiacoomes told the Indians that he didn't fear the thirty-seven Indian gods or the powwows. He explained that he was preserved through the great illness because of his fear of the great God only. Hiacoomes would come to share with them many of the sins that the Indian commits, such as having many gods and going to the powwows, wherein the non-believers would become aware through Hiacoomes that they were sinners.

Soon thereafter, Mr. Mayhew held a public meeting to make known to the other Indians the word of God. Mayhew did understand though that most of the Indians were held back because of the powwows witchcraft, as it was believed by the powwows and sachems that the introduction of Christianity lessened their strength.

Powwows are what the Indian priest and medicine men were called and these powwows influenced all the stages of life, religion, peace, war, and health, as they were the most dominating position within the Indian's life, upholding a strange and powerful influence over their superstitious fellow tribes-men. Among exorcism and charms, they were also recognized with the ability to relinquish many problems. One is reported to have made water burn, rocks move, and trees dance. Their great fear was that they would lose all their power if their tribe would convert.

The powwows demonstrated their gift through healing, or adversely, through physical harm, mental pain, torture, or even distraction of mind. Their greatest influence was psychological. The superstitious Indian lived in such great fear of the powwow's power that once told by a powwow he was cursed, the most terrible mental pains and bodily symptoms would occur.[152]

With conversion, however, the humbled Indian would learn from the white man the self-governing laws of man. Upon the island, the Indian no longer wanted to live as a subject to a single dominating ruler. The Indian was willing to pay tribute to Mayhew rather than a sachem, and was encouraged to do so by Mayhew, but he insisted that the tribute or tax should be put into the best interest for Indian development.

Mayhew Jr.'s selfless labor continued to win the attention of an ever-increasing amount of the island Indians. He did not mind spending so much of his time on the uncivilized as persistence prevailed through wet and cold. He lodged in their houses and expected no rewards. Nevertheless, there were still many obstacles, but there were three major things that brought most of the Indians toward conversion. They wanted to know what wealth they would obtain by becoming Christians, if the sachems would approve of it, and what curse the powwows would perform.

With Hiacoomes example, Christian meetings would continue with the Indians and in the year 1647 a great convention was held. At this meeting there was both Christian Indians and those who were in doubt. The dangerous power of the powwows was debated the most of all matters. Many felt their power could kill. Others asked, "Who doesn't fear them?"

Some replied there isn't a man that doesn't. It was only Hiacoomes who rose to his feet, faced the large room, and challenged the powwows, "though the powwows might hurt those that feared them, yet I believed and trusted in the Great God of Heaven and Earth, and therefore all the Powwows could do me no harm, and I feared them not."[153]

The crowd then awaited the wrath of the thirty-seven Indian gods to punish Hiacoomes. Minutes passed, but nothing happened. Thus the Indians began to question everything they believed. The power of the powwows weakened and many Indians stepped forward to profess belief in the white man's God. They asked Hiacoomes to explain what his great God wished of them. Hiacoomes would then share fifty sins committed by the Indians. Committing so many ill acts amazed and touched their consciences and by the end of the meeting twenty-two unchristianized Indians resolved to walk with God.

When Hiacoomes' disrespect of the powwows reached those not in the conference attendance, the entire island powwow population became enraged and destruction of Hiacoomes was threatened. One powwow interrupted a meeting one Sunday where Hiacoomes was preaching and challenged the converts. The powwow called three of them by name and the angered powwow told them they were deceived, for the powwows could kill any Christian Indian if they set the effort forth. Hiacoomes responded that he could stand in the center of all the powwows on the island safe and without fear and they could do him no harm.

For a significant amount of time Hiacoomes was the sole object of the curses. Powwows used every trick in their effort to ruin him, but all to no avail, as Hiacoomes was immune to the psychological warfare of the heathen priests. One powwow would later confess of using one of his own gods in the form of a snake to kill Hiacoomes. His efforts proved worthless and in time chose to worship the Englishman's God with Hiacoomes.

As a result of this widespread movement, Rev. Mayhew was quick to expand the mission through the downfall of the powwows. He increased his services as he traveled many times about the island to preach at various Indian locations with no consideration of fatigue. In smoky wigwams at night, by the flickering light of a tent fire, he would relate to a crowd of primitive children the ancient stories of the Bible, and the Indians listened in wonder. Christian meetings continued on to the joy of some Indians, and the envy of the rest.[154]

The efforts of Thomas Mayhew, Jr., on the Vineyard and John Eliot, a fellow missionary on the mainland of Massachusetts, began to interest persons of wealth in England. These men would ultimately foster money for the propagation of the gospel among the Indians in the New World. Interest within England had been inspired by letters written November 18, 1647 by Mayhew describing the missionary work. Something moved the "hearts of some godly Christians in England to advance a considerable sum for encouraging the propagating and preaching of the gospel to the Indians within New England"[155]. Nevertheless, Mayhew had spent the previous eight years with no aid. Moreover, Mayhew Jr. would continue three more years before receiving a regular salary.

At first, donations were from individual sources, but as reports brought positive news, it was decided to unite their charities. Thus, the Long Parliament, July 27, 1649, passed an act establishing a corporation for the propagation of the gospel in New England, consisting of a president, treasurer, and fourteen assistants, called "the President and Society for the Propagation of the Gospel in New England;" later to be known as the New England Company. Oliver Cromwell led a general fund amounting to thousands of pounds that was gathered throughout England and Wales for this corporation, and then invested in land.

The corporation was the only Protestant missionary society in the world, wherein the New England Commissioners of the United Colonies were the local representatives in the management of the corporation's affairs and distribution of funds.

Thomas Mayhew, Jr., performed his missionary labors with no financial compensation up to that point. Co-proprietary of sixteen islands, and son of an English governor, he could easily have bought and sold tracts of land. Instead he chose to help the uncivilized and live a modest life.

133

His modesty prevented any mention of his own undertakings, whereupon he established the first permanent English mission to the Indians. During the early years of his missionary efforts, the commissioners from the powerful Massachusetts Colony overlooked him. Martha's Vineyard was no part of a larger colony or the United Colonies, and there may have been ulterior motives for ignoring Mayhew- open land of new regions within Massachusetts for certain planters involved with the Society for the Propagation of the Gospel in New England. Much less attention was spent on a petty island compared with the attention John Eliot received on the mainland, wherein laid the abundance of western Massachusetts unclaimed Nipmuck land.

The Indians on Martha's Vineyard, however, were in good hands. Mayhew, Jr. formed a covenant in the Indian language, which he read and made understandable to the Indians, who consented with it, and promised to follow it faithfully.

The covenant was as follows:

We the distressed Indians of the Vineyard that beyond all memory have been without the True God, without a Teacher, and without law, the very servants of sin and satan, and without peace, for God did justly vex us for our sins; having lately through his mercy heard of the name of the true god, the name of his son Jesus Christ, with the holy ghost the comforter, three persons, but one most glorious god, whose name is Jehovah: We do praise his glorious greatness, and in the sorrow of our hearts, and shame of our faces, we do acknowledge and renounce our great and many sins, that we and our Fathers have lived in, do run unto him for mercy, and pardon for Christ Jesus sake; and we do this day through the blessing of God upon us, and trusting to his gracious help, give up ourselves in this covenant, we, our wives, and children, to serve Jehovah: and we do this day choose Jehovah to be our God himself, and to trust in him alone for salvation, both of soul and body, in this present life, and the everlasting life to come, through his mercy in Christ Jesus our Savior, and redeemer, and by the might of his holy spirit; to whom with the father and son, be all glory everlasting. Amen.[156]

In choosing rulers under these guidelines, the Indians chose those with goodness and those most likely to remove wickedness. This set in motion the Indian church in Martha's Vineyard, which the senior Mayhew was to fully organize with Indian officers and a pastor eighteen years later. There were 282 converts in 1652, not including children. Eight of these were previously powwows. The mission on the Vineyard created six small villages, containing about a hundred and fifty five families, and about eight hundred souls. Each of these villages held an Indian preacher.[157]

The work of the Vineyard mission was growing every year and gaining acclaim. With John Eliot asking for assistance and a publication of Mayhew's letter of 1647 to the Society for the Propagation of the Gospel, the two would finally obtain financial support. Thomas Mayhew Jr., would become a salaried missionary of England around 1654. During the years before financial recognition the mission by Mayhew had been supported entirely from the private funds of the Mayhew's.

At a yearly meeting of the commissioners of the United Colonies held in September of 1654 it was voted to allow Thomas Mayhew, Jr., for his labor this year the sum of forty pounds, and for a schoolmaster to the Indians and other employees the sum of ten pounds apiece per annum. However, Mayhew did feel his income did not compare with others involved in the same matters.

Circumstances for Mayhew also had changed. Instead of depending upon his family's private purse, which was not enough to support the work, Mayhew, Jr., was now receiving an annual salary from the society. In 1656 the Vineyard mission had been in existence fourteen years, and it was becoming well improved. Mayhew Jr., felt he could now leave for a short trip to England, where the estate of his wife and her brother commanded his attention.

By 1656, Mayhew, Jr., asked the commissioners for permission to make the trip to England. They felt however that the mission would decline by his leave and they advised him to send someone else. Permission, nevertheless, would be given the following year. This trip would also give Mayhew the chance to show the English people a proper understanding of the positive missionary work in New England, contrary to how he had minimally portrayed it through letter. A trip to England would also allow him to gain instruments for the further advancement of Indian conversion.

Prior to his departure, Thomas organized a farewell meeting with his native worshippers and peers, which brought those close to a distant meadow. There a most peaceful service was performed, as he asked all to be dedicated in their practices during his absence. His followers, didn't want to leave him, they followed him during his travel to the east end of the island for his departure by ship. The numbers grew at each meeting place until we reached the Old Mill Path. "Here a great combined service was held, and the simple children of this flock heard their beloved Shepard give a blessing to them and say the last sad farewells to them individually and as a congregation. It was a sad occasion, long held in memory by those who participated."[158] For myself, I try not to dwell on this day all the too often.

It was the final ceremony the Indians heard from Thomas. The ship would make its final departure from Boston and head for Old England with Thomas, his brother-in-law, and an Indian convert aboard it. Nevertheless, word quickly came to the island that Master Garrett and his ship was missing, whilst no one heard or saw any type of disaster that would have taken the ship Mayhew was on. "Weeks passed into months. Hope in time gave way to fear."[159] Mayhew Jr., was never to be heard of again.

The tale of death upon any man, be it a friend or foe, leaves a feeling indescribable to any great poet. The death of Mayhew is a very tragic circumstance for the true mission.

Mayhew's father took full responsibility for the Indian mission whilst everyone waited praying for Thomas' return. It seemed that each man on the island had dropped a stone upon the site where Mayhew last spoke- in both honor and as superstition for return. Return, however, never came.

Thomas Mayhew Sr., was an amazing man as his son, yet, he was much older. I greatly admire all of their sacrifice toward the natives. Nevertheless, the new path for the mission would lead away from the success of the island mission, wherein trouble would become uncontrollable in Massachusetts with the promotion of Christianity upon the Natives.

Could Christianity be brought upon the Indians with Massachusetts? Springfield was one of the most important of the plantations along the river, as Springfield's busy mills and bulging barns were a result of the valley soil.[160] Springfield was above the navigable waters of the river, with hundreds of inhabitants, its location at the junction of the Valley Trail and the Bay Path gave it importance in the valley second only to Hartford.[161]

"At this point in time, Springfield established itself as the commercial, political and social hub. As early as the late 1630s, [crops], meat products and furs from Springfield were being shipped out from William Pynchon's Windsor, Connecticut warehouse to Boston. By the 1650's, Springfield had its own active trade contacts with Hartford and Boston. In addition, Springfield functioned as the primary distribution point for goods moving into or out of the mid and upper portions of the Connecticut River Valley." [The Massachusetts Historic Commission][162]

Springfield

Were any missionaries similar to Mayhew in Springfield? in Massachusetts? The gospel, in response, made little advancement among the Mohegans and their northern neighbors in the Connecticut River Valley.[163]

The colonization of Springfield obviously brought great change for the native. The meeting-house was located in the small civic district, an area that also housed a county courthouse and jail- all located on Center Street. Few Indians held importance here.

By the middle of the seventeenth century, Springfield was clearly bustling with colonial fervent. Indians, as was the case in Wethersfield, had been placed in the blissful distance ignorance provides. One figure in Springfield, John Pynchon, had learned the skill of the natives through the family's fur business. However, at this time, fur held little value.

"After the mid 1650s, however, Pynchon's operation underwent a relatively steady decline. (...) The declining beaver population along with the decreased market value for beaver pelts, signaled the demise of the fur trade in the river valley." [The Massachusetts Historic Commission][164]

John Pynchon also did a lot of trade with the Indians, who lived in small communities along the banks of the Connecticut. Uncas certainly played a role in the area. The "tedious and harassing hostility" Miantanomo's death brought about was drawing a close with the Narragansett after fifteen years in 1658. Uncas' uneasy temper did not cease however. The Mohegan tribe was very active in the area west of Narragansett and those Puritan officials were annoyed with the reports of his activity. Uncas was up to his old trickery. From the vantage point of his outpost in Springfield, John Pynchon told John Winthrop Jr. that peace would not exist as long as Uncas held no control over himself.

On one occasion, Uncas denied the Podunk Indians to return to their dwellings and live in peace and safety, without molestation from him or his, unless they paid him tribute. In the spring of 1657, Tontonimo the Podunk sachem appealed for help, calling upon the Pocumtucks and Narragansetts to protect him from the Mohegan sachem. The Podunk sachem also called upon the Connecticut English, and offered at this time to cede a portion of his lands around Hartford to the River Colony in exchange for their services.

Pynchon was a major figure in the Connecticut River Valley and a man of importance in the village of Springfield, but also in the colony of Massachusetts, where he served as a magistrate. Amicable ties existed as he fostered relations between the local English and nearby Indians. He made certain oaths of allegiance by freemen were required in the Puritan colonies. Similar oaths were also sought from Indians, but Pynchon did not serve as their missionary.

John Pynchon called the Agawam, Pocumtuck, Pojassic, Wissantinnewag, and Nalwottog Indian tribes "Our Indians", meaning they were aligned with the English. Pynchon's Indians worked to enforce English trade laws with other Indians—especially of guns, liquor, furs, and foodstuffs—to maintain authority in the region. [165]

Inquiry followed for a few months, but I failed to find any missionary efforts to convert Indians in the Springfield area. Eliot travelled into the Connecticut River Valley but to no avail.

Eliot's failure with the Podunk tribe must be discussed, as "The Podunks were the first Indians of Connecticut who had an opportunity of listening to the preaching of the gospel. (...) John Eliot being at a council of ministers in Hartford during the year 1657, anxiously sought an opportunity of declaring the truth to the natives of that vicinity. As the Podunks lived only on the opposite side of the river, they were persuaded by some some of the principal inhabitants to assemble and listen to the preacher. He spoke to them in their own language, and, when he had finished, put the question whether they were willing to accept of Jesus Christ, the Savior, as he had now been presented to them. The sachems and old men scornfully and angrily answered, 'No.' The English, they said, had already taken away their land, and now they were only attempting to make the Podunks their servants." [166]

Coastal Massachusetts's tribes, on the contrary, had made considerable progress converting toward Christianity. In consideration of this success, even with the failure to convert Connecticut Indians, Missionary Eliot would owe gratitude toward the man who all but made funding the mission possible. Subsequent to uncovering this influential man, it was quite surprising to me who it was- none other than Edward Winslow, former Plymouth Governor.

In actuality, the missionary effort on the mainland seemed to be a bit fabricated in comparison to what occurred in Martha's Vineyard. Missionary practices actually seemed to be a component of New England's conquest for land, as Indians unfavorable toward Christian conversion were becoming segregated from the general public, aside from the Mohegans.

Winslow stated that ministers were hesitant in donations, being that prior funds allocated to transport children to New England, had wrongly been used. The converts, too, were negatively divided. The praying Indians were placed in court-sanctioned praying villages, as their ancestral land was submitted to the colony and in return they were granted allotted bounds. In these villages the Indians were to follow English customs, labor, and religion.

The semblance upon the mainland was far different than the great progress in Martha's Vineyard. I understand that according to the royal patent of Massachusetts, the principal end of this plantation was to win and incite the natives of the country to the knowledge and obedience of the only true god and savior of mankind and the Christian faith. Despite the intentions, the more I discovered about the mainland mission the more it seemed that the primary function of the mission was to make an impression in England. The mainland was such a vast wilderness that taming an entire species that roamed through it seemed near impossible. Conversion seemed likely for certain Indian tribes disbanded by disease, but there were many proud tribes that still had no intentions of aligning to colonial religion or order.

It was claimed that if England were to accept the unchristianized Narragansetts, they would hinder the work of John Eliot, as he had preached to and successfully converted the Massachusetts Indians who had submitted to the colony.

Eliot was a man true to the mission and held a great hope in expanding conversions, but the Indians of Rhode Island, were different from the Indians participating in Eliot's mission. The agent overlooking the Massachusetts Bay and Plymouth interest in England was Edward Winslow. It was said of Plymouth Governor Winslow that no one took better care of English children oversees than he, albeit he was mostly concerned with those unfavorable Englishmen within Rhode Island bounds.

Winslow, the Bay Colony's appointed representative, arrived in England in 1646. There he sought to challenge the Gortonists' title to Shawomet whilst promoting the Massachusetts mission. [167]

Once removed to England, Winslow would never return to New England, whilst amid his final years overseas, nevertheless, he continued to influence public affairs over here. His main premise was to present Massachusetts as a great victim of Gorton and his associates. Winslow presented to parliament that Gorton threatened the poor Indians that submitted themselves in 1644. Therefore, if parliament was to favor Gorton they were to destroy the divine beginnings of the mission among the Indians. It was not considered or mentioned by Winslow that the Narragansett Indians, who Gorton defended, held great hatred toward the Massachusetts and Connecticut colonies for the ill justice they performed upon Miantonomo.

Winslow, on the other hand, was most focal in making it part of his business in London to solicit the parliament of lords and commons in producing the incorporation of the "Society for the propagation of the Gospel among the Indians of New England," meeting the needs which the labor of Eliot and Mayhew had required. [168]

Before Winslow removed to England, the Massachusetts Bay Colony had become disappointed that the overseeing

Warwick commission in England had awarded Roger Williams a charter and confirmed Gorton's title within Rhode Island- the commission sided with two heterodox Rhode Islanders.

It was in May 1646 when Gorton won his case before the Warwick Commission, as he argued that in September 1643 the Massachusetts Bay General Court sent an expeditionary force to Shawomet to arrest Gorton and his disciples, who, according to the results of the hearing, resided within the jurisdiction of Massachusetts Bay all because of Pomham and Sacononoco's submission. In October, the Gortonists were tried and convicted for blasphemy and contempt for civil authority, and were sentenced to perform manual labor, in leg irons, in various towns around Boston. Some six months later, the court, convinced that the Gortonists were seducing others to their views, changed the sentence to banishment from the colony, including Shawomet, on pain of death. The Gortonists then returned to Shawomet to test the Bay Colony. After receiving a threatening letter from Winthrop, they moved to Aquidneck Island, where they planned their next course of action.

Thus, in 1646, Gorton and his associate, Randall Holden, felt action from a higher power was necessary and boarded a ship for England, whereupon arrival they would tell of the attacks upon themselves and the Narragansetts. Gorton published another manifesto toward the colony, which parliament read:

SIMPLICITIES DEFENCE
against
SEVEN-HEADED POLICY.

Or Innoceny Vindicated, being unjustly Accused, and sorely Censured, by that Seven-headed Church-Government United in New-England.

Or That Servant so Imperious in his Masters Absence Revived, and now thus re-acting in New-England.

Or The Combate of the United Colonies, not onely against some of the Natives and Subjects, but against the Authority also of the Kingdome of England, with their execution of Laws, in the name and Authority of the servant, (or of themselves) and not in the Name and Authority of the Lord, or fountain of the Government.

Wherein is declared an Act of a great people and Country of the Indians in those parts, both Princes and People (unanimously) in their voluntary Submission and Subjection unto the Protection and Government of Old England. (from the Fame, they hear thereof) together with the true manner and forme of it, as it appears under their own hands and seals, being stirred up, and provoked thereto, by the Combate and coursed above-said.

Throughout which Treatise is secretly intermingled, that great Opposition, which is in the goings forth of those two grand Spirits, that are, and ever have been, extant in the World (through the sons of men) from the beginning and foundation thereof.

Whilst the two grand spirits exists, which stands for good and which stands for evil! Or can we find the balance.

Certain members of parliament grew concerned that the United Colonies were plotting against England. Whilst the king was upon removal, powers within would not relinquish the prowess within the colonies. Gorton and Holden thereupon completely submitted along with the Narragansetts, without any hassle, which was a highly favorable move within parliament. Massachusetts, on the other hand, had overstepped their bounds, wherein they received word of the unfavorable proceedings.

Prior to his departure, Plymouth's former Governor Winslow warned Governor Winthrop of parliament's knowledge of Massachusetts' actions toward Gorton and the Narragansetts within Rhode Island. Thereupon, the most intriguing circumstance unfolded. Gorton remained in England, whilst his fellow heretic, Randall Holden, sailed directly into Boston on September 13, 1646. This act of the boldest dissent received great acclaim throughout. It was believed Holden was banished and if he would step foot in the colony he would receive death. Nevertheless, he appeared wearing no mask. He gladly shared Parliaments letter of protection, which commanded the colony to halt any misdoings upon his and Gorton's associates. The Bay held no power to intervene, but it was determined that they must strengthen their reputation in London. In response, the Bay magistrates felt divinity would propel their standing among the hierarchy, whereupon, the colony felt it necessary to send one of their finest- Edward Winslow. The mission upon the Indians would thus spawn a great significance for the purpose of the Bay Colony, wherein John Eliot would emerge. Sadly his emergence was not genuine as that of Mayhew. The Bay felt it was necessary to display the mission as that of pure Christian motives, not an act to obtain credibility.

This pretense would make the mission much more meaningful and influential, as the divine motive to Christianize the Indians would require financial support from England.

Missionary Eliot

Whilst the men who were guiding the affairs of Massachusetts distinguished that it was most necessary to send one of their own to England, greater effort was to be spent upon parliament's acceptance of the mission rather than upon the very redmen who were to be converted. It is true that a hesitation for the mission arose, as in 1643 donations were received to fund young scholars to learn the language of the redmen and carry the light among them at Harvard College. However, the money disappeared.[169]

Therefore, unrest was arising in England as it was acknowledged that the authorities within the Bay received money collected by their agents from English churches from which they had already borrowed money. As word spread, the agents would not return to the churches from which they borrowed. Nevertheless, upon Winslow's arrival, he sought Parliament to solicit funds in all the churches throughout England. Answers were sought toward the continuous slander that claimed the money given for New England had never been accounted for. One appeal for financial help for the colonies involved monies collected to send over poor children, yet no children arrived and the money collected could not be accounted for.

Therefore, it became a public service in England to promote the mission within Massachusetts, albeit Massachusetts itself refused to finance it. Thus the agent was chosen in England to see what could be done to get help for the New England colonists. Not one loud powerful voice would question the promotion for the gospel amongst the natives.

Parliament selected an agent whom they could trust following the execution of the King, which were weeks filled with nervous tension. Winslow was to "Act for the promoting and propagating the Gospel of Jesus Christ in New England." Parliament authorized that a collection begin that would canvas house to house in every parish to continue the mission in New England. Donations were small, but the sum collected surprised those filled with doubt.

> The organization was completed by providing "That the Commissioners of the United Colonies of New England in New England for the time being, by themselves or such as they shall appoint, shall have hereby Power and Authority to receive and dispose of the moneys brought in and paid to the said Treasurer for the time being, or any other moneys, goods and commodities, acquired and delivered by the care of the said Corporation at any time; . . . which said Commissioners are hereby ordered and appointed to dispose of the said moneys in such manner as shall best and principally conduce to the preaching and propagating of the Gospel of Jesus Christ amongst the Natives; and also for maintaining of Schools and Nurseries of Learning, for the better education of the children of the Natives.

The Corporation within mentioned, desire all men to take notice, That all such whom God shall stir up to contribute to help forward this great worke, may repair to Coopers Hall in London, where the said Corporation sitt, and there if they please at any time may have the sight of their bookes, how the Moneys collected and received for the use above-said, are from time to time disposed and improved, according to the true intent and meaning of the said Act. [Publications of the Prince Society, 1920][170]

Nevertheless, some were to say the work of the Company was but a plain cheat and that there was no such thing as Gospel Conversion amongst the Indians presently.[171] Hugh Peter, minister at Salem, called the mission a hoax and claimed that the mission was a fraud.

In England, Edward Winslow disguised Mayhew's effort as that of Eliot's. He first presented that the mission was helpless without financial support, as it was unable to furnish clothing, tools, spinning wheels, hoes, mattocks, shovels, salaries of teachers, or wages for Indian laborers in March 1647/8.[172] The date for the first reading of the bill was continuously set back until it was thrown out altogether. A second bill was read on July 27, 1649, which made quick progress and was ordered to be printed. Letters of Eliot's and Mayhew's were now published in London which produced great interest.

Shamefully, it became known to many that Winslow altered persons and places regarding the mission in Massachusetts. In particular, he disguised the labors of Thomas Mayhew, Jr., as if they were done by Eliot- Winslow fabricated Mayhew's work as to be that of Eliot's. Many were misled by the agent in whom they trusted, who dates the beginning of

Mayhew's labors as 1648, or 1649. Unbeknownst to parliament, "Thomas Mayhew was not only himself preaching to the Indians in Martha's Vineyard before Mr. Eliot began to first preach to those at Nonantum, but that he already had an Indian convert, Hiacoomes, who was at the same time able to preach, and who did preach with him with great acceptance."[173]

The Mayhew's sincerely began their mission one year subsequent to the planting upon the island, whilst Massachusetts had waited sixteen years following its founding. Moreover, the Bay didn't perform sermons upon the Indians until three years after Mayhew.

On one occasion, Eliot even enhanced his own reputation at Mayhew, Jr.'s expense. In November 1648, the Apostle told Edward Winslow in a letter published, "Our Cutshamekin (the Massachusetts sachem) has some subjects on Martha's Vineyard, and they hearing of his praying to God, some of them do the like there, with some other ingenious Indians, and I have entreated Mr. Mayhew, who preaches to the English there, to teach them; and he does take pains with their language, and teaches them not without success." This letter formed a false idea that Eliot had formed the Vineyard mission, which had truly began three years before his own.[174]

In defense of Eliot he did have great respect for the Mayhew family. He wrote:

> If any of the human race ever enjoyed the luxury of doing good, if any Christian ever could declare what it is to have peace, not as the world gives, but which surpasses the conception of those who look not beyond the world, we may believe this was the happiness of the Mayhews.

Winslow also left out the fact that wampum tribute extracted by Massachusetts from various Indian tribes would have financed a considerable portion of the missionary effort. Winslow, however, represented the colony as too poor, and he made it appear that the Bay struggled to support Eliot's work without English help, wherein funds received were spent on arms, ammunition, and the edifice of Harvard College.[175] He also left out the statement by Eliot himself calling the Indians the dregs and ruins of mankind.[176] This comment will stick to Eliot forever sadly. He felt such a pity for these lost people, nevertheless he chose a disparaging discription.

The question arises; did the mainland mission do any good?

Its foundation being built through fraud has corrupted its growth.

Eliot influenced some, but he had not influenced the majority of Indians he dealt with. It must be noted that in 1634, Eliot opposed the treaty with the Pequots- he did not hold what Mayhew held within. There are many reasons for this. Eliot and the local men of importance held a value for Indian converts as a tool for expansion. He sent leading converts as messengers to the Nipmucs and other non-converted tribes and these messengers were used as instruments repeatedly. They were supplied with powder and shot for their defense in times of danger in the remote parts of the country where Eliot was trying to alter the souls of the morally dark that were not willing to be changed. [177] Eliot wrote in his narrative, "I find a blessing, when our Church of Natick doth send forth fit Persons unto some remoter places, to teach them the fear of the Lord."[178]

It is hard to understand the mission Indians of the mainland, because different bands took to different sides whilst some changed their stance. It also is just as hard to understand what intentions the planters truly had for the Indians overall. The magistrates favored praying villages, yet the township's people wanted all neighboring Indians banished.

Survival and then progress held the Bay Company officials absent from the conversion of the natives for many years. Nothing came to be for a decade and a half after settlement until it became a strong possibility for Puritan leaders. It wasn't an easy matter to propagate the Gospel among natives on the mainland for there were many issues as to why it took so long.

To begin, there was no leadership within the New England Puritan Church to direct the mission or be held accountable. Another factor was that there were not enough resources, most importantly money and manpower, as there weren't enough ministers. Also, the difference of dialect was a hindrance toward spreading religion upon the natives. The few Indians who knew the English language weren't always dependable, wherein there was no way for Englishmen to know if messages were translated correctly.

The opposition held by the sachems and powwows was also another great problem as it was on the island. They saw that religion would take away many followers and remove their honor and tribute.

The most challenging issue for the mission, moreover, was the Puritan church mandate, which asked for more than just religious awareness and consistent attendance at church for conversion. It was necessary for each candidate to take part in and fulfill a number of requirements in order to obtain acceptance. Completion of church membership was an intense and extended program of instruction and study. Subsequent to completing this conversion process, the candidate was required to show, in front of church elders and leaders, a deep Bible understanding and a complete knowledge of the Puritan creed. The majority of planters, ironically, didn't even achieve this feat. How were Indians, who didn't know any of the dialect, supposed to reach membership?

Throughout the 1630s and into the 1640s there had been no plan to convert the natives, but what unintentionally brought the conversion for the Indian into reality was the voluntary submission of weaker tribes of Rhode Island, tributaries to the Narragansetts. Thus the submission by Sacononoco and Pumhan in 1643, who requested Massachusetts troops be sent against Gorton, brought neighboring tribes to the same end. Albeit there was no mention of conversion between Sacononoco and Pumhan, officials within the Bay colony were quick to identify the importance of this uncommon event and took full advantage of other submissions in the year to follow.

It must be understood that the submissions in 1643 and 1644 still didn't form a converted Indian. It was simply a beginning for government officials and religious leaders to begin to compel the Massachusetts General Court into mandating their own laws upon the Indians. The Puritans decided that before any effort was made to convert natives, they were first to change the Indians into civilized men. The Indians were expected to change their means of life and develop a civilized conduct- living in permanent towns, cutting hair, dressing in the manner of the English, and working some type of meaningful employment.[179]

Magistrates did feel that faith be formed by the word, not the sword. Whereas, the Indians weren't to be forced to worship the white man's god, but law stated they could worship no other. If convicted of worshipping another, they would be fined and if the fine was not paid, they would be imprisoned for a period of time. These restrictions would eventually cause anger in many honorable Indians.

For these laws to work they had to be consistently prosecuted, in which the praying Indians were placed under the authority of an English officer who was appointed by the English commissioners to enforce the laws made by the colony. The Massachusetts authority elected officials such as Daniel Gookin to travel from village to village to consider criminal cases and to also educate the Indians on laws, ethics, justice, and equity; whilst it was still the sachem's responsibility to enforce fines for smaller crimes. The fines collected were successfully used for the education of the Indian children, building public meeting-houses, or other tasks.

Bay Indians had shone minimal interest in the knowledge of the white man's god, but were prohibited from Christian instruction by the five ruling sachems of the Massachusetts tribe. Eliot first preached among one of the ruling sachems at Dorchester Hill (Neponset) on September 15, 1646 under Massachusetts sachem Custshamekin. This date if of great significance as it was two days after Holden arrived in Boston!

This service upon the Indians clearly indicated the Bay was distraught by the favorable reception Gorton received in London. Ironically, This first effort for the mission at Dorchester Hill was a failure, wherein Eliot did not consider it a Christian meeting. In Eliot's words, "They gave no heed unto it, but were wary, and rather despised what I said."

John Eliot, through failure, decided that if they were gathered at a neutral location, out from under the control of their leaders and the threats of violence, he would be able to influence the majority and convert them. He had felt confidence in his knowledge of their dialect as he had been talking with Indians for more than ten years before his first Indian sermon.

Eliot's first successful religious services upon the Indians took place on October 28, 1646, when he conducted a service in Indian tongue at Nonantum, what we call Newton. This service was under the leadership of Thomas Waban, who wasn't a sachem. Eliot avoided the five ruling sachems after his first failed attempt; who were the very rulers of the people in Nonantum.

Eliot credited Waban with leading the Massachusetts tribes' interest in the Puritan faith, in which Waban actually went against his sachem Cutshamekin's opposition toward the Christian religion. Governor Winthrop defined Waban as a new sachem. What a great insult! The governing body felt they held the right and prudence to assign sachems among the Indians.

Nevertheless, Waban's people organized a place of worship in the town at Nonantum by means of English order. Eliot wanted Waban to bring his friends, in which Waban summoned the people of the village to gather at his wigwam. Thomas Shepard who was present with Eliot at Nonantum wrote:

> Four of us having sought God, went unto the Indians inhabiting our bounds with desire to make known the things of their peace to them.

Four men came to Waban, a man holding no tribal stature, on a five mile horseback journey from Boston. They were greeted by six chief men who led the party to Waban's wigwam. Once assembled, the minister and the other members of the company were introduced to the gathering. Eliot greeted the redmen as friends and then raised his arms as he opened the meeting with prayer in English. After the prayer, Eliot began with a reading of the Ten Commandments. Each Commandment was presented first in English and then in Algonquian, followed by a brief explanation. He asked if they understood him and a loud positive group responded. At the end of the sermon in Waban's wigwam Eliot was asked, "How do we believe what eyes cannot say?"

"When you see a big wigwam," Eliot answered, "do you think the raccoons built it, or the foxes, or that it built itself? Certainly not."[180]

156

His manner of teaching them was, first to begin with prayer, and then to preach briefly upon a suitable portion of scripture; afterwards to admit the Indians to propound questions;-and divers of them had a faculty to frame hard and difficult questions, touching something then spoken, or some other matter in religion, tending to their illumination;-which questions Mr. Eliot, in a grave and Christian manner, did endeavor to resolve and answer to their satisfaction.[181] [Daniel Gookin]

It was a subtle beginning that brought hope to the four that rode away from Nonantum to their homes, which was a far different reaction from the reception at Dorchester Hill (Neponset). October 28, 1646 planted the seed for praying villages as the Massachuestts Indians would discover sermons. By the third meeting on November 26, more wigwams were put up with more Indians awaiting Eliot's words, in which he was asked many questions. It was also presented that they desired a town of their own, whilst the women also desired to learn the craft of spinning. At the fourth meeting held December 9, Indians were now coming from other villages. The Indians now too wished for their children to be educated by the English, in which the English responded that a school was already planned for. Eliot would grow more dedicated to this cause as he travelled through snow and rugged trails to perform his sermons. He would also begin to preach regularly at Neponset.

Within a short time of these first attempts many Indians were now meeting together to hear Eliot's services. Answers were also sought for their curiosity as to why the Nonantum Indians were cutting their hair or if the powwows would lose their spiritual presence. Most Indians first attended regularly at Nonantum because of curiosity, not Providence.

Nevertheless, with each visit they became more trustful. In Neponset and Nonantum Eliot preached these two lectures for several years with good success, which were locations within four miles near Eliot's Watertown home.

Besides his preaching to them, he framed two catechisms in the Indian tongue, containing the principles of the Christian religion; a lesser for children, and a larger for older persons. These also he communicated unto the Indians gradually, a few questions at a time, according unto their capacity to receive them. The questions he propounded one lecture day, were answered the next lecture day. His manner was, after he had begun the meeting with prayer, then first to catechize the children; and they would readily answer well for the generality. Then would he encourage them with some small gift, as an apple, or a small biscuit, which he caused to be bought for that purpose. And by this prudence and winning practice, the children were induced with delight, to get into their memories the principles of the Christian religion. After he had done the children, then would he take the answers of the catechetical questions of the elder persons; and they did generally answer judiciously. When the catechizing was past, he would preach to them upon some portion of scripture, for about three quarters of an hour; and then give liberty to the Indians to propound questions (...) and in the close, finish all with prayer.[182] [Daniel Gookin]

In the interest of Eliot, there is no doubt, these praying Indians discovered and used Christian principles that thousands of Englishmen still do not understand. Eliot, however, continued to hold concerns toward the conduct of the redmen, "shewing them how uncapable they be to be trusted therewith, whilst they live so unfixed, confused, and ungoverned a life, uncivilized and unsubdued to labor and order."

In the spring of 1650 arguments were presented to Eliot from his impatient red followers of Nonanetum in regards to civil order. It was recognized that Nonanetum was not suitable for a plantation. Thus, by the summer of 1650, Eliot and several Indians began to search locations for a central plantation. The settlement would have to be remote from the English, but close enough for Eliot to visit regularly and practice the word and other elements of the Christian lifestyle. His search for an area ended the moment Eliot took a knee to pray for God to show him the way. An Indian arrived as he prayed on his knees and told Eliot this would be home.

In October 1650, they had selected Natick, an unimproved area along the Charles River. The land held fertile fields, woods, a river, and enough area to grow without interfering with English bounds. That same month, the General Court assigned Natick 2,000 acres of land to the north of the river. The first town of praying Indians was thus in Massachusetts known as Natick. The name meant a place of hills- eighteen miles south west from Boston. This land was granted to the Indians, through the action of Mr. Eliot, by the general court of Massachusetts and in the year 1651, a number of the converts united and formed in this town. The purpose of the first dwelling house was to store furs, clothing and provisions, whilst there was a small room for Eliot to board in if he were to stay over. Eliot recounted, "I pay them wages carefully for all such works I set them bout, which is a good encouragement to labour."

Whilst the Indians had built up their settlement, Mr. Eliot formed a civil government and on the sixth of August, about one hundred of them met together, and chose one ruler of a hundred, two rulers of fifties, and ten rulers of tens. This place, Natick, would become the greatest name among the Indians, and also where their chief courts were held.[183] This first praying town would also be where teachers and preachers would train in preparation for the towns that followed.

The converts would thereupon discover education. Eliot "took great care, that schools should be planted among the praying Indians; and he taught some himself to read, that they might be capable to teach others; and by his procurement, some of the choice Indian youths were put to school with English schoolmasters."[184] However, "if any should sinfully neglect Schooling their Youth, it is a transgression liable to censure under both Orders, Civil and Ecclesiastical, the offence being against both."[185]

Nonantum Indians were pleased with the location, whilst Eliot would implement laws. Fines in the value of two to five shillings were set for offenses, such as men having long locks, women showing their chest, cracking lice between teeth, or if any man was idle for a week. Ironically, the Praying Indians were far away enough from the English, to learn the Puritan way. They also conformed to English gender roles: the men tilled the fields and raised the livestock, and the women learned to spin and weave once the men had grown enough hemp for the purpose in the mid-1650s.[186]

With the vision of an improved life compared to the life spent within a wandering band, many would-be converts first came to Natick. Large numbers of Nipmucks would come to hear Eliot preach on a consistent basis, in which Eliot would visit with all these interested souls at two-week intervals in the preceding five years.

The Indian town was increasing in audiences as Indians traveled a long way to hear him, while chiefs invited him to their villages to preach. During the following years, Eliot went into the interior of Massachusetts to visit the Nipmuck tribes and converted many of them. The increase of the great distance traveled by Indians because of interest in conversion made Eliot come to the conclusion that the solution was for more Christian Indian towns where those who wished to convert could live.

Whilst the converts increased in numbers, the resources within Natick could not support the population, additional towns were obviously necessary, and as long as Indian leaders accepted management and daily maintenance, new towns would succeed as Natick had. Therefore, Natick set the precedent. In October 1652, the General Court ruled that "if upon good experience, there shall be a competent number of the Indians brought on to civility, so as to be capable of a township, upon request to the General Court, they shall have grant of lands undisposed of for a plantation, as the English have." The formation of the Praying towns also served as a means to avoid any disagreement between Indians and colonists over boundaries, as well as, to designate an area where the Indians were to live.[187]

1654 was an important year for the mission's ability to grow, as Eliot requested that the Boston General Court form three new Indian communities: Hassanamesit (Grafton), Nashobah-'The Place between the Rivers' (Littleton) and Okommakamesit- 'The Plowed Field Place' (Marlboro). The apparent success of these towns would allow for more growth.

Okammakamesit would become one of the principal praying towns that was established. In May of that year, the General Court asked to award land, free from any challenge of an English interest, for the Nipmuck Indians of Okommakamesit. The Court's grant to the Indians in 1654 was prior to the land grant made to the English on land that would be called Marlborough. The English, nevertheless, found to their disappointment that the Indian land granted, was to be in the same location as a portion of their own grant. Yet, the praying town was to be respected by the planters if they wished to stay in Marlborough. This is a great example of fairness shown by the Massachusetts Authority, as their members were civil in their position with the praying Indians at the outset.

These Indians at Okammakamesit were a branch of the Wamesit tribe, and had submitted to the Massachusetts Colony as early as 1643, receiving assurance for the protection of their rights. They were self-supporting, peaceable, and were becoming industrious and thrifty, yet were nevertheless not trusted by many of the neighboring English, who resented their grant of six thousand acres.[188]

The surrounding English community, known as Marlborough, was developed in 1656 overlapping Okommakamesit. Marlborough was a growth off of Sudbury, one of the first frontier townships, which the court blindly awarded even as a portion of the land had already been occupied by the Okommakamesit Indians. Thereafter, the population of the English town grew so fast, which the Indians weren't prepared for.[189]

Eliot thus continued to look west toward the Indians of the Nipmuck country, as the praying town of Hassanamesit, within Nipmuc bounds, was peaceful. John Eliot wrote in 1654, Hassanamesit had become the central point of civilization and Christianity to the whole Nipmuck country. School was established and the Bible was read and studied in the Indian language. Young men were here educated and sent into the neighboring towns to preach the gospel. A regular government was created, and the forms of law were strictly observed.[190]

Another praying town shaped in 1654 called Punkapaog-near the town of Canton. The Indians that formed this town were of the Neponset Tribe originally from the Boston area. Punkapaog was fourteen miles south of Boston, and the new town was necessary because "poor Indians were much molested in these places." The name is taken from a spring that arises from red earth. The Indians that settled in Punkapaog were removed from Neponsitt mill and Ahawton was their ruler. The praying town of Wamesit would also develop which had a ditch dug around it in 1665 in order to divide it from Chelmsford.

The Indian praying towns had no sooner expanded when Eliot put future expansion on hold. His Roxbury parish was rapidly growing with white men, wherein he had to spend more time on church matters as well as his family. At this time also, the commissioners of the United Colonies in Boston were annoyed by his continuous demands for more money after he had already taken the money from his allowance. Furthermore, members of the Propagation of the Gospel in New England were concerned with Eliot's inability to keep proper records and provide them with the accounting of costs and expenses. His answers were general- not exact numbers. Eliot, moreover, did not report the many gifts sent to him privately.

It became known that there was a disguised effort to combine the Christian and non-Christian groups among the Indian population records. If a sachem promised himself and his people to pray to God, which he was mandated to do under the treaties of submission signed in 1644, the entire tribe would be considered as praying Indians. All Indians subjected under the submitting sachem could now be considered converts toward the gospel, even as they opposed conversion. For that reason, the estimates of converts are misleading.

In 1671, the number of the praying Indian population within villages can be presumed as near one-hundred. Only three towns had Indians in full communion- Natick fifty, Hassanemesit sixteen, Magunkaquog eight. This total was an insignificant number of the one thousand one hundred claimed to be driven by the gospel, wherein fact, that large number simply demonstrates the amount of Indians submitted under the Massachusetts Colony.

This manipulation occurred because Eliot and Superintendent of Indian affairs Daniel Gookin must have assumed that with the greater the image of the mission, the greater the continuing support of the missionary program. If they could increase their funding, both at home and in England, the mission would expand. So Eliot and Gookin failed to document that a large number of the natives did not want to become Christians. It was imperative to present the mission in a positive way, wherein there would be no interfere with all the invested labor.[191] There was no reason to show negative results, as all of Eliot's work may have become foiled. During his time away from the expansion of the praying towns, Eliot turned his attention to a full Indian translation of the Holy Bible.

This great work of translating the Bible into the Indian language was encouraged by the honorable corporation for propagating the gospel in New England, residing in London. "Out of the revenues belonging to that flock, which then was more considerable than now it is, did pay for the printing thereof."[192] Christianizing the Indians upon consideration seemed impossible without a Bible available in their own tongue.

The legible bible provided another step in leading the Indian toward Christianity. He would finish printing the Bible in 1663, and even throughout this time of tedious labor he still used his energy on the education and training of Indian preachers and teachers at Natick. With a number of trainees within the program in the mid 1660s and the accumulation of funds assigned during the Bible project, the corporation for promoting the gospel was again willing to sponsor expansion.

Further augmentation of conversion west of Boston, most obviously, took place through the deterioration of tribes, as this change increased the procurement of land by the planters, but did not please many non-praying natives. This increase of planters had its most dramatic effect on the Indians of central Massachusetts, between the Boston area and the Connecticut River. The Indians of this region, mostly considered Nipmucks, had been isolated from the land pressures of the English, because most of the English migrants came to the Boston coastal area between 1630 and 1640, and the children in these families did not seek land independently of their parents until the 1660s when they were of age to seek land. Thus they pursued new bounds in great numbers, wherein the Nipmucks had to face a sudden influx that provided them little time to adapt.[193]

In May 1668, Nipmuc sagamores humbly submitted to the Massachusetts authority. The subjection would be placed upon those inhabiting the bounds around Mendon through Marlborough.

> We the inhabitants of Mongunkachogok, Chaubunkongkomuk, Asukodnogest, Kesapusgus, Wabuhquoshish, and the adjacent parts of Nipmuk being convinced of our great sinns & how good it is to turn unto the Lord and be his servants by praying or calling upon his name...do give up ourselves to God...we finding by experience how good it is to live under laws & good government and how much we need the protection of the English. We doe freely out of our own motion and voluntary choyce do submit our selves to the government of Massachusetts.

Praying Nipmucs were to be trained at Hassanamesit as readers, preachers and deacons, and their teachers urged Nipmucs to forsake their tribes lifestyles. No Indian town offered the success for the Christian Indian as Hassanamesit had by the year 1670. Praying Indians living within the Hassanamesit village branched out and would assist in the creation of additional praying towns. There developed seven new praying towns and the Indians of some of these towns began to open up to the gospel: Waeuntug (Uxbridge), Quinshepauge (Mendon), Packachoag (Auburn), Manchaug (Sutton), Quabog (Brookfield), Chaubunagungamaug (Dudley), and Wabaquasset (Woodstock, Ct.). During this time, on October 12, 1670 the General Court extended its claimed jurisdiction, which had previously stopped at the Nipmuc River, but subsequent to the court ruling Massachusetts claimed an additional 20 miles into Nipmuc territory.

In the praying village of Wamesitt John Eliot would visit once a year in the beginning of May, the visit was not only for the inhabitants of the village but also to take an opportunity to spread the gospel to the visiting strangers, who came in considerable numbers that time of season. The town fell on a conjunction of two rivers, the Merrimack and Concord, which drew many non-praying Indians into the area for fish. These non-praying Indians, however, ultimately eliminated a strong praying village as they provided temptation against the civil expectations.

In July 1673, Eliot and Daniel Gookin made a journey to visit some of these villages- to encourage their growth toward the ways of God. Then again on September 14th, 1674, the two set out toward new and old praying villages with six additional godly persons, who were to be presented unto the new praying villages as ministers. The visit's "design was to travel further among them, and to confirm their souls in the Christian religion, and to settle teachers in every town, and to establish civil government among them, as in other praying towns."[194]

The party traveled west over the Connecticut Path. Their first destination was Hassanamesit and the teacher of that village was named Solomon. The village was about thirty-eight miles southwest from Boston; and is about two miles eastward of the Nipmuck River. The name Hassanamesit meant a place of small stones. The town's population was not above twelve families, or about sixty people altogether.

Eliot and his group left Hassanamesit and journeyed to the town of Manchage, which fell west of the Nipmuck River. In terms of population, Manchage was around the same size as Hassanamesit. When the group arrived, Eliot found most of the inhabitants away. Eliot spoke with those present and informed them that they were assigning a young man, Wabesktamin, as minister for the town. At the time of this visit, there was yet any land granted by the general court for this or any of the new praying villages.

The next stop was Chabanakongkomun. This town was a new plantation; the Indians had gathered there about two years earlier and now numbered about nine families, or about forty-five souls. A man named Joseph, from the church of Hassanamesit, who spoke English well, was the founder and teacher of the town. His brother Sampson was the teacher at Wabaquasset, a village in Connecticut. Joseph and Sampson were the sons of Petavit, who was a ruler of Hassanamesit, but died three days before Eliot came. There was much respect held for Petavit, as he was known for God and religion. He blocked the anger and disrespect of wicked Indians in order to praise the Christian religion at a time when it was not popular-supporting religion amongst sagamores who refused it. Petavit was possibly the strongest influence for the progress of Christianity among the Nipmucks.[195]

Another visit for the missionary group was in Northeastern Connecticut at Wabaquasset, wherein Eliot and his group took up quarters in the house of the chief sachem. Wabaquasset was by far the largest of the praying towns in terms of population; it was inhabited by one hundred and fifty souls.[196]

Upon the 16th day of September, being at Wabquissit, as soon as the people were come together, Mr. Eliot first prayed, and then preached to them in their own language. Then Daniel Gookin "published a warrant or order, that he had prepared, empowering the constable to suppress drunkenness, Sabbath breaking, especially powwowing and idolatry. And after warning given, to apprehend all delinquents, and bring them before authority, to answer for their misdoings; the smaller faults to bring before Wattasacompanum, ruler of Nipmuc country; for idolatry and powwowing to bring them before me. [Daniel Gookin][197]

A number of Indian counselors came to the sachem's wigwam and joined in the religious practices. Whilst this ceremony occurred, there sat a man at the end of the long-house, watching everything. The man, at the conclusion, spoke and informed Eliot and his party that he was an agent for Uncas. He said that Uncas had authority over the people of Wabaquasset. He protested, "Unkas is not well pleased, that the English should pass over Mohegan river, to call his Indians to pray to God."[198]

Eliot told the Indian to tell Uncas that Wabaquasset was within the jurisdiction of the colony of Massachusetts and that the government of Massachusetts intended to share the Providence available to all people within their bounds- it was not Eliot's purpose to eliminate the Indian sachems' ancient entitlement over the Indians. Eliot explained that it was the design of the English to connect them with the knowledge of Jesus and to eliminate their sins.

The party then traveled to Pachackoog, which was about forty-four miles from Boston in what is now the southwest corner of Worcester. The town consisted of a population of about one hundred persons or twenty families. James Speen of the Natick church had been performing sermons there for about two years. Horowanninit (John) and Woonanaskochu (Solomon) were the chief sachems of the village. Eliot's party first repaired to Sagamore John's house.

With the arrival of Eliot and the missionaries, the sachems then grouped their people within the village for a religious service, in which Eliot gave a brief sermon. When the service was over, the first Indian court of any type in the area took place September, 28, 1674 and was held for the purpose of selecting civil and religious leaders. The two sachems (John and Solomon) were appointed civil rulers of the town and James Speen was to continue as their minister for another year. Concluding the court appointments, a man named Mattoonus, who was described as a grave and sober Indian, was to be elected as officer for the town. Then Gookin "gave the rulers, teacher, constable, and people, their respective charges, to be diligent and faithful for God, zealous against sin, and careful in sanctifying the Sabbath."[199] Ironically, Mattoonus, the elected officer, would lead the first invasion against the English by the Nipmucks during the beginning months of King Phillip's War.[200]

By 1674, there existed many praying towns. There were two other Indian towns, Weshakim and Quabaug, which were beginning to receive the gospel- making around nine praying villages in the Nimpuck country. However, Weshakim and Quabaug were not fully settled and were omitted from the magistrate's consideration.

It is true one man had been greatly responsible for the alleged conversion of near 1100 Indians, but it must be understood that a large number of that total were unconverted Indians and they were unhappy with the formation of these praying towns. Their anger, therefore, developed toward both the English and the converts. There came only two choices for the Indian- accept or deny the white man's religion.

Praying Village Published Populations:
Natick: 145
Punkapaog: 60
Hassanamesitt: 60
Okommakamesit: 50
Wamesit: 75
Nashobah: 50
Magunkaquog: 55
Manchage: 60
Chabanakongkomun: 45
Maanexit: 100
Quantisset: 100
Wabquissit: 150
Pachackoog: 100
Wacuntug: 50
Total population: 1,100[201]

For the near twenty-five years of the mainland mission not much had changed for the unchristianized Indians. However, in the early 1670s, Eliot and his adversaries told all participating Indians that the colony would begin to heavily enforce civil and criminal laws in accordance with the general court and the Puritan religion.

Foul behavior wouldn't be tolerated and there was to be strict enforcement of the policies. All converts were to put themselves, lands, and estates under the government and jurisdiction of Massachusetts, to be governed and protected by them, according to their just laws and orders, so far as they should be made capable of understanding them. Expectations were solely put upon the Indians tocarry out minor legal issues.

"Care was taken by the general court of the Massachusetts, at the motion of Mr. Eliot, to appoint some of the most prudent and pious Indians, in every Indian village that had received the gospel, to be rulers and magistrates among them, to order their affairs both civil and criminal, and of a more ordinary and inferior nature. These rulers were chosen by themselves, but approved by a superior authority." [Daniel Gookin][202]

Indians strictly obeyed the laws which they established themselves, wherein Indians would thus spy on each other. There was a report against Waban that he had a raccoon killed on a Sunday, which broke the Sabbath.

The land situation, moreover, became an unfavorable situation, for all Indians- Christian or not. The Court of Massachusetts had bounded, stated, and settled several plantations for these praying Indians and the amount of land allotted to the Praying towns was connected with the size of the group. Land for settlement, most importantly, was only allowed to those who chose the Christian faith. As more converted, the court would consider increasing a petition for land. The non-Christian Nipmucks would grow suspicious and feel excluded.

The Massachusetts Court justified this by claiming rights to the land in the colony of Massachusetts by patent from their King. Second, the English held a grant for most of the land within this jurisdiction, either by purchase or the submission from the five ruling sachems in 1644. The general court felt the only land the Indians were entitled to was the area granted to them by the court.

The court felt the treaties the tribes had formed with Massachusetts between 1643 and 1644 forfeited the Massachusetts Indian land. Once the Indians had voluntarily submitted, the colonial government expressed a standardized statement of loyalty, which on separate occasions, the statement was worded identically. The Indians agreed "to be governed and protected by Massachusetts, according to their just laws and order, so far as we shall be made capable of understanding them." Unlike the Indians living in Rhode Island, the Indians in Massachusetts seemed to be willing to be instructed in the knowledge and worship of the Puritans God.[203]

> "Whereas one end in planting these parts was to propagate the true religion unto the Indians; and that divers of them are become subject to the English, and have engaged themselves to be willing and ready to understand the law of God: it is therefore ordered, that such necessary and wholesome laws, which are in force, and may be made from time to time, to reduce them to civility of life, shall be once a year, if the times be safe, made known to them, by such fit persons as the general court shall appoint." [Daniel Gookin][204]

172

The 1643-44 treaties automatically transferred local tribes' ancestral rights of lands to the Massachusetts Colony, a most radical measure not understood to the fullest. Therefore, the only way an Indian could claim property was by a grant from the general court, which would only be ceded for a praying village. Another factor in land rights was the Land Rights Law of 1652 stating that all land within the area of the Massachusetts Patent was under the authority of the Massachusetts court, even if the land was granted or not. The Indians thus only held the title to land they worked or lived on. The law reflected the Puritan leaders' interpretation of the Old Testament, which read, "Heaven, even the heavens, are the Lord's: but the earth hath he given to the children of men." This understanding opened the door for Puritan land claims and enabled all Indian rights of ownership in Massachusetts to be observed and governed by the general court. The Puritan theory of Vacuum Domicilium states that free land is classified as open dominion- defined by Governor John Winthrop as, "all land not actually in the possession of the natives; land which lies in common and hath never been replenished or subdued."

In the planters eyes, Indian hunting grounds, the most important land to gather meat for the Indian family, was land considered vacant and awaiting occupation by those who would put it to good use. Under this opinion, the majority of Puritan leaders felt the English had a legal right to take possession of all the open or unoccupied lands within their jurisdiction. As the natives made no improvements to the territory, especially hunting grounds, the Puritans were of the opinion that they possessed natural right. Thus, private property was created from common land when labor was put forth on vacant soil or hunting grounds. [205]

The expectation of the Massachusetts Colony was to have all the Indians live within the sanctioned praying towns, therefore, eliminating tribes from using their unoccupied and unimproved lands for future use. Ultimately, these measures confined the Indians to specific locations and provide the English the authority to civilize and control Indian behavior without the Indians getting in the way of expansion. Massachusetts' Indians, therefore, became a separate body from the same Puritan government that represented them. Indians couldn't comprehend the consequences of signing the treaties. They simply thought they were going to share the land, not become removed. If they had known it was a complete subjection, I doubt they would have agreed.

The Indians began to associate the religious transformation with the system used by the Puritan leaders to seize all unoccupied or unimproved lands. The natives were beginning to discover they would have no use of their ancestral territory. The Indians would eventually have to take up residence in one of the court-sanctioned praying towns or be pushed out of their ancestral lands. The execution of these regulations caused anger in the non-Christian Indians, and it was slowly fostering violent rage toward the Puritan, which erupted in 1675.[206]

During King Philip's War in 1675, the Nipmuc dissenters toward the Puritan mission finally released their once-contained rage. They felt their rights to customary lands had been violated.[207] Anger was not only held by the non-converted Nipmucks, but it also would begin to anger the converts. A number of Christian Indians, as well as missionary Indian members, joined the colonial enemy as they believed what was happening was wrong.[208] Prior to war, Eliot, however, felt "the harvest is ripe for many more [towns], if God please to thrust forth labourers."

In all my heart I wish to express little dissent to Eliot, as he sacrificed many hours upon the redmen, but I was with Mayhew, the most humble of all, and he manipulated no truth for his purpose. To be honest, I felt a great rage whilst I was told by the old man Smith from Skipmuck about Winslow and Eliot taking credit for Mayhew's labor. Nevertheless, events hold much greater acclaim then words. The Nipmucs repaid Eliot's labor by inciting the first attack within Massachusetts in 1675.

Massasoit's son, Phillip, told some Rhode Islanders that he had a "great fear to have any of their Indians should be called or forced to be Christian Indians. They said that such were in everything more mischievous, only Dissemblers, and then the English made them not subject to their Kings, and by their lying to wrong their Kings."

It should have become apparent to the reader that the intentions of the Massachusetts Bay Company to Christianize the Heathens always stood second to obtaining freedom to practice their own form of Christianity.[209] It was only a matter time before a great war would arise between the two civilizations.

Honor may not be the proper word when defining the life of a man who is thought to have designed the most disastrous war upon the colonies, but keep in mind dear New England reader; you may now be in possession of his soil. A land his father, a man of the most peace, shared among the sick and feeble who took possession of it whilst asking for no permission to plant upon it; A land that once outnumbered the Christians by the thousands; A land where Massasoit withstood injury upon injury, theft upon theft, depredation upon depredation. Nevertheless, it was a land that the great Wampanoag Sachem revealed such a tame manner upon those of a different civilization. A civilization that claims it is the design of God to slay others, whilst the original Wampanoag conduct would bring any nation great reverence to call such honorable men their own. Why would Massasoit's son hold different standards? Were conditions so drastically grave, within one generation of planters, that Philip could not suffer any more injustice?

Massasoit and his sons were not respected by divers at the start; they were feared. There is word that if the power had been in certain hands, the Wampanoag chiefs would have been butchered in sequence. It was considered to be of the most Christian act to drive the redmen out by diabolical means. Yes, these Christians that profess all men are grateful servants, intended to treat each other as prophets, hold true intentions to destroy!

Do you think the redmen could not sense this evil within their neighbors? Emotions and knowledge rest within the redmen just as the whitemen, wherein somehow these redmen had calmly withstood years and years of wrongs, yet once these sufferers spoke one word of the terror that they received they were denounced as savages!

We must trust the word of the man exiled away from the Puritans, Roger Williams, a man of peace with the redmen, founder and inhabitant of Providence Plantation, as he declared that the cause of all their wars were about their hunting grounds!

There exists no doubt divers Indians felt the same indignation that Philip endured! Have you every heard of a case wherein Indians harmed a man that had helped them?[210]

THE
PRESENT STATE
OF
New - England,

With Respect to the

INDIAN WAR.

Wherein is an Account of the true Reason thereof,
(as far as can be Judged by Men.)

Together with most of the Remarkable Passages that have happened from the 20th of *June*, till the 10th of *November*, 1675.

Faithfully Composed by a Merchant of *Boston*, and Communicated
to his Friend in *LONDON*.

Licensed *Decemb.* 13. 1675. *Roger L'Estrange.*

LONDON.
Printed for *Dorman Newman*, at the Kings-Arms in the *Poultry*, and at the
Ship and Anchor at the *Bridg*-foot on *Southwark* side. 1675.

London, for Dorman Newman, 1675

The Beginning Of The End

All the promising efforts I have previously mentioned on the mainland would culminate into war not peace. The harvest Eliot had planted for and labored with for thirty years would instantly become spoiled. Praying villages were the great illusion that positively promoted the Indians removal by the very men cheating them out of their own land.

> "For be it remembered, although the gospel is said to be glad tidings, yet we poor Indians never have found those who brought it as messengers of mercy, but contrawise."[211]

In April 1675, Thomas Waban, ruler of the Natick village, spread rumors that an imminent conflict between white and red man was approaching. Attacks, however, had run rampant for years.

Soon thereafter war erupted, but it all started as a consequence of contingency. The whiteman's justice would play an enormous factor in inciting Indian rage from beginning to end throughout these violent times. Thus, this final war turned rumor into truth, whilst the outcome has undoubtedly secured the New England plantations from any further domestic Indian insurrections. The Indian is more or less permanently removed- they are no longer welcome.

This past Indian war of 1675 is known as King Phillip's War. This was to be a conflict, following Indian tradition, which held no immense European-styled field battles, as the method of Indian warfare was that of skulking.

At the climax of the struggle, the praying Indians participated on both sides. Some praying Indians revolted against their colony as hostile Indians, whilst others that devotedly prayed fought on behalf of the colonists- joining the colonial militia to help achieve victory. Some praying Indians, however, would change sides and become hostile to the colonies throughout the war.

The praying Indians that fought and remained with the colonies throughout the war were the most reliable soldiers. Moreover, it was difficult to say which tribe was loyal and which was not. The true standing of any one particular tribe's alliance at the time of the war is very knotty, as many smaller Indian bands shifted sides. The Wampanoags or Pokanokets, the home tribe of which Phillip was sachem, as well as the Narragansetts and Nipmucs, were the three tribes that became known as the colonial enemy. The Narragansetts, though, did not stir up any violence at the beginning of the war and were considered neutral hitherto their tribe was invaded similar to the Pequot. Furthermore, the Pokanoket and Narragansett tribes held an opposition to the offers of the Gospel as their chief Sachems strongly rejected and opposed it.[212]

The war had begun within the Plymouth colony, whilst the war also ended there. Two of the most powerful tribes, as viewed by the colonists, lived within the bounds of Plymouth or near its border. The two great chiefs, Philip of the Wampanoags and Canonchet of the Narragansetts, were the head sachems of these powerful tribes at the outbreak of war.[213]

The Nipmucs may have committed the most frequent hostile acts during the middle point of the war, whereupon the hostile portion of the divided tribe also sent messages to the Christian Indians that the English planned to destroy them all, or send them out of the country as slaves.[214]

Hitherto of Philip's war, there were branches of the Nipmucs throughout the interior as each branch had their specific region. The Quabaug Indians, for instance, lived in the territory about the town of Brookfield. Although Quabaug is Nipmuc territory, it seems to have attracted others and thereupon became made up of an assortment of bands as a result of the conflict for Indians elsewhere.

Of the Nipmuc tribes, one member, especially, in the beginning of the war, had a potent influence for the rebellion against the colonies. Mattoonus, who lived in the praying village of Pachackoog, would revolt and lead the first invasion against the English on the town of Mendon, Massachusetts, in July 1675.[215]

There are a number of possibilities that would explain Matoonas' assault on Mendon. One reason for his revolt may be that he had to revenge the death of his son at the hands of the English. It is rumored that one of Matoonas' sons was framed for the murder of Zachary Smith in 1671, whereupon he was then hung and beheaded for the apparent crime. The head would stand upon a stake for five years. If a valid tale, Matoonas must have held quite a grudge.

Whatever the case, as Daniel Gookin put it, "The Indians

here do not much rejoice under the English men's shadow; who do so overtop them in their number of people, stocks of cattle, &c. that the Indians do not greatly flourish, or delight in their station at present."

This second Puritan conquest has been named King Phillip's War or even the Narragansett War, as you will soon see why; however, the war was a collection of various conflicts involving several New England tribes. One overall fact for the Indian was that their strength had continued unraveling in the 1670s. The Indian population was around 20,000, about half of what the number of English planters in the area was; about 4,000 were Narragansetts, about 3,000 were Nipmucks, over 1,000 were Wampanoags, whilst the rest were Mohegans, Pequots, Pocumtucks, Massachusetts, River Tribes, and other bands.[216] In terms of men available for the United Colonies commissioners, it was decided while in the summer session that a thousand men respond in reaction to the first sign of an outbreak of war—by quotas, Massachusetts, 527; Connecticut, 315; Plymouth, 158. However, three times that number was to be needed."[217]

Rumor made it appear as though Philip was stirring the conflict. Wherein fact, it was the younger Indians who first became hostile, whilst some older Indians sought peace. The Wampanoag Confederacy's sachem Philip was the great Massasoit's son, and Philip would become known as the great igniter of this grave war, yet he may simply have lost control of the younger Indians. Massasoit would be the first to open the gates that would welcome in swarms of Englishmen to plant. Yet, near fifteen years after his death, his son was being accused of putting efforts forth to destroy the plantations through a united Indian force. There were, also, other tribes sachems who were important actors in the war, especially Canonchet of the Narragansett.

Canonchet was Miantonomo's son, whereupon he held the sachemship at the time and during the war. The relations on behalf of the colonies with the Narragansetts before the war was of arrogance, intolerance, and selfishness, as the agreement between the King and the Narragansetts of 1644 held no binding amongst the surrounding colonies. At the beginning of the war, Canonchet, an able and brave chief, received constant hatred and falsehood from the now elder Uncas. Yet, the Narragansett sachem had still been able to maintain neutrality with the English, always keeping in mind what happened to his father. In 1675 he was by far the most powerful chief in New England, his fighting force being estimated at over a thousand, even though the force was never united prior.[218] Subsequent to the outbreak of war in 1675, the Wampanoags and Narragansetts stance with the colonies was ever-changing. Chandler Whipple wrote:

It was in 1647 when Canonicus [Narragansett Sachem] died, a very old man. At some point thereafter Canonchet, son of Miantinomo, assumed his position as sachem of the Narragansett. In 1655 Edward Winslow of the Plymouth Colony, old and true friend to Massasoit, died. Massasoit realized that he was losing all his old friends among the English. He ordered his two eldest sons, Mooanam [Wamsutta] and Metacomet [Pometacom], to go to Plymouth and adopt English names. It would appear that he thought of this as a means of protection, of making it easier for them to take their places in the English scheme of things. At any rate, the magistrates were much impressed with the noble manner of these two handsome young men. They gave them names of Greek History: Alexander, for the elder, Philip for the younger. Then in 1661, Massasoit abdicated his sachemship, left his base at Mount Hope and moved in with his old friends and allies, the Nipmucs- into the

Quabaug village. This somewhat scattered tribe ranged from areas around Worcester as far down as northeastern Connecticut. This put Massasoit in territory very close to that claimed by Uncas, as the Mohegan sachem now concentrated on land further beyond the almost altogether conquered river tribes. The power and territorial claims of Uncas continued to expand as his influence with the colonists had. He would attack the Nipmucs.

Massasoit tried to mediate with the English, hoping they would force Uncas to make restitution for the damage he had caused. This attempt resulted in partial failure. It appears that Uncas received no punishment. Uncas was a newer and more valuable friend than the old Wampanoag Sachem Massasoit. Massasoit would soon die thereafter. [Chandler Whipple][219]

It was rumored that before the war broke out in 1675, Phillip was planning a coordinated attack with other Indian nations for some time. The River Indians attacking the settlements along the Connecticut River, the Nipmucks attacking the interior towns, and the Narragansetts and Wampanoags attacking from Boston to Providence, all simultaneously, would have driven out most of the colonists from New England.[220] However, no united Indian force attack took place and it was actually the death of a Praying Indian named John Sassamon and the trial and execution of his murderers that began the Indian war.

To understand the war I must take the reader to previous years and discuss the end of Massasoit and the peace he maintained. In 1657, Massasoit formed his final land deed with Plymouth near the age of eighty and then joined the Quabaugs to the west. The Quabaug tribe was friends to the Pokanoket, and Massasoit claimed himself the leader of them in front of

Boston in 1637. This change of residence allowed Wamsutta, his eldest, to become grand sachem of the Wampanoags and it also continued the alliance between the Nipmucs and the Wampanoags.

Massasoit died around 1661 at the age of eighty-one. He was succeeded by his son Wamsutta (Alexander). The known children of Massasoit were Wamsutta, Pometacom or Metacomet or Phillip, Sunconehew, Amie, and possibly another daughter. Wamsutta was first known as Mooanam.[221]

In the early part of 1661, before Massasoit's death, "Uncas attacked the Indians of Quabaug in the eastern part of Massachusetts, killed some, made others prisoners, and carried off property, as the sufferers alleged, to the value of thirty three pounds sterling."[222]

It was possible England could prosecute Uncas for his acts, all because Quabaug Sachem Massasoit had "gone through the ceremony of submitting to the English". A relationship Uncas claimed to be unaware of. The court left the incident with no punishment. Uncas, furthermore, may have had some role in the death of Wamsutta through his use of slander. Trouble arose for Wamsutta as he was suspected of selling land to outsiders, whilst other rumors expressed that he was trying to stir up trouble and to organize a general uprising. It was a noticeable fact indeed that Wamsutta had been selling lands for several years prior to the date of his father's death.

Some of the English settlers at Boston, having visited the Narragansetts, wrote to Mr. Prince, then governor of Plymouth Colony, informing him that Wamsutta had sought the Narragansett tribe to engage in a war against the English. Captain Thomas Willet was sent as messenger to Wamsutta, living in Mount Hope. Captain Willet informed the chief of the ill story concerning him, at whom Wamsutta seemed to take no offence, but remarked that the Narragansetts were the enemies of himself and his people, and that this was an effort of theirs to put an abuse upon him, and involve him in difficulty with the English.[223]

He was ordered to Plymouth immediately to acknowledge his loyalty. On July 7, 1662 a letter written to Josiah Winslow, Major Commandant of the Plymouth Colony Militia, describes the bearing upon Massasoit's eldest son:

> Insomuch as Alexander, King of the Wampanoags, did not appear before the duly convened Court of Plymouth on June 1 as he had promised and instead, was seen in the company of the Narragansetts on that date, I hereby call upon you to muster the Marshfield militia and march south to Pokanoket territory where you are to locate the King. Bring him straight away to Duxbury where he shall answer the two charges brought against him before the Plymouth Court, namely, that he is negotiating with the Narragansett nation to engage with him in war against Plymouth Colony and that he is selling land directly to colonists contrary to the agreement between Plymouth Colony and the Wampanoags. If he should resist, you shall force him to come in whatever way serves you best.[224]

Wamsutta would thus be forced by gunpoint from hunting grounds. He was to remove to Plymouth to discuss his actions and if he refused he was a dead man. Unfortunately, Wamsutta became sick on the way - so ill that Winslow let him go before they arrived in Plymouth. Half way before he got home, Wamsutta died.

> Alexander being sent for with armed men, and while he and his men were breaking their fast in the morning, they were taken immediately away, by order of the governor, without the least provocation, but merely through suspicion. Alexander and his men saw them, and might have prevented it, but did not, saying the governor

had no occasion to treat him in this manner; and the heartless wretch informed him that he would murder him upon the spot, if he did not go with him, presenting a sword at his breast; and had it not been for one of his men he would have yielded himself up upon the spot. Alexander was a man of strong passion, and of firm mind; and this insulting treatment of him caused him to fall sick of a fever, so that he never recovered.[225]

With the unforgivable death of Wamsutta, his brother became sachem of the Wampanoag Confederacy. We have become to know him as Phillip, as his Indian name is Metacom. Also known as Pometacom, or King Philip, he seems at first to have been desirous of continuing the friendly relations with the whites, which his father first began. The friendly relations between white man and Indian were held for forty years within his father's reign subsequent to the signing of the treaty with Governor Carver. Within a few months of Philip's succession to the great chieftaincy, he renewed the covenant that Massasoit had made with the planters, even with the death of his brother in such a manner. In the winter of 1663-64 John Eliot sent books for learning to read and to pray unto God. An act that appeared as if the English were presenting an opportunity to continue the friendship that had existed in the beginning.[226]

Plymouth ultimately wanted a contract from Phillip that eliminated any future sale of land without the Plymouth colonies' consent- In 1665 he sold New Bedford and Compton for forty dollars. In 1667 he sold to Constant Southworth and others all the meadow lands from Dartmouth to Matapoisett, for which he received sixty dollars. The same year he sells to Thomas Willet a tract of land two miles in length, and perhaps the same in width, for which he received forty dollars. In 1668 he sold a tract of some square miles, now called Swansea. The next year he sells five hundred acres in Swansea, for which he received eighty dollars.[227]

Phillip recognized, though, that the charter his land lay under pledged subjection to the king of England, not Plymouth. Philip's recognition as subject to the king thus made him feel as an equal to the authorities. During a visit to Rhode Island by the royal commissioners from England who represented the king, they were received by Philip and intervened in a dispute over land at Mount hope between the Wampanoags and Narragansetts. The royal commissioners sided with Phillip and confirmed his home of Mount Hope [Pokanoket] fell in Rhode Island bounds. Thus, Philip's knowledge of his land was in accordance to Rhode Island's royal charter of 1663.

Plymouth challenged the charter, whilst Rhode Island disputed the boundary claims. The boundary claims were a very important issue at the time, whereupon the Narragansett country was territory where Connecticut, as well as Massachusetts, was trying to place its jurisdiction. Moreover, Massachusetts, Rhode Island and Plymouth conflicted over a region where the three colonies claimed boundaries had overlapped. This area was also the edge of the Nipmuck territory.

In 1667 Plymouth's General Court established the town of Swansea. Located at the western edge of Plymouth's claims and alongside the counterclaims of Rhode Island. Most importantly it trespassed on Phillip's homeland. A year later the general court authorized expansion of Swansea for divers to purchase lands, which disregarded Phillip's plea to prevent others from seeking his lands. The Wampanoag Indians thereupon became angry, wherein they would eventually show an armed force before the Swansea planters in 1671. This act would thus force Phillip to Taunton.[228]

There were also reports that claimed many Indians were repairing toward Mt. Hope and manufacturing bows and arrows, half pikes, and setting up their guns. These rumors spread rapidly amid the plantations. Hence, there was an effort made to remove the chance of a war between Plymouth and the Wampanoags. John Eliot hoped to share the Gospel with the tribe and sent a couple Natick Indians, but Philip was not interested in giving up his life or possessions for peace with the colonies. Philip viewed his relationship to Plymouth as being one of equals, as the two parties had direct ties to the king of England and that relationship was the only avenue to settle disputes within the colony.

The Wampanoag sachem felt Plymouth was as much a subject to the king as himself, but Plymouth did not view the situation as that. Philip was correct in his stance, in all the treaties between the Wampanoags and the Plymouth Colony, subjection was acknowledged toward the king- only friendship was declared between the Wampanoags and Plymouth residents- dating all the way back to 1621.

Philip would meet with the white men in Taunton, whereupon "a very unusual scene was enacted" on April 12, 1671, in the Meeting House on Taunton Green, when the English Commissioners from the Bay and Plymouth colonies were to meet with Phillip and his leading counselors. The Indian Chieftain, with his band of warriors armed and painted as if ready for war, first approached within four miles of the town, where he established his camp. He thereupon sent messengers to the English, inviting them to meet with him for a conference.

The Governor preferred Phillip to come into town, and it was finally arranged for him to enter, which only transpired because two colonists were left with the Indians as hostages.

Phillip thereupon decided it would be safe to confront the colonists and with some of his men he approached Crossman's Hill, on the outskirts of Taunton. "Here he again became suspicious, and well he might have felt so, because some of the Plymouth men wanted to attack him then and there, but were restrained from doing so by the cautious representatives of the Bay Colony."[229]

Philip was finally persuaded by the Massachusetts men to attend the conference provided it were staged in the Meeting House, whilst he and his warriors were stationed on one side of the church and the colonists should occupy the other side. "Philip's complaint was, that the Pilgrims had injured the planting grounds of his people. The Pilgrims said that the charges against them were not sustained; and because it was not, to their satisfaction, the whites wanted that Philip should order all his men to bring in his arms and ammunition; and the court was to dispose of them as pleased." Philip was also ordered to pay for his insolent clamors he had put upon the Colony. Yet, why were the whitemen never responsible to pay the Indians for all the suffering they had committed upon them?[230]

In this conference it was proved pretty conclusively that the Indian Chieftain was arming, and not against the Narragansetts, but to oppose the whites. As the English Ambassador asked him why he wanted to make war against them and then asked him to make a treaty, Philip is said to have replied: "Your governor of Massachusetts is but a subject, I shall treat of peace only with the king, my brother; when he comes, I am ready."

On September 29, 1671, Philip and five other Sachems finally submitted, which recognized Philip as a subject to Plymouth and their laws.

Thus the claim of "King" began to be added to Phillip's name. Though the sachem of an insignificant tribe, his reputation reached a height never attained by any before.[231]

John Sassamon

It became evident to another Indian that Philip was planning to drive the English out of the land.[232] In January 1675 a praying Indian named John Sassamon traveled to Governor Josiah Winslow's house to explain that Phillip was preparing for war. He informed the Governor of Plymouth Colony that the Wampanoags were organizing a general conspiracy against the English. Sassamon was in dead earnest, and even expressed fear that his warning to the governor might cost him his life.[233]

How right he was.

John Sassamon was a mixed man—a Wampanoag by his father, a Massachusett by his mother. He became a Praying Indian by his parents' decision to convert, but he was never a permanent representative of either the English or the Wampanoag. He orphaned when his parents died of smallpox in the epidemic of 1633.

Many of the Indians stricken by illness along the coast were converted to Christianity on their deathbeds, and so, their children carried the religion and were fostered by English families. Thus, many Indian children were taught English, Christianity, and the European way of life. John Sassamon, who was around thirteen when his parents died, was one of the Indians brought up English. Sassamon would live in the home of a wealthy Dorchester resident, Richard Callicott, in which the young Indian gained an education through this family. John Eliot, the minister of the neighboring town of Roxbury visited Dorchester often, formed a relationship with Sassamon from the time of his childhood, and taught him Christian principles. Sassamon also attended an Indian School in Dorchester, where Eliot regularly taught the pupils.

As a young man, Sassamon served with his master Richard Callicott during the Pequot War under Captain John Underhill, and he was both interpreter and soldier. According to Underhill, when Pequots saw Sassamon, who was wearing English clothes and holding a gun, they asked him from a distance, "what are you, an Indian or an English?" "Come hither," Sassamon replied, "and I will tell you." As they came close enough, "hee pulls up his cocke and let fly at one of them, and without question was the death of him." After the war, they returned to Dorchester with Indian captives.

Sassamon continued his relationship with John Eliot following the Pequot War, and as a result, Eliot began to understand the Indian language more and more. Thereupon, Eliot began to use Indian translators, including Sassamon, who helped teach Eliot their language, while receiving in exchange for his labor the English and the Christian way of life. Obviously, Eliot could not translate the Bible into the Massachusett language all by himself- he had to rely on these translators.

Eliot learned the Massachusett language enough by 1646 to preach those first sermons at Neponset and Nonantum in the language. The missionary thus made Sassamon his principal aide, whereupon Sassamon served until his death. In 1651, while Eliot formed the first praying town in Natick, Sassamon was involved from the start and would become a schoolmaster.

In 1653, Sassamon studied at Harvard College through his relationship with Eliot. Nevertheless, he did not stay long and returned to Natick within a year. He continued there as a schoolmaster, but in 1654 Sassamon left Natick and joined the Wampanoag community, and whilst in Wampanoag country, he quickly became the translator for the chiefs.

Sassamon labored for Massasoit, and then for his eldest son, Wamsutta; when he succeeded his father around 1660. By this time Sassamon had a significant role within the tribe-translating treaty negotiations between the Wampanoags and Rhode Island. Whilst Philip became the chief sachem after his brother's death, Sassamon's importance grew, whereupon he became Philip's interpreter and counsel. His knowledge of English was of the most importance to Philip who could not read or write in the foreign language. During the 1660s Sassamon was a witness to Philip's pledges of loyalty to the English, whilst also serving as interpreter in treaty negotiations and in land transactions. However, controversy would arise through Sassamon's mishandling of his role, wherein conflict with Philip would arise. Sassamon's loyalty toward the Wampanoag did not compare in importance with his standing with the Bay.

As Sassamon labored for Sachem Philip Eliot became eager to convert Philip. He would use Sassamon as a tool to influence Philip, and in 1664, Eliot requested the commissioners of Plymouth colony to give support toward Sassamon in order to teach Philip and his men to read. Eliot stated that Philip, "did this winter past, upon solicitations and means used, sent to me for books to learn to read, in order to praying unto God which I did send unto him, and presents with all."

Eliot knew that Sassamon was the tool to connect Philip with the missionary work. Neither Sassamon's effort or the books Eliot sent would convert Philip though. On the occasion Eliot visited Philip and prayed for his redemption, the sachem crossly responded whilst ripping a button off Eliot's coat, "he cared for his gospel, just as much as he cared for that button."

With the failed attempt, Sassamon did not stay at Mount Hope with Philip much longer, whereupon there was one particular incident that broke the bond between Sassamon and Philip. Whilst Philip asked Sassamon to write his will, Sassamon pretended he was writing down everything Philip presented, but instead, Sassamon named himself heir to most of Philip's land. Thus Sassamon would be forced to flee when Philip discovered what his translator had done. Furthermore, Sassamon was a Christian Indian and Philip felt those kind of Indians were the most mischievous, as they were subject to no Indian and only the subject to the colony.

In the late 1660s, Sassamon rejoined the Natick Indians, whereupon his downfall began. In August Eliot directed the Natick Praying Indians to send Sassamon and two other missionaries to the Wampanoags and invite Philip to Boston. Whilst on this mission, upon sharing the invitation, Sassamon spied Philip joined with leaders of the Sakonnets and many other sachems, including some Narragansett sachems. It was assumed that the meeting was to gain support. Sassamon would bring this news back to the English and describe all the leaders present. Philip would nevertheless travel to Boston and humble himself as a subject to Plymouth and the King of England.

A meeting between Sassamon and Philip again occurred at the end of 1674, when Philip and his men were hunting around Sassamon's town, Nemasket. Sassamon chose to visit his Wampanoag relatives. Subsequent to the brief encounter, Sassamon left right away for Plymouth with a fear for his life. Sassamon would then meet Plymouth Governor Josiah Winslow at his house and disclose Philip's plan to attack the English.[234] Sassamon claimed he discovered that Philip was planning to attack the English and drive them away forever. He also now feared for his safekeeping.

As he himself predicted, Sassamon never returned to his home after his meeting with Governor Winslow. He was supposedly murdered subsequent to the meeting and was stuffed under a pond of ice. This was the court's version of Sassamon's death, whereupon the suspicion of murder was greatly strengthened by the known facts of Sassamon's life. Thus when his death at Assawompsett Pond did occur and word of it spread, the authorities had every reason to be suspicious, and drew the conclusion that Phillip was behind the murder.[235]

Behold! John Sassamon became the first Christian martyr of the Indians, as it became suspected he suffered death on the account of his Christian profession and fidelity to the English.[236] Thereupon, a praying Indian named Patuckson told authorities he had seen the murder. He named three of Phillip's men as the killers- a claim that would make the sachem responsible. Yet, not many Indians believed this claim as Phillip would have no reason to hide his role in the murder- it was the right of a sachem to order an assassination upon his own.

Three Wampanoag Indians, Tobias, Mattaschunanamoo, and Wampapaquin, were thus arrested on the words of the witness. The alleged Indians, however, claimed that Sassamon had been drowned while fishing and that the marks on his body were caused by contact with the ice.[237] It was also declared that Patuckson had a motive for accusing the three Wampanoag Indians, which was to be attributed to a gambling debt. The Indians reported that the informer played away his coat, and these men then sent him that coat, and thereafter demanded payment instead. Yet, Patuckson chose not to pay and therefore so accused them, knowing it would please the English so to think him a better Christian.[238]

"In connection with the accusation of these men [it must come to] question what authority the English assumed within the jurisdiction of the matter. There is no evidence that Sassamon was subject to them or under their special protection by reason of any treaty or agreement. The three men whom they tried for his murder were Indians, and, if they belonged in the vicinity where the crime was committed, were subjects of the sachem Tuspaquin, and the offence was against the laws of the territory of that chief. It was such acts as this, ignorance for the natives rights to deal with offenders among their own people- men who were not subject to the English and in their own territory. This superiority by the colonists was one of the great provokers to bring the Indians to war."[239]

The Plymouth authorities stirred anger in Philip for imprisoning the Wampanoag men for the murder of a Wampanoag, and I am not sure if Philip was aware of how unfair the trial of those men were.

This trial of the three Wampanoag men was far different in comparison with the records of other trials in the Plymouth Court, "the record of this trial is brief and uninformative". Six Indians were chosen to the jury along with twelve colonists. These were six Praying Indians, Indians who had rejected their Wampanoag heritage, and nevertheless, knew little to nothing of the English legal system, nor had they known enough English to understand the testimony.

Another unfair aspect of the Wampanoag trial was that there was no defense provided- a long founded rule in the English Court system. Also, unjustly, there was only one eyewitness testimony depended upon, which ignored the rule that, in trials of capital crimes, there are to be two witnesses. The punishment would then bring matters into the most ill of conditions- the Wampanoags were hung to death within a week of the verdict. In the English system, conversely, the punishment for capital crimes was carried out at least a month subsequent to the trial. Plymouth, chose a different course, and with this decision, ended the fifty years of justice between Indians and colonists, bringing about a new interpretation on how to prosecute the Indian. The colony punishing Wampanoags for any crime was a violation of treaties of ancient date.

The Wampanoag modus operandi, on the other hand, would have had the two parties involved settle the punishment amongst their own as it was a matter to be handled solely within the tribe. No third party existed as in the English system. To Phillip and his tribe, it was inconceivable that Plymouth Colony should be punishing Wampanoags for the murder of a Wampanoag. The trial and death penalty brought upon the three Wampanoag members by a separate party stirred great anger in the Wampanoags that led them "to beat their war drums".[240]

The trial and execution incited the Wampanoag warriors to madness, and thereupon began the second Puritan conquest in Plymouth Colony. About the time of their trial, Philip was said to be marching his men up and down the country in arms, which brought upon a tension that was to now spiral out of control. From all sides came reports to the authorities of hostile acts on the part of the Wampanoags. Cattle were shot, corn stolen, houses robbed; in some places, outbuildings were fired. The attitude of the warriors had become defiant, while spies reported that strange Indians were swarming into Philip's villages and the women and children were being sent to the Narragansetts. Alarm also spread among the distant settlements- including Springfield.[241]

It must be said, however, that Philip's men limited their damages to the killing of cattle and hogs and the carrying away of property, the purpose being to drive the colonists to the first acts of violence against the Indian. It was Wampanoag superstition that the first party to shed blood would be vanquished. Blood soon would result as an Indian was shot and killed in Swansea whilst committing some act of wrongdoing. This began the war, but in this war the committer of the first blow would not become vanquished.[242]

Swansea

The Wampanoag sachem, divers colonists believed,
readied his nation for war shortly after his men were executed
on June 8th, 1675. Hitherto, fear could have not but arisen in
Philip as he may have been next to be executed. Philip would
express he had no choice but to rouse his council for the
uncertainty which the future held:

*You see this vast country before us, which the great
Spirit gave to our fathers and us; you see the buffalo and
deer that now are our support. Brothers, you see these little
ones, our wives and children who are looking to us for food
and raiment; and you now see the foe before you, that they
have growing insolent and bold; that all our ancient
customs are disregarded; the treaties made by our fathers
and us are broken, and all of us insulted; our council fires
disregarded, and all the ancient customs of our fathers; our
brothers murdered before our eyes, and their spirits cry to
us for revenge. Brothers, these people from the unknown
world will cut down our groves, spoil our hunting and*

planting grounds, and drive us and our children from the graves of our fathers, and our council fires, and enslave our women and children.

As tensions increased, some of the whites in the outlying settlements abandoned their farms and hoped for safety in Plymouth; others stayed behind. On June 18th, in Swansea, some scavenging Indians invaded one of these semi-deserted villages, whereupon they took property left behind by fleeing owners. However, the planters who had remained fired them upon.

"Some Indians were seen by an old man and a lad, pilfering from houses whose owners were at church, whereupon the old man bade the young one shoot, and one of the Indians fell but got away."[243] That Indian was to be dead soon and the first blood was thus drawn by the English not by the Indians. The neighboring natives would then visit the local garrison and ask why the whitemen had shot their fellow tribesman. The English, in reply, simply wanted to know whether he had died. The Indians answered that he had, whereupon a lad of the garrison replied that the death "was no matter".

Rhode Island, alarmed at the state of affairs even before the incident in Swansea, made attempts to compromise the matter and bring Philip to an agreement. Deputy Governor Easton of the colony, and five others, including Samuel Gorton, met Philip and his chiefs at Bristol Neck Point on the 17th of June, a day before the Swansea death. The party sought to reduce the chances of a violent reaction with the execution of Philip's Indians by means of negotiation. Philip gave a humble response and nothing was resolved.

The war would soon begin after this meeting—but not through a conspiracy on the part of the Indians. Philip was hardly masterminding a campaign to drive the English out-Wampanoag actions were reactions to the injustice that was far beyond Phillip's control. The rebelling Indians would now increase greatly in numbers, some from the neighboring tribes, whilst others were strangers. Most of the women and children were sent away to the Narragansett country. It was actually the younger warriors who demanded open acts of hostility with the swift increase of Philip's following.

Rather than the presumption of King Philip as the grand conspirator, Philip may have just lost control. Wampanoag male youths wanted to take matters into their own hands on June 17th, as some settlers advanced into Phillip's country in search of horses, which had strayed away from their owners and entered into the territory of the Wampanoags. The white men would end up side by side with the Wampanoags and one of the young Indians wanted to kill an Englishman. Yet, the men in search of their horses were all released upon orders from Phillip himself. The incident shows that the Wampanoag sachem, unlike his young warriors, was still hesitant to commit violence. [244] [245]

However, the time came when Philip could no longer restrain his young men, who, upon the 24th of June, fired at the people returning from church. It is said, however, Philip did not coordinate this attack, but opposed it.

Also on June 24th, Massachusetts's envoys visited eight Nipmuck villages and thirteen of the Indian sachems there confirmed continual submission to the Massachusetts government and gave their word not to join Philip. Pocumtuck Indians along the Connecticut River also gave their word to a partnership with the English. Young Indians of these tribes may have fled to Philip, but Sachems and rulers were hesitant to lose an alliance with the English.

In July, several surrounding praying Indians from Hassanamesit, Maunkoog (Hopkinton), Manchauge (Sutton), and Chaubunagungamaug (Dudley), left their homes and gathered in the town of Marlborough. These praying Indians came into English bounds whilst trouble increased, as the English wing of Marlborough was viewed as safe. There the converts built a fort in the center of the town, not far from the church or meeting-house. The intentions were to secure themselves, but also to become more helpful to the English upon the frontier.

These Indians at Marlborough, some of them having been abroad to scout in the woods to discover the enemy and secure the place; they met with a track of Indians which they judged to be a greater number by the track, and upon discovery whereof they presently repaired to the chief militia officer of the town named Lieutenant Ruddock, and informed him thereof, who presently joined some English with them, and sent forth to pursue the track, which they did, and first seized five Indians and after two more, which were in all seven; these being seized were forthwith sent down to the magistrates at Cambridge, who examined them and found them to be Indians belonging to Narragansett, Long Island, and Pequot, who had all been at work about seven weeks upon Merrimack river; and hearing of the wars they reckoned with their master, and getting their wages, conveyed themselves away, and being afraid marched secretly through the woods, designing to go to their own country, until they were intercepted as before. This act of the Christian Indians of Marlborough was an evident demonstration of their fidelity to the English interest. The seven prisoners, after further examination before the council, told the same thing as before, were for a few days committed to prison, but afterwards released. [Daniel Gookin][246]

Orders were given to Major Daniel Gookin on July 2nd 1675 by means of the Governor and council to raise a company of the praying Indians to combat the hostile Indian force formed at Mount Hope. The Praying Indians were to be armed, furnished, and then sent to join the regiment outside of Mount Hope. The Major immediately sent for one third of all able praying Indians, who all readily and cheerfully appeared, and being enlisted were about 52, as the able men among the praying Indians at this time amounted to about 156. These men being armed and furnished were sent to the army under conduct of Captain Isaac Johnson, on the 6th of July, 1675.[247]

Prior to the conscription of the praying Indians, on June 28th, the government of Massachusetts carried an official letter to Governor Winthrop of Connecticut, also informing him of the outbreak of trouble with the Wampanoags-including an account of conditions at Swansea. The letter reached John Winthrop Jr., in New London, the following day, who read it and then sent it to his father in Hartford:

Thomas Danforth, who was then First Commissioner of the United Colonies, wrote the rough draft of Council's letter to the Connecticut Governor:

There is reason to conceive if Phillip be not soone [suppressed] he and his confederates may skulke into the woods and greatly anoy the English, and the confederacy of the Indians is larger than yet wee see. (...) Particularly we request you to use your utmost authority to restrain the Mohegans and Pequots.[248]

The position of Uncas' alliance with Connecticut continued through time and the authorities in Hartford joined the Mohegans securely to the English cause in 1675 as the Mohegans offered their assistance on July 9th. The English sent a letter to Uncas that if he sent hostages to the English for the assurance of his faithfulness they shall accept his offer.[249] Thereupon, Uncas sent six of his men to assure friendship and offer his service against Phillip or any other enemies of the English. He sent two of his sons to Boston as hostages, whilst his eldest son and successor, Oneko, he sent with fifty men, to assist the English against Philip. These Indians were sent to Plymouth under the conduct of Quartermaster Swift. They subsequently joined with the Rehoboth men in pursuit of Philip after he fled Poccasset. The Mohegans received the plunder they seized from the camp of Philip and the fleeing hostile Indians. Furthermore, Mohegan alliance may have determined the Narragansetts' reluctance to join the colonial force against Phillip.[250]

In Swansea, the contingent of praying Indians thereupon became the eyes and ears of the regiment during their brief conscription. This induction of the Indian soldiers and scouts was in accordance with the requirements upon the residing Indians' within the Bay's jurisdiction- founded on the land submission to the General Court by the Massachusetts Tribe in 1644, "wherein subjection and mutual protection were engaged."[251] They positively served as scouts, interpreters, and warriors, which adapted many white men to live and fight as the Indians fought- stealthily, rapidly, and lightly. Nevertheless, the subsequent reports from commanders describing the Praying Indians as carrying themselves well, proving themselves as courageous soldiers and faithful to the English interest, served no positive means for the redmen. By the end of July 1675 half of these soldiers were released from duty and sent home, and the other half soon followed. Indian soldiers, aside from Connecticut Indians and a handful of others, would not serve on the English side again until April 1676. The Indian removal from the force was appropriated amid complaints by English soldiers that the Indians were cowards and skulked behind trees in battles, and that they shot over the enemies' heads.[252]

On July 5th, 1675 the Massachusetts Company marched toward the Narragansett country, wherein they separated from the Plymouth Company in Swansea. It was of most importance to bring the Narragansetts into a relationship with the English by peaceful means, notwithstanding the English had a strong suspicion of the Narragansetts. This great importance for a treaty was no more than a waste of energy.

Moreover, the Narragansetts were subjects to the crown, wherein the United Colonies held the hopes of invalidating this subjection upon the King. Therefore, a treaty formed would hold no bearing, as the tribe was administered by the crown and was not permitted to enter into any such treaty. Most bluntly, this treaty was not to keep the Narragansetts out of war, the true purpose was for the submission of that tribe.

Upon arrival, the design was to put upon the tribe a necessity to declare themselves friends or enemies, and to push upon them the former articles of agreement between the English and themselves.[253] The recent orders came from Boston desiring for Major Savage's force to enforce a treaty with that powerful tribe, and prevent an alliance with Philip.

The company, however, found the country deserted on July 7th, except the few aged left behind in the villages. Again and again Captain Hutchinson sent for the sachems, yet neither Canonchet nor any of his leading Sachems could be found. The officers, nevertheless, spent several days completing a treaty with some of the old men whom they were able to bring together and form an agreement of peace and friendship.[254]

Thus, by the 15th of July a few aged and unimportant Indians were forced to sign a treaty on behalf of the Narragansett Indians. One article the Narragansett elders proscribed urged that the English should not send any among them to preach the Gospel or call upon them to pray to God. The English refused to compromise to such an article and it was withdrawn, but a peace was still concluded for that time. The Narragansetts declared that their hearts were to reject Christ and His grace offered to them.[255]

By the terms of the treaty on the 15th of July the signers on behalf of the Narragansetts agreed:

> That all and every of the said sachems shall from time to time carefully seize, and living or dead deliver unto one or other of the above-said governments, all and every one of Sachem Philip's subjects whatsoever, that shall come, or be found within the precincts of any of their lands, and that with the greatest diligence and faithfulness.

> That they shall with their utmost ability use all acts of hostility against the said Philip and his subjects entering his lands or any other lands of the English, to kill and destroy the said enemy, until a cessation from war with the said enemy be concluded by both the above said colonies.

> The said gentlemen in behalf of the governments to which they do belong, do engage to the said Sachems and their subjects, that if they or any of them shall seize and bring into either the above English governments, or to Mr. Smith, inhabitant of Narragansett, Philip Sachem, alive, he or they so delivering, shall receive for their pains, forty trucking cloth coats; in case they bring his head they shall have twenty like good coats paid them. For every living subject of said Philip's so delivered the deliverer shall

receive two coats, and for every head one coat, as a gratuity for their service.

Pettamquamscot, July 15, 1675[256]

The Narragansetts against received great disrespect from the colonies, which was evident through the request for Narragansett hostages in order to show fidelity. By July 17, twenty-one Narragansetts made the journey to Boston. Subsequent to the treaty, both Narragansetts and Wampanoag refugees were sent away and placed under the colony's protection as an assurance of sincerity. These Narragansetts, of all the New England tribes, were most deserving of sympathy, as they remained peaceful following the unjust murder of Miantonomo and continued to keep the peace in 1675, whilst receiving terms of a treaty through the threat of an armed force- signed by no sachem. Canonchet, furthermore, we will see, had no concept of this treaty and suffered at the hands of the English for breaking it. The whole conduct of Massachusetts and Connecticut against the Narragansetts had been solely unjust and high-handed.[257]

Other Indians besides the Wampanoags would also beat the war drum. On the 14th of July, a war party of Nipmucks from the praying village of Pachackoog led by Matoonas launched a sudden attack against the small frontier town of Mendon in the southern part of Massachusetts, killing six of the inhabitants while they labored in the fields. This was the first attack within the Massachusetts Colony.

The Massachusetts company, on return from the Narragansett country, heard word of the attack on Mendon, whereupon they rejoined the Plymouth forces and prepared for a potent attack against the Wampanoags. The combined force moved forward toward the Pocasset swamp country on July 19th where Philip had fled. As soon as the colonial force arrived they were immediately met with a murderous volley by a band of hostile Indians lying in wait for them in a thicket. Five of the colonial men were instantly killed and many were wounded. Undaunted by this attack, the English forces pushed on toward the great cedar swamp where the Indians withdrew.

The regiment quickly learned how dangerous it was to fight in such overgrown woods, as their eyes were blinded by leaves and their arms trapped with the thick limbs of the trees and surrounding prickers, and their feet continually bound with the roots spreading every which way. "It was ill fighting with a wild Beast in his own den," and they never were able to get their hands on the Indian warriors.[258]

The English now found themselves deep in the swamp, and obviously at a great disadvantage. Because of the terrain and the tangle of brush they were too seriously handicapped by their equipment. Night was also approaching and a swamp was no place for the large company at night. Frustration was felt throughout.

Over a week had passed and it was learned from an old Indian found in one of the neighboring wigwams that Philip was nearby. The English attempted to pursue his location, but the light was removing fast and at dusk the soldiers began to fire at every stump and waving bush, wherein many, made nervous and confused by the darkness, shot in the gloom even at their comrades. Considering that Philip was cornered and as good as captured, the main force disbanded, and Captain Prentice marched towards Mendon where the Nipmucks had attacked prior. Philip, though, was far from being taken, and, while Captain Henchman was building a fort outside the swamp, the sachem evaded the outposts during the night of the 31st of July, crossed the Taunton River and made his escape.[259] The best they could do was capture the one man who informed them that both Phillip and Weetamoo, a Pocasset noble woman and Wamsutta's former wife, had recently departed.[260]

Many bands were now beginning to sway toward Phillip's persuasion, which the Narragansetts had not chose to do at the time of the July 15th treaty. Reaction to the first Nipmuc attack on Mendon was felt through the Massachusetts colony, and the attack was especially concerning to the Governor and Council of Massachusetts. However, prior to the attack, peaceful intercourse was sought with the Nipmucs- comparable to the peace sought with the Narragansett tribe.

Ephraim Curtis

Thirty-five year old scout, trader, and hunter Ephraim
Curtis of Worcester was sent into Nipmuck territory previous
to the time of the Mendon invasion, as he was most familiar
with the Nipmucs amid his outpost encounters in the area.
Curtis was also one of the messengers in June 24-26, 1675,
who previously received confirmations of subjection to the
Massachusetts government from sachems of the Nipmuck
towns of Hassanamesit, Manchage, Chabanakongkomum,
Maanexit, Quantisset, Wabquisset, and Pachackoog- all praying
towns. Treaties were made with all of these seven principal
towns visited.

Curtis was then employed by the Bay to journey into the
Nipmuc country on the 13th of July, a day prior to the Mendon
attack, with the purpose of negotiating and spying upon the
Nipmucs.[261] An additional task was drawn into this journey,
Curtis was to join Uncas and his six men homeward as far as
Wabaquesesue, whereupon he could speak with the praying
Indians and understand their fidelity. Uncas, consequently,
had previously offered Mohegan assistance in Boston and was
on his way back to Connecticut. The important prospect for
Curtis, aside from transporting Uncas, was to discover the
motions of the Nipmucs or "Western Indians".

Governor Leverett and the Bay council were in favor of obtaining and confirming subjection of powerful tribes. It was of most importance to keep strong Indian forces from joining in the rebellion. The authorities in Boston sent three separate missions to the separate Indian tribes- the Nipmucks, Narragansetts, and Pocumtucks- as part of an overall plan to prevent a full outbreak of war, which at the time proved effective with the Narragansetts. Instead of sending an army to the Nipmucks as the colony had in the case of the Narragansetts, the authorities chose Ephraim Curtis, a young trader who owned a trading post deep in the Nipmuck country, and knew these Indians firsthand.

Curtis and a small party were chosen for the mission, whereupon he would spend his time interviewing the rulers of the various villages. At the meetings, divers of these sachems denied any of their men had gone to aid Phillip, and those that had gone away with the rebellion were promised to be recalled.[262] Yet, Curtis was not aware that an Indian village constable had already persuaded many of the Nipmucks, "those who did not become praying Indians would be killed."

These separate tribes would read to the sachems a message from Governor Leverett, receiving in turn a promise that two of their leading men would visit the governor in the near future- a promise never to be fulfilled. Upon reaching Marlborough, Curtis was informed that Matoonas, with Sagamore John, leaders of the Nimpuc party friendly to Philip, along with fifty of Phillip's men, had robbed his house at Quansigamug (Worcester). Some Indians, with whom he had traded for many years, told Curtis that it would be dangerous to continue his journey. Curtis had written an account of this predicament:

I conducted Unkeas his men safly while I com in sight of Wabquesesue new planting fielde; first to Natuck, from thenc to Marelborrow, from thenc to Esnemisco,

from thenc to Mumchogg, from thenc to
Chabanagonkomug, from thenc to Mayenecket, from
thenc over the river to Seneksig, while wee cam nere to
Wabaquasesu, wher they were very willing that wee
should leve them, and returned thanks to Mr. Governer,
and to all them that shewed them kindness, and alsoe to
us for our company. And in my jorny my chefe indever
was to inquire after the motions of the Indians. The first
information which I had was at Marelborrow att the
Indian fort, which was that my hous at Quansigamug was
robed; the Indians, to conferm it, shewed me som of the
goods and alsoe som other goods which was non of mine.
They told mee it was very daingerous for mee to goe into
the woods, for that Mattounas, which they said was the
leader of them that robed my house, was in company of
fifty men of Phillips complices rainging between
Chabanagonkamug and Quatesook and Mendam and
Warwick, and they might hapen to mett mee; and if I
mised them, yet it was daingerous to meet or see the
other Nipmug Indians which wer gathered together, for
they would be reddy to shoot mee as soon as they saw
mee. (...)

  I speak to many of them in the Governor's name,
which I called my master, the great Sachim of the
Massathuset Englesh, requiring them to owne ther
fidellyty and ingidgement to the Englesh, telling them that
I cam not to fight with them or to hurt them, but as a
messinger from the Governer to put them in mind of their
ingaidgment to the English. I think some of them did
beleve mee, but the most of them would not. [History of
Hardwick][263]

Despite the robbery of his own house and the attack on
Mendon, which confirmed that the Nipmucks were in a most

violent state. He would nevertheless continue his mission among the familiar tribe. The positive result of the Curtis missions not only had the English authorities reach the ears of the Nipmucks with their message of peace, but unfamiliar information was also exposed.

Written assurances were provided by Nipmuc sachems not to assist Phillip, as the document was signed by Piamboho and Wawas (James the Printer) who were the rulers of Hassanamesit; John of Packachoog; Conkeaskoyane, sachem of Quabaug; Black James of Chonbonkongamaug; Pocamp, Nashowonea & Shockoi of Manexit; Willasksoupin of Manchachage.

Curtis traveled back to Boston on the 16th of July satisfied that he made some progress toward repairing the Indians' anger against the English. He reported on July 24th that the tribe was in better spirits and they "promised that Keehoud and one more of their principle men would come to the Massachusetts Bay within four or five days and speek with their Great Sachem."[264]

The Council waited in vain for the Nipmuc embassy. None came, and, thoroughly alarmed, they determined to force matters to an issue. Captains Hutchinson and Thomas Wheeler, with twenty troopers, were accordingly sent from Boston, July 28th, to demand the reasons why the promised Indian embassy had not been sent, and to warn them that unless they delivered up Matoonas, his accomplices and all hostile Indians who came among them, the Council would hold them as aids and abettors. [Ellis and Morris][265]

Boston, 27 July, 1675. The Council, beeing informed that the Narraganset Indians are come downe with about one hundred armed men into the Nipmuck country, — Do order you, Capt. Edward Hutcheson, to take with you

Capt. Thomas Wheeler and his party of horse, with
Ephraim Curtis for a guide, and a sufficient interpreter,
and forthwith repaire into those parts, and ther laubour
to get a right understanding of the motions of the
Narraganset Indians, and of the Indians of Nipmuck; and
for that end to demand of the leaders of the Narraganset
Indians an account of the grounds of their marching in the
country, and require an account of the Nipmuck Indians
why they have not sent downe their Sagamore according
to their promise unto our messenger Ephraim Curtis.
[History of Hardwick][266]

During the time of Phillip's initial revolt, the Nipmucks
became divided into a tribe for war and a tribe against war,
many turned hostile as those that didn't join the English were
coerced by the rebels. The colonies instant support of each
other, as hysteria increased toward local Indians, showed all
the Massachusetts and Rhode Island Indians that an alliance
with the English meant nothing; Englishmen from any colony
would stick together against any Indian.

Curtis' return to Boston yielded no harvest. No Nipmuc
Sachem appeared. The council thereupon sent Captain Edward
Hutchinson, escorted by Captain Thomas Wheeler and his
mounted Company, with Curtis as guide, to find the Indians
and bring them to terms.[267]

The authorities were now presenting demands upon the
Nipmuck sachems that Matoonas and the other Indians who
had taken part in the murders at Mendon be delivered up to
justice, as well as, a guarantee of peace. Captain Edward
Hutchinson, having just returned from the treaty mission to the
Narragansetts, was given the responsibility of trying to obtain
those desired commitments.

On July 28th Captain Wheeler, with about twenty of his troop and Captain Hutchinson, reported to the Council and thereupon marched from Cambridge to Sudbury, and thence the next three days into the Nipmuck Country. Ephraim Curtis and three friendly Natick Indians who served as guides and interpreters, also marched. Traveling toward their destination they passed through a number of Indian villages that were empty, which meant the Nipmucs were at a central location not living scattered as in times of peace. Hutchinson and his party of mounted men then rode into the small town of Brookfield, which housed twenty families. Thereupon, they learned the great body of the Indians were at a place about ten miles northwest of Brookfield.

On August 1st Captain Hutchinson sent Curtis and a few other men to arrange a parley with the defiant Nipmucs. Ephraim Curtis led the group- two were Brookfield men, and the fourth was one of the Indian guides.[268] The group would meet with the Quabaug Indians near a swamp, whereupon the company would inform the Indians that they had not come to do harm but to send a message. The messengers found the atmosphere at the Indian camp anything but welcoming, the young warriors were threatening at first, nevertheless, their sachems agreed to meet Captain Hutchinson and his party next day at eight o'clock. Curtis reported the Quabaugs, whose leader was Mattaump, agreed to come next day to a plain some three miles from Brookfield.[269]

The company was now surrounded by the foreign wilderness of the Nipmuc, whilst violence was not on their mind as they set out for the place of rendezvous the following day. Captain Hutchinson, accompanied by the troopers, scouts, and three of the chief men of Brookfield, went to the meeting place, but no Indians appeared. At which point the officers suspected betrayal, and were warned by the Indian guides not to go on; but the Brookfield men that came along, were so confident of the good faith of the Nipmucks, that they urged to trust the local natives, whereupon undertaken with persuasion, the party marched on.

The audacity led the group toward the Indians in a swamp several miles away which was in accord with the report as to where the Indians were previous. The path to the swamp was, at one point, narrow and difficult- having an impassable swamp on one side and steep rocky hill on the other. Here with their skill the Quabaug Indians had placed their ambush, which was a defensive measure.

The company first entered where a wooded hill rose suddenly from the edge of the swamp- covered with thick brush and tall grass. The English were forced to take a single file in consideration of the narrow trail, whereupon the entire company unbeknownst passed the first lines of the ambush, which immediately closed to cut off a retreat. Whilst the foremost of the troopers had ridden forward some sixty or seventy rods, the Indians, from their hiding places on either side along the narrow path, poured in upon them a sudden and terrible volley. Eight men were killed at the instant.[270] Unable to retreat by the way they had come, a few of the company, dismounting, held the savages from rushing and overpowering them in a hand-to-hand conflict until the rest rallied.[271]

The company was unable to move forward because of the ground, whereupon the men turned and fled the way they came in, yet the Indians closed in behind them. With great confusion and eight men dead and more wounded, inexplicably, the three Indian scouts knew the way to Brookfield without following the main trail. The safe journey back to Brookfield was solely the result of the Nipmucks lacking horses. After a difficult ride of ten miles, the troopers rode into Brookfield, where they set out an alarm and fortified one of the largest houses. The alarm immediately spread through the town, and the inhabitants left their own houses and fled to the house held by the company.[272] The return of the defeated and wounded men made clear the deadly force that was now approaching the little settlement. The frightened residents of Brookfield prepared to defend themselves against a Nipmuc attack, setting the stage for the battle of Brookfield.

Barely had the preparations for the garrison's safety been completed whereupon the Quabaugs poured into the village, plundering and burning the deserted houses and surrounding the garrison on all sides. Thus reinforcements were crucial for Brookfield's survival. Ephraim Curtis and Henry Young mounted their horses and attempted to travel east to Marlborough to notify the garrison there. Yet Indians were spied whilst the two barely reached the further end of the street and thereupon returned to the garrison, which the Indians began to attack.

The Indians were well supplied with ammunition, wherein they shot through the walls of the garrison. Whilst the attack went on, the strength of the enemy seemed to grow. Ephraim Curtis made another attempt to get help, but again was forced back. On August 3rd, he tried a third time, crawling through the darkness on his hands and knees. Finally, he would make it through the lines of the Quabaugs and safely arrive at Marlborough thirty miles away exhausted. News of the Nipmuck attack on Brookfield reached Marlborough earlier than Curtis arrived by travelers who were making way towards Connecticut; they saw the burning houses and the killing of some cattle, and thereupon turned back and spread the alarm at Marlborough. Immediately, Major Williard was sent for and spotted by messengers on his march from Lancaster to Groton that day.[273] Help finally was approaching. It was a long ride to Brookfield, but the troopers covered the distance quickly.[274]

In Brookfield, the Nipmuck warriors continued the attack and shot flaming arrows into the roof of the garrison house as the Brookfield men fired back at the Indians. The people were wise inside and cut holes in the roof, putting out the flames before they spread. The Quabaug bullets occasionally pierced the walls of the garrison house, whilst they inflicted few casualties among the fifty women and children and the thirty-two men within.[275]

By the 4th of August, the siege had been under way for near forty-eight hours, whereupon the Nipmuc would receive large reinforcements. The invading Indians proceeded to fortify the meetinghouse nearby and also the barn belonging to the overtaken house, which served as proper protection from the Brookfield muskets. In short time, they invented a weapon of war, of a style unheard of before or since in warfare. It was a sort of rolling cart fourteen rods long, a pole cut through the heads of a barrel for a front wheel, and for a body, long poles spliced together at the ends and laid upon short cross-poles, and truckle wheels placed under. They constructed two of these war carriages and loaded the fronts with flax and candlewood to serve as combustibles. The war wagon was almost completed, whereupon, a heavy shower fell and wet all their combustibles, wherein the threat was eliminated.[276]

In the meantime, Major Williard and his force arrived, whilst so intent were the Indians about the machines, that Williard's company, coming about an hour after dark, positioned the force outside the garrisoned house before the enemy received them. There was a large body of Indians posted about two miles away, on the road by which the Major's company had passed, and another party of over one hundred nearer the garrison, yet the Indian watch post had let the company pass unharmed, most likely depending upon the larger group to strike the blow; whilst these Indians of closer proximity depended upon the others from a distance for an alarm, which was not heard. Thus both groups missed the opportunity to attack Williard's company. As soon as they saw their mistake the Quabaugs attacked Major Williard's party with fury, but without much avail, thereupon the additional men were safely within the garrison house. The Indians seeing their devices defeated and the garrison reinforced, set fire to the barn and meetinghouse they occupied, and in the early morning of August 5th withdrew[277] and disappeared into the forest.

Were the Quabaugs wrong in ambushing unwelcomed men, whom they knew held capabilities so grave to eliminate the entirety of the whole?

Thus, the Brookfield battle made it clear to the planters that a complete abandonment of the town was necessary. On the other side, growing confidence by the Brookfield success led the Indians to lurk more about those western towns, whilst Philip, for some time, was among them:

He had met the Quabaugs retiring from their invasion of Brookfield in a nearby swamp, on the 5th of August, and, giving them wampum as a pledge, praised their success. He told their chiefs how narrow his escape from capture or death in the fight at Nipsachick had been. Two hundred and fifty men had been with him, besides women and children, but they had left him; some were killed and he was reduced to forty warriors and some women and children. After this encounter, aside from rumors, there is little heard of Philip for some months. [Ellis and Morris][278]

October 5, 1675 The Springfield Invasion

Frenzy now spread into neighboring towns with news of the Brookfield attack. The English chose to seize the guns from the Pocumtuck tribe, who neighbored the Brookfield affair. The Pocumtucks thereupon chose to flee instead of losing their defensive means, while some rebelling Pocumtucks stayed behind and took part in more devastating attacks. Despite the violence, there were few Wampanoags participating in any of the August attacks, as it was the Nipmuc and Pocumtuks that increased the hostility within Massachusetts.

Whilst the war was now spreading through the region, enemy Indians were reported south of the Merrimack River, whereupon the frontier villages in that vicinity pleaded for help. On the 22nd of August, violence broke out at Lancaster when a group of unidentified Indians killed seven inhabitants of that town. At first, suspicion fell upon the local praying Indians then residing at Marlborough, but the truth seems to be that surrounding Nipmucks, encouraged by the presence of Philip in their country, were extending the field of war.[279]

Things growing to this height among the English, the governor and council, against their own reason and

inclination, were put upon a kind of necessity, for gratifying the people, to disband all the praying Indians, and to make and publish an order to confine them to five of their own villages, and for them not to stir above one mile from the center of such place, upon peril of their lives. The copy of which order here follows:
At a council held in Boston, August 30th, 1675.

The council judging it of absolute necessity for security of the English and Indians in amity with us, that they be restrained their usual commerce with the English and hunting in the woods, during the time of hostility with those that are our enemies; do order, that all those Indians, that are desirous to approve themselves faithful to the English, be confined to the several places underwritten, until the council shall take further order, and that they so order the setting of their wigwams that they may stand compact in one place of their plantations respectively, where it may be best for their own provision and defense, and that none of them do presume to travel above one mile from the center of such of their dwellings unless in company of some English, or in their service, excepting for gathering in their corn with one Englishman in company, on peril of being taken as our enemies, or their abettors. And in case any of them be taken without the limits aforesaid except as above said, and do lose their lives, or be otherwise damnified by English or Indians; the Council do hereby declare that they shall account themselves wholly innocent, and their blood, or other damage by them sustained, will be upon their own heads. Also it shall not be lawful for any Indians, that are now in amity with us, to entertain any strange Indians, or to receive any of our enemies' plunder, but shall from time to time make discovery thereof to some English that shall be appointed for that end to sojourn with them, on penalty of being accounted our enemies, and to be proceeded against, as such.

Also, whereas it is the manner of the heathen that are now in hostility with us, contrary to the practice of civil nations, to execute their bloody insolences by stealth, and skulking in small parties, declining all open decision of the controversy, either by treaty or by the sword; the council do therefore order, that after the publication of the provision aforesaid, it shall be lawful for any person, whether English or Indian, that shall find any Indian travelling in any of our towns or woods, contrary to the limits above named, to command them under their guard and examination, or to kill and destroy them as they best may or can. The council hereby declaring, that it will be most acceptable to them, that none be killed or wounded, that are willing to surrender themselves into custody.

The places of the Indians residence are, Natick, Punquapog, Nashobah, Wamesit, and Hassanamesit. And if there be any that belong to other places, they are to repair to some one of these.

By the Council

Edward Rawson, Secretary[280]

By this order, the Christian Indians would have undergone even greater changes- formerly hindered from their hunting, securing their corn from the cattle and swine, laboring among the English to get food and clothes. The converts would be subject to being slain or imprisoned daily, if found outside their sanctioned bounds, whilst planters also took away their guns and kept them, which left the Christian Indian defenseless.

The result of what the committee presented to the Court for consideration, that those Indians of Natick be removed to Noddle's Island; Nashobah Indians to Concord; Hassanamesit,

Magunkog, and Marlborough Indians to Mendon; Punkapog Indians to the Dorchester neck of land, resulted in nothing, for the English inhabitants refused to admit them to live so near them. The Court declined the consent to the committee's proposals.

Therefore the Court took another means. Divers were angered at the committee on how they dealt with the Indians, and it was said "some men were more a friend to the Indians than the English. To this man, however, it was no strange thing for men's reason to be darkened, if not almost lost, when material and temptation do prevail."[281] It was thus ordered and intended by the Council, that two or three Englishmen should be kept at each of the Indian plantations, to judge their conduct.

Only a few men, nevertheless, were willing to live amongst these praying Indians. Inspection was brought upon the Indians at Punkapog, conducted in particularly by Quarter-Master Thomas Swift, who testified concerning the Praying Indians living there. It became obvious to him that the jealousies and suspicions upon the Christian Indians were unsupported. Another man appointed to live among the Red Puritans was named John Watson, who, before he lived with these Christian Indians, judged all Indians with prejudice and displeasure. Yet, whilst he had lived with them, he received such joy, and became aware of his prior false judgment, he was ashamed of himself for his former accusations of them all because of common rumors. The good John Watson testified this good fare before the governor, general court, and divers that wondered how the Indians conducted themselves.

Despite the testimony of these English witnesses on behalf of the Christian Indians, the hatred among the divers grew daily. The anger was not only against those Indians, but also towards the English who chose to be charitable toward them. Many harsh speeches were made against Major Daniel

Gookin and Mr. John Elliot, even as Gookin held the highest of representation backing his efforts. He had been appointed to rule and govern by the authority of the General Court of Massachusetts and the Honorable Governor and Corporation for Gospelizing those Indians for twenty years, whilst Eliot had been their teacher and minister about thirty years. Anger should have only been justified if these men did support and protect those hostile toward the English.[282]

On the other side of the war, many hostile Indians were gathered in great numbers on the west side of the Connecticut River in Massachusetts, whilst under the direction of Philip- although it is unknown if he took part in any of the assaults. Small parties were constantly lurking near the frontier towns, Hatfield, Northampton, and as far south as Springfield, where, on September 26th, they burned the farm-house and barns of Major Pynchon on the west side of the river.

Hitherto, the Springfield Indians had been friendly and remained quiet in their large fort on the east side of the river near Longmeadow. Just below Springfield, upon the river bank, there had been a village for many years of the Agawams. It had existed when the first planters of Springfield selected the site for their town, and the redmen had lived on friendly terms with the planters for forty years.[283]

Some change, though, had been noticed in those Agawams, and Major Pynchon had turned to the commissioners about disarming them. The Connecticut Council advised against the measure, and suggested rather to take hostages from them. The plan was accepted and the hostages would be sent to Hartford, for security, but the Agawams, excited by the successes of the revolt in Western Massachusetts, whilst being encouraged by agents of Philip, decided to join the war against the English. They somehow facilitated the escape of their hostages, and waited for an opportunity to strike a significant blow.

On Monday, October 4ᵗʰ, a large body of the enemy had been reported some five or six miles from Hadley, and immediately all the soldiers were withdrawn from Springfield. We were defenseless.²⁸⁴

Much uneasiness fell upon the planters in Springfield. It is true the Agawams and Springfield residents enjoyed excellent relations for a long time, mostly a result of the fair John Pynchon. For as long as I could remember, the local natives were living in a sort of fort about a mile below the town, where they could be closely supervised by local officials. Most men in Springfield refused to believe that the sachem, Wequogan, and his people could wrong us.²⁸⁵

There would, however, be terror in Springfield by these same Indians.

The burning of Springfield by the Indians October 5, 1675, nearly forty years after its settlement, has been the most horrific event witnessed there. With open hostilities spreading amid the river valley prior to the horror- Hadley, Deerfield, and Northfield had previously been invaded- Major John Pynchon had gone to Hadley with a small force on the 4ᵗʰ of October because of reports of a large body of Indians. Springfield was left unprotected. Divers had not been happy to see the troops march out of town on the 4ᵗʰ of October, whilst the very next evening these same people, as they rummaged through the ruins of the town, were shouting, "We told you so!"²⁸⁶

On Long Hill in the south part of the town, overlooking the valley, a fort had been constructed for the protection of the friendly Indians, who were dwelling in peace in the neighborhood. Into this a large number of hostile Indians, including some who had previously been on terms of intimate friendship with the whites, had secreted themselves. Toto, a friendly Indian, who was living with Henry Wolcott, Jr., a Windsor farmer, revealed a violent Indian plot by the Agawams to Wolcott, and that night the

226

farmer named Wolcott risked his life and rode swiftly into Springfield bringing the warning, which roused the inhabitants and cautioned them of the threatened danger. Everyone was notified who had not gone to Hadley with Major Pynchon, and immediately took refuge in the three fortified houses. Among the numbers were some of the older men of the community including:

Deacon Samuel Chapin
Rev. Pelatiah Glover
Jonathan Burt
Lieut. Thomas Cooper
Thomas Miller
and others.

A messenger was dispatched to Hadley to notify Major Pynchon of the great danger that was reported by Toto, but the morning of the 5th opened without any indications of an attack upon the town, and Toto's statements began to be discredited. Lieutenant Thomas Cooper, long engaged in this region, set out on horseback for the Indian fort. Thomas Miller accompanied him. They had approached Mill River, within less than a half a mile of the Indian fort, when the Indians fired upon them. Miller was instantly killed and Cooper severely wounded. Cooper's horse galloped back to town and stopped in front of Major Pynchon's house and at this point Lieut. Cooper fell dead to the ground. The Indians then followed up this attack, and soon the dwellings which had been temporarily deserted by the residents of Springfield, for places of greater safety, were set on fire and destroyed. My dwelling was far enough away to be insignificant.

Pentecost Mathews, wife of John Mathews, was shot and killed in the south part of the town, and her house set on fire and consumed. Whilst the work of destruction *unfolded, the Indians in this most tragic attack were recognized as familiar spirits. They proved to be some of the friendly Indians—one of them an old Sachem who had been on the most intimate terms of friendship, almost from the time of the first settlement. The house of correction, some of Pynchon's mills and many other dwellings and barns, were burned to the ground. Major Pynchon, hurried back from Hadley as soon as informed of the contemplated plot, but did not arrive until the town was in ashes and witnessed around thirty houses burnt.*

During the attack Edmund Prygrydays and Nathaniel Brown were severely wounded and both died soon after. Major Treat of Connecticut who had been stationed at Westfield with an armed force, and Major Pynchon and Captain Appleton with their two hundred soldiers all arrived and prevented further destruction. [287]

Subsequent to October 5th, the morale of the people in the upper Connecticut Valley, especially Springfield, reached a new low. The inhabitants and soldiers were now living crowded together in the houses. Divers were shocked at the local Indians, who had long been considered among the most peaceable and dependable. Now, their dissent caused increased suspicion of neutral or praying Indians everywhere, which made the lives of such Indians even more difficult than ever before. [288]

This was Springfield's first introduction to blood in this Indian war, and although they were greatly disheartened, they thereupon set about repairing our broken estates. Such great destruction of life in a single year reflects the danger that existed within the western plantations. With the destruction of Springfield and the other Hampshire County towns, great concern was now directed toward the intent of all Indians:

At Brookfield August 2- 13 killed

Above Hatfield, August 25- 9 killed

At Deerfield, September 1 and after- 2 killed
At Northfield, September 2- 8 killed
Near Northfield, September 4- 16 killed
At Deerfield September 18- 71 killed
Of Captain Mosley's Company September 18- 3 killed
At Northampton, September 28- 2 killed
At Springfield, October 5- 4 killed
At Hatfield, October 19- 10 killed
At Westfield, October 27- 3 killed
At Northampton, October 29- 4 killed [Henry M. Burt][289]

Deer Island

The attacks upon Springfield in October worsened matters for all Indians, with the exception of the Mohegans. The attack not only led to the removal of Christian Indians from their dwellings, but it also prompted the United Colonies' invasion of the great swamp fort in the Narragansett territory. Because the Indians who had assaulted Springfield had for so long showed their loyalty, their actions left the English confused and suspicious of Indians who held a neutral position. Divers in Springfield actually blamed the Praying Indians for this attack, wherein distrust grew upon those who previously trusted those Indians.[290]

Thereupon an incident then occurred to decrease trust throughout. Around the end of October, the General Court received a complaint from the officials of Dedham claiming that some of the praying Indians of Natick were responsible for setting fire to a house and barn in that town. It was, however, suspected by the Superintendent of Indian Affairs Daniel Gookin that the rundown structures, which he said were deserted and of no use to the owner, had been burned purposely by some of the residents who wanted the local Indians banished. They assumed the accusation upon the Natick Indians of such a crime would force the General Court to have them removed. Whilst hearing the evidence, court officials voted toward an immediate removal of Natick Indians to a desolate island in Boston Harbor named Deer Island.[291] Deer Island would be used as a place of detention as early as October 1675. Subsequently, the island would come to house about five hundred Praying Indians following months of war.

These praying Indians faced hardships so severe that only the devil could administer, yet, nevertheless, continued to hold the most divine nature. The non-converts thought of the converts as untrustworthy apostate and the planters to whom they submitted and whose religion they had adopted were also distrustful of them. Furthermore, those Indians who were hostile to the English made attempts to create trouble between the praying Indians and the planters, wherein many false accusations were made. The praying Indians knew of this hatred and placed their hopes and reliance upon the English neighbors. The planters, however, were in a struggle for their very own existence and chose not to trust any Indian. All Indians were to be regarded with such suspicion, wherein the General Court passed severe regulations that none should be allowed to enter any town unless under the guard of two musketeers, and anyone found without such a guard might be arrested. The praying Indians, therefore, had the support of neither side.

The question arose if the English should have trusted the praying Indians more and made greater use of their fighting prowess, and knowledge of both methods of warfare and their home landscape. The natives often said that in action they had the advantage of their white enemies in several ways; they themselves in their marches and battles always spread out, whereas the English usually kept "in a heap together," so that it "was as easy to hit them as to hit a house."

On the contrary to the attack by Matoonas and the Nipmucs, the Natick Indians behaved particularly well on behalf of the colony in one of the first encounters with Philip. Incredibly, the Natick Indians fought against their own, yet, some in their company accused the Naticks of skulking and of shooting over the heads of the enemy, and although some of them brought four Indian scalps as proof of their loyalty, they were still distrusted and would be punished for false accusations made by the townspeople. There is no doubt that in several cases the fires were set and damage was done by inhabitants living near the Praying villages- either the Englishmen who hated these Indians and desired their removal or the hostile Indians who were skulking about. The hostile natives knew they had much more to fear from the praying scouts rather than from all the troops of the English.[292]

Upon the 26th of October, the reports were raised and stirred up against the Christian Indians of Natick, upon pretence that some of them had fired a house or old barn at Dedham, not worth ten shillings. This house, all probability, was set on fire on purpose by some that were back friends to those poor Indians; thereby to take an occasion to procure the removal of all those Indians from Natick; the engineers of which well knew that the magistrates generally were very slow to distrust those poor Christians, this trick was therefore used to provoke them. Hopefully one day the consciences of those persons that have been active to defame and trouble those poor innocent Christians, without cause, will transform into a mind clear of prejudice and hatred. The body of them, the Naticks, were always true and faithful to the English; and I never saw or heard any substantial evidence to the contrary. Besides this burning of the house, there was other false information presented at the same time to the General Court, to stir them up to a sharp procedure against those Indians.

This scheme against the Natick Indians achieved what it was designed for, the passing of an order in the General Court to remove them from their place unto Deer Island; having first obtained the consent of Mr. Samuel Shrimpton, of Boston and owner of Deer Island. In pursuance of this order, Captain Thomas Prentice was commanded to bring them down speedily to a place called the Pines, where boats were appointed to be in readiness to take them on board, and take them to the aforesaid Island.[293] [Daniel Gookin]

Whilst those Indians at Natick became aware of what was contemplated, they first sent a petition requesting the court to show them respect. They asked the court to disregard the false charges against them. They also suggested that either more Englishmen should be sent to live among them as witnesses of their proper behavior, or else that the tribe should hand over some of their leading men as hostages.

They would beg not to be taken from their wigwams just as winter was approaching, whilst the island would bring impossible conditions for the aged and ill. They would declare innocence and loyalty to the colony. These proposals seemed fair, but the divers became still more angered. The General Court thus passed a vote in October that all the Natick Indians be sent for, and disposed of to Deer Island, which would serve as their present residence. It was first necessary to get the permission of the owner of the island, Samuel Shrimpton, of

Boston, who would grant permission provided no wood should be cut or any of his sheep killed.

An Englishman named Captain Prentice, of Roxbury, who was a friend to the Indian people, carried out the removal of the Naticks, who were to be marched down to the Bay with the aid of several others Prentice brought along. Upon reaching Natick he told the Indians of the decision for their removal, and in an hour they gathered a few possessions and left in a quiet sadness. The group of two hundred men, women and children started forth with six carts carrying their possessions along with the ill, first to a place called "The Pines," on the banks of the Charles River.

Good Mr. Elliot, that faithful instructor and teacher of the praying Indians, met them at the Pines, where they were to be embarked, who comforted and encouraged and instructed and prayed with them, and for them; pushing them to patience in their sufferings, and confirming the hearts of those disciples of Christ; and encouraging them to continue in the faith, for through many tribulations we must enter into the kingdom of heaven. There were some other Englishmen at the place called the Pines with Mr. Elliot, who were much affected in seeing and observing how submissive and Christianly and affectionately those poor souls carried it, seeking encouragement, and encouraging one another with prayers and tears at the time of the departure, being, as they told some, in fear that they should never return more to their habitations, but be transported out of the country; of this I was informed by eye and ear witnesses of the English nation that were upon the place at the time. In the night, about midnight, the tide serving, being the 30th of October, 1675, those poor creatures were shipped in three vessels and carried away to Deer Island, which

234

was distant from that place about four leagues. [Daniel Gookin][294]

The landing place on the island was bare. There was no shelter until wigwams were built, whereupon a time when winter was setting in. The Island was bleak and cold, as would be the wigwams. The clothes were few and thin as the corn was. Their own corn supply was ordered to be collected from their own plantations, which was brought to them in small quantity. The irony of this struggle is that these poor souls withstood these wicked conditions, yet still conducted themselves as the most decent Christian.

The great uproar raised against the Naticks for burning an empty barn was the tool that devastated them, nevertheless, it also was justified by the authorities and the friends of these Indians as the best means to get them away from the incensed.

If only the people of Massachusetts understood the value and faithfulness of these praying Indians, there would have been far fewer deaths sustained by the colonial forces upon the Massachusetts frontier. These Praying Towns were so located that they might have formed a line of defense for the greater part of the Massachusetts towns upon the frontier; and it was proposed and urged by those who knew most about these Christian Indians that the forts, which in most cases they had built for themselves under the direction of the English, should now be garrisoned by them, with English officers and about one third of the garrison English soldiers; and that these would be a great asset in scouting and guarding the frontiers. There is little doubt that this course would have saved most of the destruction and bloodshed which took place in Massachusetts during the war; but there was a furious popular prejudice against all Indians, and the majority of the population had no confidence in any attempt to employ Indians in [the company's] movements. [Bodge][295]

The magistrates were in a troubling state throughout the war. They had to negotiate between planters certain that the neighboring Christian Indians were enemies, and, the supporters of the Christian Indians—John Eliot and Superintendent of Indian Affairs Daniel Gookin. The magistrates attempted but could not please both sides. They spoke of justice, whilst at the same time they paid no attention to the pledge of 1644 for mutual protection.[296]

With the grave destruction from the hands of friendly neighboring Indians, the fate of the Christian Indians and the neutral Narragansett Tribe would be a matter of most importance.

The Swamp Massacre

Canonchet, the great Narragansett Sachem, son of Miantonomo, stood distant from participation in both the war and the July 15th treaty, hitherto, until, he would be summoned to Boston in September 1675, ordained to reconfirm the July treaty. He appeared before the Council and received the same threats from the Council as those brought about in July from the previous treaty. He was to sign a treaty guaranteeing his tribe to fight against the hostile Indians, and to seize and turn over all those in his territory who had taken part in the war. This demand was impossible for him to perform; nevertheless, he finally accepted the terms on October 18th. The English gave Canonchet the deadline of October 28th to deliver all hostile Indians.[297]

He signed the treaty on October 18th agreeing to surrender Weetamoe within ten days, wherein he was rewarded a silver-trimmed coat. The surrender of all Philip's subjects, including women and children, who took refuge with the Narragansetts, was also agreed upon by Canonchet. The July treaty was not adhered to by Canonchet for a long time, yet on the demand of the commissioners of the United Colonies, Canonchet confirmed to deliver all the Wampanoag men, women, and children to the Governor or Council at Boston before October 28th.

If peaceful Indians did not receive trust, a neutral tribe, such as the Narragansetts, was not to be considered favorable; waiting for a justification for war upon the Narragansetts had became the colonial approach. Neutrality with the colonies, which was pursued and achieved by previous Narragansett Sachems Canonicus and Pessacus, was soon to become broken. Nevertheless, previous attempts at submission and subservience had not influenced the Narragansett, nor had it made the English less industrious in furthering their own interests and those of Uncas.[298] Whilst news reached Narragansett of Phillip's men murdering planters on June 24, 1675, the commissioners in Boston were told that the Narragansett Tribe professed to hold no agreement with Philip.

Nevertheless, this promise was not adequate. On the 2nd of November, it was decided that the Narragansetts failed to obey the agreement as refugees were not delivered within the specified time. Thus the United Colonies agreed the Narragansett sachems had violated their solemn engagements with the English, and accordingly Plymouth Colony officials sold 144 of the Narragansetts and Wampanoag refugees who had previously come in as security- whilst it was known that they had nothing to do with the hostilities. They were sent to Cadiz, Spain, and averaged a price of two shillings and two-pence each.[299]

The distrust of the Narragansetts along with the temper of the young warriors had not gone away, and the commissioners of the United Colonies called an emergency meeting to discuss the situation. It was decided, rather than to be patient, the best course of action would be to destroy the Narragansett people immediately- before the tribe could join Philip.[300] "On November 12, 1675, the commissioners of the United Colonies unanimously agreed to discipline the Narragansetts for their defiance of the treaty formed on October 18 which ordered the tribe to provide Wampanoag refugees to the English. Canonchet had no intent on keeping his treaty obligation, as his experience with the English left him no trust in the English word.[301]

Whilst the Narragansetts being people not so acquainted with such ways as handing over refugees from a different tribe, the United Colonies raised [over] a one thousand man army under the command of Josiah Winslow to march into Narragansett country and demand that they hand over all Indians who had sought their shelter."[302]

"The [colonist also believed the] Narragansett Indians favored Philip and seemed on the point of joining his alliance. Intelligence was also received that the hostile Indians with Philip were retreating towards the south and to winter quarters amongst the Narragansetts. Unbeknownst of the true circumstances, the Narragansett's had gathered their winter's provisions and fortified themselves in the center of an almost inaccessible swamp[303]."

Thereupon the veteran troops of the plantations were recalled and reorganized; small towns in various parts of the colonies were garrisoned, and an army of one thousand men was equipped for a winter campaign. General Josiah Winslow, Governor of Plymouth Colony, was appointed commander-in-chief of the Army; Major Samuel Appleton was to command the

Massachusetts regiment, Major William Bradford that of Plymouth, and Major Roger Treat that of Connecticut.

General Winslow, upon his appointment as the command of the army in this expedition, rode to Boston for consultation with Governor Leverett and the Council. Thence on Thursday December the 9th, he rode to Dedham, having Benjamin Church as aid.

On December 18th, this, the largest army ever assembled in the colonies, after a day of fasting and prayer on the 2nd, whilst the people were told by the government of the Bay Colony that they were suffering judgment for their sins of frivolity, [they] started at daylight for the Narragansett swamp where some 1,200 warriors were fortified with their women and children. And it was Sunday.

In this December, the Narragansetts did not follow the old winter tradition of separating into "smaller bands and hunting-camps". The number of refugees with them, as well as the lack of food, made this impossible. Instead, the Narragansetts gathered themselves with huge stores of corn at a hidden village in the Great Swamp near Kingston, Rhode Island. Narragansett families assumed safety within the fort as it was out of sight. Their concealment was a clear sign that they had no intention for warfare.[304]

Peace would grow further from possible, as tragedy for either side occurred nearly every week. Land! For this is what divers crave, but it is a great farce- an artist has sculpted a work emerging as something it is not. All this folly! All to claim ownership, and we are the undertakers in this absurdity.

Hartford no less than Boston can count this as one of the gravest moments in its history. As they marched, three feet of snow would cover the ground before the night was through. Upon arrival at the edge of the swamp, the English encountered a party of Indians who quickly returned the fire of the Massachusetts army's advance troops, and then withdrew into the swampland. The leading companies followed into the swamp after the retreating lookouts. Fortunately for this regiment, the cold of the past few weeks had completely frozen the muck and water of the swamp, so that the English were able to advance across land which under warmer conditions would be impassible.[305]

The onrushing troops suddenly saw before them within the swampland a small piece of upland and upon it a great Indian village secured behind a wall. The wall itself was constructed of tall impenetrable wood of almost a rod in thickness set upright in the ground, and around its perimeter was piled a thick mass of tree limbs and brush several yards thick. The fort had been raised upon an island of four or five acres of rising land in the midst of a swamp. Its place of entrance could only be reached over a long tree stretching over a small body of water. The bridge was made up of a long log laying four feet from the ground over which men could enter, whilst there was a block-house opposite to it. The English thus filed into this area as it was the only means of cover and entrance. From the block house, as well as within the entrance, they were shot down nearly as fast as they arrived.[306] It is true the English were shot down at first, but they continued to pour in.

As fate would have it, the first English troops to arrive found the one vulnerable spot in the entire structure, at the one corner of the palisade that was not complete, there was a gap which had been temporarily blocked by the trunk of a tree placed in a horizontal position.[307]

Within the palisade, the Indians began to fall back as the company continued to enter, as the colony was now somewhat protected by the sharpshooters in the nearby blockhouse, but many men still continued to fall, and the Narragansetts, rallying again, began to pressure them violently, whereupon the Connecticut force suffered from the enemy's fire. A short time later, the Plymouth men made their entrance. Little by little the attack of the English finally had driven the Narragnsetts out of the village, whilst they still hung on the outskirts of the swamp, firing continuously at the English from the shielding woods.

Either through chance or deliberately fired by an English hand, the Indian wigwams caught fire, and the wind swept the fire in a mighty wave of flame through the crowded fort. Great flames indicated that the victory had been won, but the price paid had been heavy.[308] The many weary troops were thus forced to march back through the snow, carrying their wounded, to the head quarters, where they had departed in the morning. The suffering was incredible.[309] The numbers of Indians that had escaped, and were still in the woods close at hand, were unknown, but supposed to be several thousand-one report told of a thousand in reserve about a mile distant.[310]

How many Indians had perished was not determined, but it must be assumed that the Narragansett force had been greatly reduced. At least twenty from the colonies were killed.

Consequently, the number of Indians killed has been greatly exaggerated. One thousand perished I have been told by some.[311] "The Naragansetts had lost at least 97 warriors and between 300 and 1,000 women and children is told by another account."[312] However, divers of the Narragansett warriors escaped enraged, and now chose to join the Nipmucks.[313] The colonies did not comprehend that their mishandling of thousands of peaceful neutral Indians eliminated the greatest asset of all- friendly Indians. The invasion ironically turned the Narragansetts toward an alliance with Philip, wherein violence would now spawn more violence.

Meanwhile, contrary to rumors, Philip wasn't in Narragansett, nor was he with the Nipmucs. He had left for New York sometime around December 1675, wherein he was with a band of warriors to recruit Mahicans and descendants of prior Puritan massacres- north of Albany.

Philip, with the remnant of his Wampanoags and Pocassets, had spent the late fall and early winter at Quabaug, but in December, joined by his own followers and a following from the upper river tribes, went west and established winter quarters, some twenty miles northeast of Albany.[314] It is probable that in New York he was there negotiating with the Mohawks for their cooperation in a spring campaign, as well as, to speak with a mediator outside of New England with royal authority. It is believed that he had assurance from the French of ammunition and arms, together with a body of Canadian Indians to re-enforce him.[315] The removal from the scene of war let Philip gain apparent advantages: communication with the French and Mohawks; and also access to the Dutch traders for supplies of powder, who ignored bans on sales to hostile Indians. However, many of the traders refused to sell direct, but the Mohawks took the furs from Philip's warriors and traded them off as their own, in exchange for powder, lead, and guns.

On January 5, 1676, New York Governor Edmund Andros received word of Phillip's whereabouts and was urged to send Mohawks to attack Phillip. Philip had the ability to cause hostility in New York and the Mohawks accepted Governor Andros' encouragement to attack. They fell upon their old enemies in a brutal surprise attack that broke and scattered the great force that Philip had collected to ravage New England during the spring. The Mohawks altogether killed fifty of Philip's men; driving Philip and the surviving force back to New England.

The Death of Philip And The Indian

In New England, success for the colonies began to show amid several expeditions, especially in that of the Narragansett Swamp. The Indians, on the other hand, were distressed for want of food, whilst their ammunition began to disappear. The sudden reverses of fortune on both sides abundantly shows how quickly the advantage in war can change. Accordingly, the spring of 1676 would open with terror as Philip and his diminished force would return east.

Philip and his force were weakened whilst they returned to the upper Connecticut River Valley, the existing hostile Indians, conversely, had increased. A new violent and destructive energy was now within the Indian spirit. The scouts and advanced parties of the Narragansetts began to come among the Nipmuc tribe subsequent to their retreat from the swamp, altogether, conveying news of the destruction of their swamp fortress.

There was no cooperation between Nipmucs and Narragansetts at first. The Rhode Island were not believed, nor were they received by the Nipmucks. The Narragansetts had stayed neutral with the English throughout, which was viewed as a union. The great leader Canonchet and his tribe chose for Narragansett indifference in all the great war councils for the support of Philip. Consequently, these bands fleeing for their safety, whilst they came to the camp at Menamest carrying English scalps and heads, were rejected and their messenger shot at. Accusations of friendship with the English was the justification. Yet, when larger bands came, bringing more proofs of the same kind, whilst confirmation was delivered from other bands, there was great rejoicing that the Nipmucs had acquired the assistance of the strongest tribe in from the south along with their chief. Last to choose violence against the plantation, their reasons for hatred and revenge would become deepest.[316]

The praying Indians remaining on the mainland and interned on Deer Island had no intention to join the hostile Nipmucs and Narragansetts whilst they were living in dire circumstances. Divers praying tribes upon the mainland, however, would join the Naticks on Deer Island in the winter. The same logic that interned the Naticks was applied to other peaceful tribes. Near the end of December, orders were issued to have the Indians of Punkapoag interned on the Boston Harbor islands, as they were sent to the island for as little a cause as the Naticks were.

Near the end of February, 1676, the peaceful tribe from Nashobah was also removed to Deer Island. The citizens of Concord found the Nashoba Indians unbearable and feared an Indian attack, whereupon the town quietly sent for Samuel Mosley- a man known for his ill conduct upon the redmen. Whilst Samuel Moseley arrived he entered the congregation in Concord with a company of volunteers as the town was performing worship. He entered the church and waited until the Minister finished his sermon. Moseley then addressed the Concord people and offered to remove the town's Indians, wherein he received praise. As soon as the services were finished Moseley and his men marched to a local resident's house where the Indians lived. Moseley and his company were followed by divers of the congregation—"a hundred or two of the people, men, women, and children." There would be an armed mob outside the home where the Indians lived that night, whereuponhe townspeople thus entertained themselves with foul speeches toward the Indians.

The next morning, Moseley stated that he was to take the Nashobahs to Boston. Mr. Hoar, who housed the Nashobah Indians at his residence, insisted that Moseley show an order from the Council for their removal from his land. Moseley felt that his commission to kill and destroy the enemy was justification enough for the Indians removal. Hoar, in turn, protested that the Nashobahs were not foes, but friends sanctioned under his care. Nevertheless, Moseley ordered his men to break down the door and remove all the Indians.[317] The Indians were taken, whereupon Moseley's soldiers would steal all the Indian belongings. The Nashobah's were then marched down to Boston, where the court would send them to Deer Island in February of 1676.[318]

Sufferings on the island during this winter was very severe, for their rude shelters were inadequate, their clothing scanty and their food, consisting chiefly of shell-fish and clams, was unhealthy and also insufficient- in spite of almost continuous fishing and digging. There was little wood because they were prohibited by the owner of the place from cutting any of the standing timber. Many of course died, whilst they uttered few complaints. John Eliot often visited Deer Island to comfort the prisoners and to look after their wants. This interest caused the white men to condemn Eliot severely.[319]

Other praying tribes had faced far different conditions. About the first of November 1675, an enemy force of nearly three hundred armed Indians came down to Hassanamesit and pressured the Christian Indians to go away with them. The Indians living within the Hassanamesit Praying village had already been disarmed and threatened by their English neighbors that some had already left to join the enemy willingly.[320]

These Christian Indians at Hassanamesit were gathering their crop of Indian corn into barns whilst they were told that the band would steal what corn they had and leave them to starve if they didn't satisfy the requests. The enemy Indians explained to the Christian Indians that if they followed the English, they would suffer as those Praying Indians of Natick. The good Christians were unable to combat the enemy, whilst, also, in fear of future sufferings by the English; many of them at last chose to follow the enemy into their quarters, under their promise of good treatment and protection.[321] Thus, the broken Indians of Hassanamesit joined the enemy's quarters about Wenimesset (Tewksbury), where portions of the Nipmuck, Quabage, and Wesakam Indians now would keep their rendezvous.

And so, finally, it became evident that the praying Indians were the essential tools to overcome the hostilities. Subsequent to the Narragansett swamp fort destruction, the English were anxious to gain information relative to the Narragansett bearing. Thus, the employment of praying Indians removed upon Deer Island was thought necessary, wherein they were to be used as spies amongst the Nipmuc and Narragansett bands. Two Indians were chosen, whilst they received five pounds apiece. Gookin wrote on the matter:

> In the early months of internment on Deer Island, King Philip was successful in his warfare and many

dissenters befell the English settlements and after the fight which was between the English and the Indians at Narragansett, December, 1675, the Council of Massachusetts were very desirous to use means to gain intelligence of the state of the enemy; and, in pursuance thereof, passed an order empowering Major Gookin to use his best endeavor to procure two persons of the Praying Indians, from Deer Island, to undertake that service, and to promise them a reward for their duty. Accordingly, upon the 28th of December, Gookin went down to Deer Island, and advising with two or three of the principal men, they approved the design [for spying on the enemy] and of the persons he had pitched upon for that employment of intelligence, if they could be procured, Job Kattenanit and James Quannapohit. These, being spoken to by the Major about this matter, answered, that they were very sensible of the great hazard and danger in this undertaking; yet their love to the English, and that they might give more demonstrations of their fidelity, they being also encouraged by their chief men, they said, by God's assistance, they would willingly adventure their lives in this service. The same day, the Major brought them up with him, and conveyed them privately, in the night, to his house at Cambridge, and there kept them in secret until all things were fitted for their journey, and instruction and orders given them.

Upon the 30th of December, before day, they were sent away, being conducted by an Englishman unto the falls of Charles River, and so they passed on their journey undiscovered. These spies, Job Kattenanit and James Quannapohit, [carried] themselves in this service prudently, and faithfully brought the intelligence which might have conduced much to the advantage of the

English had their advice been wisely believed. They first fell among the enemy's quarters about Wenimesset, where the Nipmuck, Quabage, and Wesakam Indians kept their rendezvous, among whom were most of the praying Indians that were captivated from Hassanamesit, as was previous mentioned. These spies were instructed to tell a fair, yet true story to the enemy during their labor; that they were some of the poor Natick Indians, confined to Deer Island, where they had lived all this winter under great sufferings; and now these being gotten off, they were willing to come among their countrymen and find out their friends that had lived at Hassanamesit, and to understand the numbers, strength, unity, and estate of their countrymen, that were in hostility with the English, that so they might be the better able to advise their friends at Deer Island and elsewhere, what course to steer, for the future; and that one of them had all his children among them. Upon the 24th day of January, James Quannapohit returned, and was led to Major Gookin's house, from the falls of Charles River, by an Englishman that lived near that place.

The main matters of the enemy described to Gookin was that the enemy quartered in several places this winter and Philip and his soldiers were not far from Fort Albany. They intended a general rendezvous in the spring of the year, and then they would prosecute the war vigorously against the English, burn and destroy the towns. They heard of the fight between the English and the Narragansetts, and rejoiced much at that breach, hoping now to be strong enough to deal with the English, when the Narragansetts and they were joined. That there were messengers sent from the Narragansetts to the Nipmucks, that quartered about them, declaring their desire to join with them and Philip. That the enemy gloried much in their number and strength, and that all this war their loss of men was inconsiderable. They seemed to be very high and resolute, and expect to carry all before them. He said, they lived this winter upon venison chiefly, and upon some corn they had got together before winter from several deserted plantations. The enemy boasted of their expectation to be supplied with arms and ammunition and men from the French, by the hunting Indians. He declared the enemy purposed, within three weeks, to fall upon Lancaster. [Daniel Gookin][322]

The two spies remained near a month amongst the enemies, wherein they had viewed Matoonus at the time he joined the two praying Indians with the hostile group, as he led a train of followers in war dances. Walking eighty miles through deep snow James Quanapohit returned to the Falls of the Charles. He reported to the Council that he had met the enemy beyond Lancaster, and under the false pretense of getting information for their friends on Deer Island, he learned considerable news, including the intended attack upon Lancaster, which proved true. The spies also discovered the Sachems and old men were inclined for peace whereas the young men were too proud and vain to pursue peace.

James escaped from the enemy with the aid of Job, but Job remained, as he could not carry his children away yet. James escaped whilst Job and he pretended to go out hunting, killed three deer quickly, and, went over a pond and lay in a swamp till before day; and, after they had prayed together, James ran away.[323] Job would later, wherein his children would also join him on Deer Island.

It was understood that these two spies were to return to their prison camp in spite of the valuable service they had rendered. In fact, they were accused of bringing in false information, albeit they predicted the attack on Lancaster and voluntarily returned to Deer Island. Although they had risked their lives, and executed such important service, it was nevertheless said that they held correspondence with the enemy, whereupon their betrayal was assumed as the only reason why they came back to the island safe.[324]

Amid the early winter months of 1676 the war continued on violently. The magistrates found it necessary to make still further use of the interned Indians on Deer Island. The General Court voted in February 1676 to raise an army of six hundred men, whereupon Major Savage was chosen Commander-in-Chief. Before the General Court adjourned, which was not until the 28th of February, Major Thomas Savage, as Commander-in-chief, wouldn't accept the duty until Christian Indians interned upon Deer Island were sent with him for guides.

In the months of February, March, and April, the enemy Indians were very violent in their attempts and assaults upon all the frontier plantations, burning several villages or part of them, and murdering many people in the pathways- Warwick, Lancaster, Medfield, Weymouth, Groton, Marlborough, Rehoboth, Providence. Divers places were among those destroyed or damaged. Almost daily, messengers with sad news were brought into the Council. A deep fear existed that seed time and harvest would be hindered and result in a famine. These thoughts upon the minds of those at the head of government, along with the need to end the success of the enemy, brought the Council to arm and send in a company of the Christian Indians that were living on Deer Island. The praying Indians throughout had appeared very desirous and willing to engage against the enemy.

Captain Daniel Henchman was appointed by the Council to look to the Indians at Deer Island and to put them upon employment. This gentleman made motions to the Council of his readiness to conduct these Indians against the enemy; declaring that he had great confidence in God, that if they were employed they might, with God's blessing, be instrumental to give check to the enemy and turn the alarm; testifying that he found them very willing and desirous to serve the country, and leave their parents, wives, and children under the English power, which would be rational security to the English for their fidelity. But those motions were not accepted at first. The people generally distrusted those praying Indians, and were not willing to have any of them employed to serve the country; which was the principal reason why the Council complied not with those and former motions of this nature, for many of the Council were otherwise opposed to it. Though afterwards the motion to arm and employ the Christian Indians was embraced and put in practice. [Daniel Gookin][325]

Captain Henchman, who had been chosen to look after the interned Indians, urged the magistrates to permit him to lead a small company against the enemy. His recommendation at first wasn't accepted, but later, towards the end of April, the Council voted to arm and send out a Company of seventy men under Captain Samuel Hunting and Lieutenant James Richardson, who knew the Indians well. Arms could be procured for only forty and as soon as the men were selected and gathered they headed out on April 21 first reaching Charlestown on their way to Chelmsford.

Upon the 21st of April, Captain Hunting had drawn up and furnished his company of forty Indians, at Charlestown. They were ordered by the council at first to march up to Merrimack river near Chelmsford, and there to build a fort near the great fishing-places, where it was assumed the enemy would come at this time to fish. This fort was to keep their scouts about daily and to seize upon the enemy. If they should be overpowered by greater numbers out in the field, their fort was also for their retreat, until assistance might be sent them. However, for just as those Indians soldiers were ready to march, upon the 21st of April, about mid-day came many messengers, they expressed that a great body of the enemy, who had gathered around fifteen hundred at Wachusett Mountain, had assaulted a town called Sudbury that morning, and set fire on houses and barns. Thereupon the force joined with Praying Indians would change their plans and be called upon the scene of a great disaster.

Whilst the townspeople deserted from Groton, Billerica, Lancaster, and Marlboro, it was Sudbury that had become the important frontier town of the Bay settlements. Situated on the east bank of the Sudbury River it was a point of considerable importance, the roads were opened to the settlements, north, east, south, and west. Small parties of soldiers with supplies were continually passing through on the way to and from the valley.

Captain Samuel Wadsworth was dispatched by the Council with a company of foot to relieve the garrison at Marlboro. Unfortunately, the full force assigned to him could not be collected, whereupon many of those impressed into the war failed to appear, wherein he began his march with only seventy troops, many of them boys. The advance parties of the Indian warriors were already in the woods about Sudbury, when Wadsworth, on the evening of the 20th of April, passed through the town unmindful of the large number of Indians near by, for during the day, some of the Sudbury planters had been fired upon, whilst a house or two upon the distant outskirts had been burned. It was believed, however, that this was the work of only a small party, and Wadsworth was ignorant that over five hundred warriors, Philip among them, was waiting in ambush.

These soldiers that had been sent from Boston, under Captain Samuel Wadsworth of Milton, who, on their way toward their destination to Marlborough, took the trail of Philip, and followed it through the woods to Sudbury, whereupon within a mile of the town, they discovered a body of a hundred Indians. These Indians fled as if through fear, leading the Massachusetts Regiment into a place convenient to be surrounded by five hundred savages, who, thereupon, sprang forth and destroyed them. Near seventy men were slain; but a few of them were left alive to be tortured.[326]

Following the massacre, Captain Hunting with his Indian company, being on foot, got to Sudbury around nightfall, thereupon, the enemy had retreated unto the west side of the river of Sudbury at the time of the praying Indian companies arrival. Upon the 22nd of April, early in the morning, forty praying Indians stripped themselves and painted their faces alike to the enemy. They traveled over the bridge to the west side of the river without any Englishmen- the Indian soldiers soon felt a great grief as they witnessed divers dead.[327]

It was the hostile Indians typical manner to remove themselves and celebrate "when they had done any mischief, lest they should be found out; and so they did at this time. They would travel three or four miles; and there build a great wigwam, big enough to hold a hundred Indians; which they did in preparation to a great day of dancing." (Mary Rowlandson)

The hostile Indian demeanor was still weak even with such a great victory in Sudbury according to a female captive. The cause of this melancholy may be a reaction to what the outlooks for the hostile Indians saw following the massacre- Praying Indians. They would witness Christian Indians fully armed on the side of the English. Christian Indians bearing arms was the last enemy the hostile Indians wanted to face, as the Christian Indians knew their method of warfare, and were great at lurking and scouting.

From this time forward, the Christian Indian soldiers were constantly employed in all expeditions against the enemy, while the war lasted; and after the arrival of the ships from England, which was in May, arms were bought to furnish the rest of the able men; and then Captain Hunting's company was made up to the number of eighty men; those did many services in the summer, 1676. During this summer, the company destroyed or captured a very large number of the enemy and performed most effective work in the closing operations of the war. [Ellis and Morris][328]

Still, the sufferings of the four hundred or so older men, and of the women and children who were left on the islands continued, although spring with its warmer weather had already arrived. In this condition of want and sickness they were, after their men were sent for to fight in the wars. It was until mid-May when the Lord must have been pleased to satisfy the hearts and minds of men towards them, little by little; partly because of the true reports brought to the General Court, of their distressed estate, and the great unlikelihood they were to plant or reap any corn at the Islands; and partly from the success God was pleased to give their brethren, abroad in the country's service. The hearts of many were in a degree changed to those Christian Indians; and the General Court then sitting passed an order, giving liberty to remove them from the Islands, cautioning their order, that it should be done without charge to the country. This liberty being given, Major Gookin, their old friend and ruler, by the authority and encouragement of the right Honorable "The Corporation for Gospelizing the Indians", residing in London, and by authority of the General Court of Massachusetts in New England, immediately hired boats to bring them from the Islands to Cambridge, not far from the house of Mr. Thomas Oliver, a virtuous man, and of a very loving, compassionate spirit to those poor Indians; who, when others were shy, he freely offered a place for their present settlement upon his land, which was very commodious for the situation, being near Charles River, convenient for fishing, and where was plenty of fuel; and Mr. Oliver had a good fortification at his house, near the place where the wigwams stood, where they might retreat for their security. This deliverance from the Island was a jubilee to those poor creatures. [Daniel Gookin][329]

Providentially for these poor souls, the excellent record of the fighting men from Deer Island caused the English to close internment and in May, as aforementioned by Gookin, the General Court passed an order for their removal to Cambridge by hired boats. In Cambridge the Indians were much relieved, especially as some were ill at the time. Thereupon Eliot and others provided the sick ones with food and medicine and all recovered.

The war was now nearing its end and the help of the Mohegans and Christian Indians contributed much towards bringing it to a close. The colonists had suffered the loss of about six hundred of their best men, thirteen towns had been destroyed, and six hundred dwellings laid low, whilst destruction would have been much worse had it not been for their Indian converts, who, through their knowledge of the country and the method in war, were able to offer such precious services. The war was a sad blow to the cause of Christianity among the natives, many of them seemed to disappear or desert, chiefly from the more recent Nipmuc Praying Towns; some became heathen again, some were killed in conflict, some died on the islands during captivity and were buried there, some proved untrustworthy and were executed as rebels, and some died of starvation.

It has been estimated that four hundred of the colonies Indian Allies were either captured or killed, nevertheless, the converts killed over three hundred of their very own. Their fidelity to the colonies is rather to be marveled at, particularly when one considers their treatment and that they were drawn against their own kind. Grateful testimonials do exist that were made by some of the English officers serving over them. The Christian Indians conducted themselves well, and proved themselves courageous soldiers, faithful to the English interest. They must be judged as a great influence of the positive outcome for the United Colonies.[330]

The outcome of war for the bands of hostile or neutral Narragansetts, Wampanoags, and Nipmucs was not favorable. Canochet, the son of Miantonomo, and the chief sachem of the Narragansetts, had escaped the destruction of his principal fort, and had many brave fighting men under him in the early spring of 1676. Some time in March he had ventured down from the north to Seekonk, near the seat of Philip, to get seed-corn with which to plant the towns upon the Connecticut River that had been deserted by the English. [331] Necessity brought Canonchet and a band of Indians to plant corn upon vacant lots, for it was a hungry winter.

This past spring Connecticut was conducting independent military operations of her own, mostly in the Narragansett country. From time to time, parties of Narragansetts made their way down into the Connecticut Colony in search of food, wherein these Indians became the objects of Connecticut's military efforts east of the Pawcatuck. These expeditions were well manned with company volunteers, together with Mohegan, Pequot, and Niantic Indians.[332]

In the sad fate that would be pressed upon the Narragansetts, it would be a combined force of whitemen, Pequots, and Mohegans, who discovered the location of Sachem Canonchet. In a raid around Seekonk and Pawtucket, Canonchet was spied crossing the Blackstone River, whilst his foot slipped, he was thrown into the water, wherein his gun became too wet that it became useless. This misfortune so weakened him that he was overtaken by a swift-footed Pequot who was accompanied by a pursuing party of whites and Indians. Thereupon his capture, the first Englishman to approach him was very young. Whilst this young man attempted to interrogate him, Canonchet replied, "You much child. No understand matters of war. Let your brother or your chief come. Him I will answer." His capture occurred on March 27th, whereupon he was taken to Connecticut.[333] Canonchet, son of Miantonomo, would soon share a similar fate as his father.

To the offer of his life if he would secure peace, Canonchet replied that he wished to die before his heart was made soft and before he had spoken unworthy of himself. On April 8, the council at Hartford formally acknowledged the receipt of his head from the Mohegans and Pequots to whom he had been turned over for execution."[334] Thus as Canonchet's father was killed by Uncas, the son of Uncas superintended the execution of the son of Miantonomo.[335]

The death of Canonchet was the true death-blow of the war for the hostile Indian and the turning point for the colonies. For he was the real leader of all active operations in early 1676, as Canonchet led many devastating attacks on English towns from February through early March. Philip was still considered chief instigator, however, following Canonchet's death, more than before, he became the controlling mind of a larger number than ever before.[336]

The success gained through such a major blow to the enemy, which the Connecticut troops had performed because of their use of the Mohegans and Pequots, may make it appear that the conduct used by Massachusetts during the majority of war was a great folly. For the numerous disasters Massachusetts withstood, how many could the Christian Indians have prevented if they had been trusted and employed sooner?[337] The Mohegans may have been accused of being untrustworthy, nevertheless, Connecticut continued to use Mohegan services, wherein the colony never once demanded seizure of their arms, as the Mohegans were completely faithful. Not one town in Connecticut was destroyed in this war.

The remaining operations of war in these parts mostly became, simply, the hunting down of near defenseless bands. The authorities eventually issued a proclamation calling all those Indians who had been engaged in the war to come in and surrender- submitting themselves to the judgment of the English courts. Divers bands sought to take advantage of this, but were captured upon their approach and were treated as captives.

Following this proclamation which had been made for the peaceful surrender of all Philip's supporters, the squaw sachem of Saconet, an ally of Philip, had first sent three messengers to the governor of Plymouth, asking for life, promising, under that proclamation, submission; and accordingly surrendered herself and tribe to Major Bradford. But, sad to tell! They were slain, the entire one hundred and ten, that very day.[338]

It may be said in truth, that God made use of these poor, despised, and hated Christians, to do great service for the churches of Christ in New England, in this day of their trial; after the Indians went out, the balance turned in favor of the English side; for after the attack of Sudbury and the addition of the Christian Indian soldiers, the enemy went down the wind; and, about July, one hundred and fifty surrendered themselves to mercy to the Massachusetts government, besides several that surrendered at Plymouth and Connecticut. [Daniel Gookin][339]

Philip and his warriors at this point had become greatly weakened by a combination of disease, starvation, and attacks; whilst the settlers began to have much optimism. By June, most Indians had no intention of war and most large groups scattered. It was finally a force of English and Indians under Benjamin Church that found and killed King Philip to end the war in New England.[340] Church had discovered the perfect kind of company for dealing with the scattered remnants of the enemy- a small, volunteer company comprised of Indians and English. Captured enemy Indians were even sometimes given the opportunity to join Church's band, and these traitors made excellent scouts and preying soldiers.

The force, which finally got a hold of Philip, was volunteer, as the men pressed into the war during the later stages were solely conscription for defense of local garrisons. The colonies source for offensive power came from the special companies like Benjamin Church's Plymouth-based volunteer company. Church had come to value the Indians' skulking way of war and adapted it to English custom. The companies of colonial volunteers, as Connecticut men had, were convinced to join because of promises of wages, pillage, and bounties.

It was in July when Captain Church's mixed band captured Philip's wife and nine-year-old son. Yes dear reader, they took one of the King's incipient son's and made a slave of him! When he got the news, Philip, it is said, was ready to die. Philip's family being captured at last and his force surrendering, he fled, broken-hearted, to his old home.[341] King Phillip, who had been a deadly inciter, that had once three hundred men barbarously inclined, was reduced to ten.

Philip hid in a swamp on Mount Hope Neck, with his little party, yet unfortunately for the Wampanoag Sachem, one of his Indians being discontented with him made an escape. This defector located Church and informed Captain Church of Philip's whereabouts. The Wampanoag deserter spoke of Philip's condition, as Philip had killed the Wampanoag exile's brother for advising surrender. This Indian offered to pilot the English to Philip's hiding-place.[342] How the contemptuous men have presented the conclusion of this great war - 'twas not the brilliance of the whiteman that conquered Philip, but the treachery of his very own that conquered the great chief.

The company held the required weapons and supplies necessary to combat the great chief as they had the understanding of where King Philip hid. Captain Church and his company fell upon the swamp, which was very mucky, whilst the ground so loose, that the men sunk and the passage was too difficult. Nevertheless, in the dark, the party of men crawled into position and came within sight of the enemy's camp. An order was made to lie hidden until daybreak, and then open the day with a surprise attack. Instead of taking patience outside the Wampanoag camp, one of the company fired a shot at an Indian who appeared as if he glanced at Church's party.

While they were at first overwhelmed with difficulties in this attempt, the providence of God wonderfully appeared, for by chance the Indian guide and the Plymouth man being together, the guide spied an Indian running for his very life and bids the Plymouth-man shoot, whose gun went not off, only flashed in the pan. With that, on August 12, 1676, the Indian looked about, and was going to shoot, and shot the enemy through the body, dead, with a brace of bullets; and approaching the place where he lay, upon search, it appeared to be King Philip, to their no small amazement and great joy.

A Plymouth Man and the guide named Alderman had been stationed by Captain Church at a point where Philip was thought likely to appear, and according to Church it was the guide whose shots took effect, causing Philip to fall upon his face in the mud and water, with his gun under him.

This seasonable prey was soon divided. They cut off his head and hands, and conveyed them to Rhode Island, and quartered his Body, and hung it upon four trees. One Indian more of King Philip's company they then killed, and some of the rest they wounded, but the Swamp being so thick and miry, they made their escape. [Charles Lincoln][343]

Sadly in the end, over a thousand Indians were sent into slavery in the West Indies with the closing of the hostilities. Thus, Philip's forces had become very small, as so many were tricked away by the whites. It was the most unfortunate situation for all Indians, the Wampanoags for instance, who surrendered to Plymouth, were all sold out of the country as slaves. This action would thereafter force many peaceful Indians not to surrender and turn to other hostile Indians for security. Philip, however, chose death over surrender.

The moment of fatality for Philip paralleled the rapid decrease of hostile Indians still in the open frontier. Cotton Mather wrote on July 8, 1676: very many of the Indians are dead since the war begun; and that more have died by the hand of God, in respect of deseases, fluxes and fevers, which have been amongst them, than have been killed by the sword.

Indians would begin to surrender under white flags carrying such a weak condition. In consideration of such depravities, we must also consider that the English held no mercy in war whilst the redmen's weapons were useless.

Prior to Philip's death in June 1676, Massachusetts and Plymouth claimed mercy to Indians who surrendered, yet nevertheless chose to execute or deport those innocuous souls. Philip's Indian brethren thus deserted his cause and submitted themselves to the English by the hundreds. On July 17, Sagamore John of Pachackoog and one other Nipmuck sachem, with four braves, came in seeking peace. John and his followers were ordered by the court to be put under supervision of the Cambridge village. The Nipmucks may have not wanted to dishonor themselves by surrendering to the English, but the possibility of death at the hands of the English made self-preservation the only option.[344]

One young fellow starting anew came into the shop and described the actions of Sagamore John and the fate of Mattoonus:

> Sagamore John, of the Indians on Pakachoag Hill, who had been induced by the wily King Philip to join with his men in the war against the white settlers, alarmed at the dangerous condition of affairs, (...) prudently sought safety by timely submission to the colonial authorities. July 13, Sagamore John ventured to visit Boston to deliver himself up and make terms for his men. The Governor and Council had issued proclamations offering pardon to the Indians who voluntarily came and surrendered.
>
> Sagamore John expressed sincere sorrow for taking part against the English, promised to be true to them in the future, received assurances of security and protection, and was permitted to depart. On the 27th of July he returned, bringing with him 180 of his followers. To propitiate favor and purchase peace by an acceptable offering, he had treacherously seized Mattoonus and his

son Nehemiah and brought them down bound with cords to be given up to justice. Mattoonus, having been examined, was condemned to immediate death. Sagamore John, with the new-born zeal of a traitor and turncoat, in order to signalize his devotion to the cause he adopted by extraordinary rancor against the cause he deserted, entreated for himself and his men the office of executioners. Mattoonus was led out, and being tied to a tree on Boston Common, was shot by his own countrymen, his head cut off and placed upon a pole opposite to that of his son. [The Nipmuck Indians][345]

Were they true Christians? citizens for the community? They did not desire what we desired, until we corrupted them. We are the one's motivated by temptation, greed, and lust, not the redman. He is a man of family and community. There is no defining word that describes their God. They accepted the all-knowing infinite creator as he was, as he is, and as he will be. They did not ask or beg for anything until enabled. If they needed it, it would be naturally provided. We are the ones that made rules that could be manipulated only to favor certain men. I ask myself often if peace would have existed on the mainland if compromise and respect to the Indian culture had existed there as it had in Martha's Vineyard- where there was not one Indian revolt during this war. Or was the vast wilderness of Massachusetts an impossible land to tame?

Preserving their people and land, as Massasoit and Uncas have tried, became of no option for proceeding Indian generations. Indians that chose the most peaceable relationship with the white men were still sent to an isolated Island. Would there be a change in history if the Indian conduct had been different throughout the two Puritan conquests?

If Christ's divinity is available to all men, wherein no man holds judgment towards another, and simply wishes to help all men, the mission was surely the work of God's Will. However, why did the mission fail on the more emphasized mainland rather than on a little island? Was the devil's sinister influence of greed and temptation the reason for failure?

It is clear that the past Indian wars have eliminated any chance at furthering the gospel amongst the Indians on the mainland. The great irony in all this is that the loss of Indian authority in New England didn't strengthen the Puritans in Massachusetts, instead, the Puritans, as a group, became looked upon as servants for the Crown of England. Thus, the Indians were all considered servants and now so were the Puritans. It's unfortunate that a universal understanding of true Christian conduct could not be the most important interest of all nations. With that being said, I do not overlook the many men in London who held the highest divinity and shared their purses in order to sponsor an effort to share Christianity with the Native.

The idea of faith does not serve any purpose if man does not evolve his spirit toward the divine principles which faith defines. The solution for greed and delinquency will be found in religion, if used in accordance with the true intentions of the gospel. Unfortunately, a parasite has arisen that craves excess. Expansion of property, expansion of wealth, expansion of power, have become the precedent set during the building of the Unified Colonies. The enhancement of one's own material wealth has become imperative, with the natural well being of the whole becoming denied. What is the value of our peace and prosperity when it comes at the expense of another man?

And what is peace! The use of force will continue to increase by any means with land within reach! Representation by a single theology will increase! Private property will increase! These matters are all circumstances that incite the greatest rage within men who do not wish for change in their homeland. An everlasting sense of invincible expansion had become the direction of the United Colonies Commissioners. Even the Indians who have joined this cause have been enslaved, killed, and imprisoned onto a village, but most importantly, they lost their homeland, never to be returned. And the land that was first to be taken was always the most valuable.

I will close in the words of the man who opened the gates for the very men who closed the gates for his very own. Chief Massasoit has spoken: "It cannot be the earth for the earth is our mother, nourishing all her children, bears, birds, fish and all men. The woods, streams, everything on it belongs to everybody and is for the use of all. How can one man say it only belongs to him."[346]

I will conclude by asking you one simple question.

Would you prey or pray?

Bibliography

A Brief History of the Pequot War, John Mason

A Brief History of the Unites States, Joel Dorman Steele and Esther Baker Steele, American Book Company

A History of the Indian Wars with the First Settlers of the United States, to the Commencement of the Late War, Daniel Clarke Sanders, 1828

After King Phillip's War: Presence and Persistence in Indian New England, Colin G.Calloway, University Press of New England, 1997

Cotton Mather: The Puritan Priest, Barrett Wendell, Harbinger Books, 1963

Epochs of American History: The Colonies 1492–1750, Reuben G. Thwaites, Longmans, Green, and Co., 1894

Eulogy on King Philip, William Apess

Flintlock and Tomahawk, Douglas Edward Leach, Parnassus Imprints 1958,

Historic & Archaeological Resources of the Connecticut River Valley, The Massachusetts Historic Commission, 1984

Historical Account of the Doings and Sufferings of the Christian Indians in New England in the Years 1675–1677, Daniel Gookin

History of Hartford County, Charles W. Burpee, S. J. Clarke Publishing, 1928

History of the Indian Wars of New England, with Eliot the Apostle Fifty Years in the Midst of Them, Robert Boodey Caverly

Indian History, Biography and Genealogy: Pertaining to the Good Sachem Massasoit, Ebenezer Weaver Peirce & Mrs. Zerviah Gould Mitchell

Indian Wars of New England: Topography of Indian Tribes, Herbert Milton Sylvester

John Eliot Apostle to the Indians, Ola Elizabeth Winslow, Hooughton Mifflin Company, Boston, 1968

King Phillip's War: Civil War in New England, 1675–1676, 1999 James D. Drake

King Philip's War, George W. Ellis & John E. Morris, Grafton Press, 1906

Leift Lion Gardener His Relation of the Pequot Warres, Lion Gardener

Massacre at Hurtleberry Hill: Christian Indians and English Authority in Metacom's War, Jenny Hale Pulsipher, The William and Mary Quarterly, 1996

Massasoit of the Wampanoags, Alvin Weeks, 1920

Missionary register, Volumes 2-3 By Church Missionary Society

Mystic Fiasco: How the Indians Won the Pequot war, 2010, David Wagner and Jack Dempsey, 7-8

Narratives of The Indian Wars 1675–1699, Charles H. Lincoln, Charles Scribners's Sons, 1913

New England Frontier: Puritans and Indians 1620-1675, Alden T. Vaughn, 1965

New England on Fire! Margaret Barton, Poppet Publications, 2008

News From America; or A New and Experimentall Discoverie of New England; Containing, A True Relation of Their War-Like Proceedings These Two Yeares Last Past, With a Figure of The Indian Fort, or Palizado, Captain John Underhill, 1638

Of Civil Government Second Treatise, John Locke, A Gateway Edition, 1955

Other Indian Events of New England, Allan Forbes, State Street Trust Company of Boston, 1941

Roots of American Racism: Essays on the Colonial Experience, Alden T. Vaughan, Oxford University Press, 1995,

Rhode Island's Founders: From Settlement to Statehood, Patrick T. Conley, History Press, 2010 18–20

Roger Williams: Prophet and Pioneer, Emily Easton, Houghton Mifflin Company, 1930

Soldiers in King Philip's War, George M. Bodge, 1891

Springfield, Massachusetts: Volume I, Henry M. Burt. Printed and Published by Henry M. Burt, 1898

Stories of Wethersfield, Nora Howard, White Publishing 1997

The Beginnings of New England, John Fiskes, Houghton Mifflin Company, 1902

The Beginnings of New England, John Fiskes, 1889,

The Colonial Mind, Main Currents in American Thought Vol. 1 1620–1800, Vernon Louis Parrington

The Enslavement of the American Indian, Barbara Olexer, Library Research Associates, 1982

The Gentle Radical: A Biography of Roger Williams, Cyclone Covey, The Macmillan Company, 1966

The History of Ancient Wethersfield: Volume 1, Sherman W. Adams & Henry R. Stiles, New Hampshire Publishing Company, 1904

The History of Connecticut, From the First Settlement of the Colony to the Adoption of the Present Constitution Volume 1, G. H. Hollister, 1857

The Indian and The White Man, Chandler Whipple, The Berkshire Traveller Press, 1974

The Indian Land Titles of Essex County, Massachusetts, Sidney Perley

The Indians of the Nipmuck Country in Southern New England, 1630–1750, Dennis A. Connole, MacFarland & Company, 2001

The Invasion of America, Francis Jennings, Norton and Company, 1975

The Indian Wars, Robert M. Utley & Wilcomb E. Washburn, American Heritage Publishing/Bonanza Books, 1977

The Memorial History of Hartford County, Connecticut, 1633–1884. Volume 1, edited by James Hammond Trumbull

The New England Company

The New–   –   By Justin Winsor,

The Nipmuck Indians, Caleb A. Waei., Esq., 1898

The Pequot War, Alfred A. Cave, University of Massachusetts Press, 1996

The Puritans, A Sourcebook of Their Writings, Edited by Perry Miller and Thomas H. Johnson,

The Puritan Dilemma: The Story of John Winthrop, Edmund S. Morgan, Longman Inc., 1999

The Reformed Doctrine of Predestination, Loraine Boettner

The Story of Connecticut Vol. 1, Charles Burpee

The United States to 1865, Michael Kraus

Thomas Hooker: Preacher, Founder, Democrat, 1891, George Leon Walker, Dodd, Mead, and Co.

Thomas Mayhew: Patriarch to the Indians, Lloyd C. M. Hare, AMS Press, 1969

Uncas: First of the Mohegans, Michael Leroy Oberg, Cornell University Press 2003

[1] A Historical Account of the Indians of New England, Daniel Gookin, 170
[2] John Eliot Apostle to the Indians, Ola Elizabeth Winslow, 1968, 72
[3] John Eliot Apostle to the Indians, Ola Elizabeth Winslow, 1968, 80-81
[4] The Beginnings of New England, John Fiskes, 1889, 258–59
[5] Cogely, 238
[6] A Praying People, Dane Morrison, 1995, Peter Lang Publishing
[7] John Eliot Apostle to the Indians, Ola Elizabeth Winslow, 1968, 86
[8] King Philip's War, George W. Ellis & John E. Morris, 23
[9] The Memorial History of Hartford County, Connecticut, 1633–1884. Volume 1, edited by James Hammond Trumbull, 11–15
[10] Cave, 50
[11] Thomas Mayhew: Patriarch to the Indians, Lloyd C. M. Hare, 8–9, 1932
[12] Thomas Mayhew: Patriarch to the Indians, Lloyd C. M. Hare, 8–9, 1932
[13] Ibid, 11–15
[14] The Indian Wars, Utley & Washburn, 45
[15] The Gentle Radical, A Biography of Roger Williams, Cyclone Covey, 1966, 15
[16] The Story of Connecticut Vol. 1, Charles Burpee, 16
[17] The History of Ancient Wethersfield: Volume 1, Sherman W. Adams & Henry R. Stiles, New Hampshire Publishing Company, 1904, 56–60
[18] Of Plymouth Plantation 1620-1647, William Bradford, 302
[19] The Story of Connecticut Vol. 1, Charles Burpee, 28–78
[20] Thomas Hooker: Preacher, Founder, Democrat, 1891, George Leon Walker, Dodd, Mead, and Co. 40–51
[21] The Story of Connecticut Vol. 1, Charles Burpee, 87
[22] The Connecticut, Walter Hard, 1947, 37-38
[23] The Gentle Radical: A Biography of Roger Williams, Cyclone Covey, The Macmillan Company, 1966, 150
[24] Deforest, 82-83
[25] G. H. Hollister, 27
[26] Historic & Archaeological Resources of the Connecticut River Valley, The Massachusetts Historic Commission, 1984
[27] Historic & Archaeological Resources of the Connecticut River Valley, The Massachusetts Historic Commission, 1984
[28] Stories of Wethersfield, Nora Howard, White Publishing 1997 12–13
[29] Hollister, 113–114
[30] Adams & Stiles, 60
[31] Roots of American Racism: Essays on the Colonial Experience, Alden T. Vaughan, Oxford University Press, 1995, 201–203
[32] The Indian and The White Man in New England, Chandler Whipple, 155
[33] Adams & Stiles, 62–65
[34] Ibid, 201–203
[35] Hollister, 54
[36] Adams & Stiles, 23
[37] Cave, 136–137

[38] Hollister, 127
[39] History of the Indian Wars of New England, with Eliot the Apostle Fifty Years in the Midst of Them, Robert Boodey Caverly, 78
[40] Covey, 95
[41] History of the Indians of Connecticut from the Earliest Known Period 1850, John William De Forest, 1853, 86
[42] Deforest, 85-86
[43] Cave, 57–68
[44] The Indian Wars of New England, With Eliot the Apostle Fifty Years in the Midst of Them, Robert Boodey Caverly, 83
[45] The Indian Wars of New England, With Eliot the Apostle Fifty Years in the Midst of Them, Robert Boodey Caverly, 83
[46] Hollister, 44
[47] Francis Jennings, 196
[48] Ibid, 70–71
[49] Deforest, 81
[50] The Indian and The White Man in New England, Chandler Whipple, 213
[51] Hollister, 20
[52] Vaughan, 117
[53] Underhill, 63–64
[54] History of Hartford County, Charles W. Burpee, S. J. Clarke Publishing, 1928, 44
[55] The Story of Connecticut Vol. 1, Charles Burpee, 48
[56] Cave, 100–101
[57] Cave, 95–100
[58] The Indian and the White Man, Chandler Whipple, 218
[59] The Indian and The White Man in New England, Chandler Whipple, 220
[60] Underhill, 56–57
[61] Covey, 159–160
[62] Underhill, 61–62
[63] Ibid, 161
[64] Covey, 162
[65] Covey, 162
[66] Covey, 162
[67] History of the Indian Wars of New England, With Eliot the Apostle Fifty Years in the Midst of Them, Robert Boodey Cavalry, 73
[68] Covey, 163–164
[69] John Winthrop Journal, 190
[70] John Wintrhop Journal, 192-195
[71] Introduction to John Mason, A Brief History of the Pequot War, Thomas Prince, iii
[72] The Story of Connecticut Vol. 1, Charles Burpee, 51
[73] The Story of Connecticut Vol.1, Charles Burpee, 51
[74] Adams & Stiles, 71
[75] The Story of Connecticut Vol.1, Charles Burpee, 52
[76] The Story of Connecticut Vol. 1, Charles Burpee, 52
[77] The Story of Connecticut Vol. 1, Charles Burpee, 52

[78] The Story of Connecticut Vol. 1, Charles Burpee, 52
[79] Hollister, 54–55
[80] Mason, 21
[81] Wagner and Dempsey, 42
[82] Ibid, 38–49
[83] Underhill, 51
[84] Hollister, 55–56
[85] The Indian and the White Man, Chandler Whipple, 227
[86] Hollister, 57–58
[87] The Indian and the White Man, Chandler Whipple, 228
[88] Hollister, 57–58
[89] Ibid, 60
[90] Cave, 98–141
[91] Mason, 26
[92] Mason, 27
[93] Ibid, 139
[94] Mystic Fiasco, Dempsey & Wagner, 90
[95] Hollister 61–62
[96] Mystic Fiasco, Wagner & Dempsey, 117
[97] Ibid, 107–109
[98] Underhill, 82–83
[99] Ibid, 113
[100] Ibid, 133
[101] Hollister, 64
[102] Underhill, 84–85
[103] Mason, xix
[104] Sanders, 32–33
[105] Hollister, 147
[106] Cave 158–160
[107] Wagner and Dempsey, 139
[108] Mason, (John Fiske, Beginnings of New England) xviii
[109] The Story of Connecticut Vol. 1, Charles Burpee, 53
[110] Mason, 37–40
[111] Ibid, 163
[112] Vaughan, 340–341
[113] Weeks
[114] John Winthrop Journal, 171
[115] The Indian and The White Man, Chandler Whipple, 238
[116] The Indian and the White Man, Chandler Whipple, 238
[117] Adams & Stiles, 69
[118] Vaughn, 205
[119] Deforest 184-185
[120] The Journal of John Winthrop, 211
[121] The Journal of John Wintrhop, 211-213
[122] Steele, 57

[123] Roger Williams, Emily Easton, Houghton Mifflin Company, 1930
[124] Ibid, 227
[125] Rhode Island's Founders: From Settlement to Statehood, Patrick T. Conley, The History Press, 45–46 2010
[126] The Story of Connecticut Vol. 1, Charles Burpee, 111
[127] Odberg, 102
[128] The Indian and The White Man, Chandler Whipple, 164
[129] Weeks
[130] King Philip's War, Ellis & Morris, 32
[131] The Journal of John Winthrop, 237
[132] Hollister, 124
[133] Alvin Weeks
[134] Hollister, 123–124
[135] King Philip's War, Ellis & Morris, 33
[136] Jennings, 260–263
[137] Forbes, 8,12
[138] Jennings. 255
[139] Easton, 228
[140] Indian Wars of New England: Topography of Indian Tribes, Herbert Milton Sylvester, 457
[141] Indian Wars of New England: Topography of Indian Tribes, Herbert Milton Sylvester, 472-473
[142] The Indian Land Titles of Essex County, Massachuestts, Sidney Perley, 36–37
[143] The Story of Connecticut Vol.1, Charles Burpee, 165
[144] Historical Collections of the Indians of New England, Daniel Gookin, 202
[145] Hare, 27–28
[146] Hare, 62–63
[147] Ibid, 64
[148] Ibid, 41
[149] Ibid, 116–117
[150] Hare
[151] Sabbath at Home, Volume 2, Illustrated Religious Magazine, 1868
[152] Ibid, 58–59
[153] Hare
[154] Hare, 98
[155] Mathew Mayhew, Hare 101
[156] Hare, 108
[157] Historical Collections of the Indians in New England, Daniel Gookin, 206
[158] Hare, 111
[159] Hare, 112
[160] Leach, 18
[161] King Philip's War, Ellis & Morris, 9
[162] Historic & Archaeological Resources of the Connecticut River Valley, The Massachusetts Historic Commission, 1984

[163] Odberg, 167

[164] Historic & Archaeological Resources of the Connecticut River Valley, The Massachusetts Historic Commission, 1984

[165] Drake, 39–41

[166] De Forest, 252

[167] Cogely, 28–30

[168] The New–   –   By Justin Winsor, 12

[169] Jennings, 233

[170] The New England Company of 1649 and John Eliot, Publications of the Prince Society, 1920

[171] The New England Company

[172] John Eliot Apostle to the Indians, Ola Elizabeth Winslow, 1968, 114

[173] Sabbath at Home, Volume 2, Illustrated Religious Magazine, 1868

[174] Cogely, 178

[175] Jennings, 210

[176] Leach, 6

[177] Jennings, 249

[178] A Brief Narrative of the Progress of the Gospel amongst the *Indians* in *New England,* in the Year 1670, given in by the Reverend Mr. JOHN ELIOT, Minister of the Gospel there, in a LETTER by him directed to the Right Worshipfull the COMMISSIONERS under his Majesties Great-Seal for Propagation of the Gospel amongst the poor blind Natives in those United Colonies. *LONDON,* Printed for *John Allen,* formerly living in *Little-Britain* at the Rising-Sun, and now in *Wentworth street* near *Bell-Lane,* 1671.

[179] Connole, 88–89

[180] John Eliot Apostle to the Indians, Ola Elizabeth Winslow, 1968, 93

[181] Historical Collections of the Indians in New England, Daniel Gookin, 168-169

[182] Historical Collections of the Indians in New England, Daniel Gookin, 169

[183] Historical Collections of the Indians in New England, Daniel Gookin, 180-181

[184] Historical Collections of the Indians in New England, Daniel Gookin, 169

[185] A Brief Narrative of the Progress of the Gospel amongst the *Indians* in *New England,* in the Year 1670, given in by the Reverend Mr. JOHN ELIOT, Minister of the Gospel there, in a LETTER by him directed to the Right Worshipfull the COMMISSIONERS under his Majesties Great-Seal for Propagation of the Gospel amongst the poor blind Natives in those United Colonies. *LONDON,* Printed for *John Allen,* formerly living in *Little-Britain* at the Rising-Sun, and now in *Wentworth street* near *Bell-Lane,* 1671.

[186] Cogely, 105–107

[187] Cogely, 140

[188] Bodge

[189] Connole, 141–144

[190] The Nipmuck Indians

[191] The Indians of the Nipmuck Country in Southern New England, 1630–1750, Dennis A. Connole, 109–110
[192] Historical Collections of the Indians of New England, Daniel Gookin, 172
[193] Drake, 94–95
[194] Historical Collections of the Indians of New England, Daniel Gookin, 189
[195] The Indians of the Nipmuck Country in Southern New England, 1630–1750, Dennis A. Connole,109–111
[196] The Indians of the Nipmuck Country in Southern New England, 1630–1750, Dennis A. Connole,112
[197] Historical Collections of the Indians of New England, Daniel Gookin, 192
[198] Historical Collections of the Indians of New England, Daniel Gookin, 191
[199] The Nipmuck Indians
[200] The Indians of the Nipmuck Country in Southern New England, 1630–1750, Dennis A. Connole, 113
[201] Historical Collections of the Indians of New England, Daniel Gookin, 195
[202] Historical Collections of the Indians of New England, Daniel Gookin, 177
[203] Drake, 50
[204] Historical Collections of the Indians of New England, Daniel Gookin, 177
[205] Ibid, 118–119
[206] The Indians of the Nipmuck Country in Southern New England, 1630–1750, Dennis A. Connole, 118
[207] Ibid, 120
[208] Connole, 84–121
[209] The Indian and The White Man, Chandler Whipple, 157
[210] William Apess
[211] The Eulogy of King Philip, William Apess, 20
[212] Gookin, 439
[213] Bodge
[214] Gookin, 462
[215] Connole, 113
[216] Leach, 1
[217] The Story of Connecticut Vol.1, Charles Burpee, 214
[218] Bodge
[219] The Indian and The White Man, Chandler Whipple 170–171
[220] Barton, 48
[221] Weeks
[222] De Forest, 256
[223] Indian History, Biography and Genealogy: Pertaining to the Good Sachem Massasoit, Ebenezer weaver Peirce
[224] Ibid, 5
[225] Apess, 15-16
[226] Weeks
[227] William Apess
[228] Jennings, 289–293
[229] Forbes, 45–48

[230] Eulogy of Philip, William Apess, 29–30
[231] Forbes, 45–48
[232]Epochs of American History: The Colonies 1492–1750, Reuben G. Thwaites, Longmans, Green, and Co., 1894, 170–171
[233] Leach, 31
[234] Vaughan, 76–85
[235] Leach, 31–32
[236] Gookin, 440
[237] King Phlip's War, Ellis & Morris, 48
[238] Jennings, 294–295
[239] Weeks
[240] Barton, 48–49
[241] King Phlip's War, Ellis & Morris, 49
[242] Weeks
[243] King Phlip's War, Ellis & Morris, 57
[244] Drake, 70
[245] Leach, 35
[246] Gookin, 441–444
[247] Gookin, 441–444
[248] Bodge
[249] Bodge
[250] Leach, 44–45
[251] Pulsipher, 466
[252] Pulsipher, 466
[253] Gookin, 439
[254] King Phlip's War, Ellis & Morris,70–71
[255] Gookin, 439
[256] King Phlip's War, Ellis & Morris, 72
[257] King Phlip's War, Ellis & Morris, 73
[258] King Phlip's War, Ellis & Morris, 77–78
[259] King Phlip's War, Ellis & Morris, 77–78
[260] Leach, 50–69
[261] King Phlip's War, Ellis & Morris, 84
[262] Leach, 40–41
[263] History of Hardwick, Massachusetts with a Genealogical Register, Lucius R. Paige, 1883
[264] History of Hardwick, Massachusetts with a Genealogical Register, Lucius R. Paige, 1883
[265] King Phlip's War, Ellis & Morris, 84–89
[266] History of Hardwick, Massachusetts with a Genealogical Register, Lucius R. Paige, 1883
[267] Bodge, xiii
[268] Bodge
[269] Bodge, xiii
[270] Bodge

[271] King Phlip's War, Ellis & Morris, 90
[272] Bodge
[273] Bodge
[274] Leach, 77–84
[275] King Phlip's War, Ellis & Morris, 92
[276] Bodge
[277] Bodge
[278] King Phlip's War, Ellis & Morris, 96
[279] Leach, 84
[280] Gookin, 450–451
[281] Daniel Gookin, 470
[282] Gookin, 451–453
[283] King Phlip's War, Ellis & Morris, 117
[284] Bodge
[285] Leach, 89
[286] Leach, 95
[287] Springfield, Massachusetts: Volume I, Henry M. Burt. Printed and Published by Henry M. Burt, 1898, 130–135
[288] Leach, 96
[289] Springfield, Massachusetts: Volume I, Henry M. Burt. Printed and Published by Henry M. Burt, 1898, 130–135
[290] Pulsipher, 465–466
[291] Connole, 174
[292] Bodge
[293] Gookin, 469–474
[294] Gookin, 469–474
[295] Bodge
[296] Pulsipher, 467
[297] Bodge
[298] King Phlip's War, Ellis & Morris, 136
[299] Olexer, 57–58
[300] Connole, 178
[301] Bodge
[302] Burpee, 118
[303] Steele, 58–59
[304] Mystic Fiasco, David Wagner & Jack Dempsey, 95
[305] Bodge
[306] History of the Indian Wars of New England, with Eliot the Apostle Fifty Years in the Midst of Them, Robert Boodey Caverly, 186–87
[307] Leach, 129
[308] King Phlip's War, Ellis & Morris, 151–152
[309] Bodge
[310] Bodge
[311] Ibid., 58–59
[312] Drake, 119

[313] Jennings, 312
[314] King Phlip's War, Ellis & Morris, 165
[315] Bodge
[316] Bodge
[317] Pulsipher, 472
[318] Ibid, 175
[319] Gookin, 486-488
[320] Bodge
[321] Gookin, 475-476
[322] Gookin, 486-488
[323] Gookin, 489
[324] Gookin, 491
[325] Gookin, 500-507
[326] History of the Indian Wars of New England, with Eliot the Apostle Fifty Years in the Midst of Them, Robert Boodey Caverly, 205
[327] King Phlip's War, Ellis & Morris, 207-208
[328] King Phlip's War, Ellis & Morris, 212
[329] Gookin, 516-517
[330] Forbes, 57-64
[331] Hollister, 282
[332] Leach, 171
[333] Weeks
[334] Burpee, 131
[335] Hollister, 284
[336] Soldiers in King Philip's War, Bodge
[337] Bodge
[338] History of the Indian Wars of New England, Col. Robert Boodey Caverly, 73
[339] Gookin, 513-519
[340] Zelner, 215-216
[341] Ibid., 59
[342] Bodge
[343] Lincoln, 104-105
[344] Connole, 208-212
[345] The Nipmuc Indians
[346] Barton, xxiii

Made in the USA
Charleston, SC
30 November 2015